S0-AVX-150

The Ritualization of Mormon History

and Other Essays

The Ritualization
of Mormon History
and Other Essays

Davis Bitton

University of Illinois Press
Urbana and Chicago

© 1994 by the Board of Trustees of the University of Illinois
Manufactured in the United States of America

C   5   4   3   2   1

This book is printed on acid-free paper.

Library of Congress Cataloging-in-Publication Data
Bitton, Davis, 1930–
    The ritualization of Mormon history and other essays /
Davis Bitton.
        p. cm.
    Includes index.
    ISBN 0-252-02079-0
        1. Church of Jesus Christ of Latter-Day Saints—History.
    2. Mormon Church—History.   I. Title.
    BX8611.B537   1994
    289.3—dc20   93–28931
                                                            CIP

Contents

Introduction

THIS COLLECTION of articles, some previously published, others appearing for the first time, is intended to convey something of the excitement and variety of Mormon history. The pieces separately should be self-explanatory, and readers are of course free to read only those that arouse their interest.

When I say "self-explanatory," I may be too sanguine. It is not everyone who knows the rudiments of Mormon history. For those wishing an introductory treatment, may I be so presumptuous as to recommend Leonard J. Arrington and Davis Bitton, *The Mormon Experience: A History of the Latter-day Saints* (1979; rev. ed., University of Illinois Press, 1992)? Or a good encyclopedia article may provide the necessary factual scaffolding.

For those unmotivated to engage in such outside preparation before reading the volume in hand—and I imagine myself in the same situation—let us review Mormon history in a few broad strokes. The Mormon Church (officially the Church of Jesus Christ of Latter-day Saints) was organized in upstate New York in 1830. The founding prophet, then twenty-four years old, was Joseph Smith. During the previous ten years or so, young Smith, according to Mormon tenets, had experienced heavenly visions. In the first of these, when he was a teenager, God the Father and Jesus Christ appeared, assuring him of the forgiveness of his sins and informing him that no Christian church on earth was wholly acceptable. Later, young Joseph was visited by an angel, who told him of the location of a set of buried metal plates, left there many centuries earlier by the surviving leader of a people descended from Hebrew immigrants to the New World. Smith translated these records into English and in 1830 published them as the Book of Mormon.

In the 1830s and early 1840s the new religion attracted adherents not only in the United States but in Great Britain and other countries abroad. The converts "gathered" to be with the prophet. Meanwhile there was persecution, for not everyone was in favor of these latter-day zealots who claimed to have the one true religion. From New York Smith and other leaders moved to Ohio, at the same time establishing a gathering place in western Missouri. By the end of the 1830s, they had been forced to flee both Ohio and Missouri. It was then that they established their city on the eastern bank of the Mississippi River at Nauvoo.

The Nauvoo phase was also short-lived, however, for anti-Mormon sentiment continued strong. In addition to religious, political, and economic differences, there was now the practice of polygamy, or plural marriage. Practiced by a small number of leaders and devoted followers, polygamy could not be kept secret. It added oil to the flames of anti-Mormon vigilantism. In 1844 Joseph Smith was lynched by a mob.

The leadership was assumed by the council of Twelve Apostles, with Brigham Young as president (in 1847 he was sustained as president of the Church). His main challenge at first was to lead his people to a place of refuge. In an impressive display of resourcefulness and organizational skill, he formed the refugees into companies that then moved westward hundreds of miles to establish a new center at Salt Lake City in the Rocky Mountains. It was the Mormons' exodus. Brigham Young was their Moses.

While a few splinter groups appeared in other locations, the largest of these eventually taking shape as the Reorganized Church of Jesus Christ of Latter Day Saints, the center of most Mormon history for the remainder of the century was in Utah and surrounding states where settlements were established. A campaign against polygamy was launched by the federal government in a series of statutes. Although there were individual prosecutions, the campaign enjoyed only limited success until Supreme Court decisions starting in 1879 opened up the way for more vigorous measures during the 1880s. By 1890 Mormon leaders were ready to throw in the towel. Polygamy was abandoned. Actually, matters were not this simple, for some new polygamous marriages continued to be performed surreptitiously. By 1904, however, a determined effort to cut off these new marriages was generally successful. With the exception of die-hard "fundamentalists," excommunicated when discovered, polygamy was no longer part of Mormon experience.

In the twentieth century Mormonism has seemed less eccentric. Gone were the "distinctives" of polygamy, communal economic organization, and a one-party system that for a time aspired to political supremacy. Whether all of this was an advance or a step backward, a slight

adjustment that retained the essentials of what Mormons call the restored gospel or a fatal betrayal of the core message, depends on one's
point of view. Both positions have been argued. What cannot be easily
disputed is that twentieth-century Mormonism continued to expand,
steadily between the wars, more rapidly with the resumption of full-
scale missionizing after World War II, and explosively from the 1960s
on to the present. A church that finally attained a membership of one
million around 1950 has soared upward to over eight million. Much of
this growth has been in Latin America, Asia, and Africa.

Ironically, such success seemed to bring not acceptance but criticism.
Public response was actually rather complex, ranging from admiration
through indifference and on to an outspoken hostility. One Mormon
leader recommended a studied ignoring of the criticism. The Latter-
day Saints should not waste their time bickering with their enemies,
he said, but should concentrate on their responsibilities of proclaiming
the gospel and living lives of Christian service. "The dogs bark but the
caravan moves on."

In short compass, these are the main contours of Mormon history.
Some of my fellow Mormons will no doubt think my account too
detached, failing to convey the fervor of Mormon conviction. Anti-
Mormons will be disdainful of a flat exposition that fails to highlight
what they see as sinister. To both groups my reply is simple. My purpose
here is the limited one of sketching in a schematic backdrop. Anyone is
free to read more widely, perhaps even works that do not fit prior prejudices. In the meantime, on to the present series of articles.

"Early Mormon Lifestyles" gives the reader a look at how the Mormons of the past century lived their lives. It should not be surprising to
discover that, like everyone else, they spent much of their time in the
struggle for existence, or that, when possible, they took the opportunity
for recreation, following the different forms of the period. In many ways
they were not very different from their contemporaries, but, as I hope
my essay demonstrates, in some ways they were unique. Their patterns
of activity were not unaffected by their own community standards and
publicly proclaimed goals, much less by the experiences that gave these
early Mormons a strong sense of "differentness" from the larger society.

Polygamy among the Mormons is a large subject in itself. For most
modern readers, one assumes, the system is patently backward and op-
pressive. It occurred to me some years ago that nowhere did we have a
convenient summary of the Mormon defense of their peculiar institu-

tion. Hence the article "Polygamy Defended." It seems to me so obvious as to require no further explanation, but, having been misunderstood in the past, I will state anyway that I am not here offering my own defense of polygamy. What the Mormons were saying in defense of what they fully realized was an unpopular, despised marital system is itself part of history, as of course is the case on the other side. In an effort to enhance our understanding of the minds of this past generation, as others have done, for example, with the pro-slavery argument, I offer to the reader a handy summary.

Most accounts of pioneering pay little attention to children. The journey itself was not only dangerous but disruptive. In the new environment the struggle for existence had inevitable priority. Through all of this some Mormons did manage to raise children well, giving them a decent education. But other young people, right up through the teenage years, had time on their hands and were anything but models of deportment. I have examined this hitherto neglected phase of the heroic pioneer generation in "Zion's Rowdies."

Historians studying the Mormon past have exploited many kinds of primary sources: diaries, letters, government documents, sermons, newspapers, and others. But practically no attention has been given, it seems to me, to early poetry as historical source. To find out what such material can tell us I have examined the verse of Charles Lowell Walker, an articulate diarist whose occasional poems were very popular on the Dixie frontier, so called, of Southern Utah.

Mormons were often thought to live in isolation, and indeed to a degree that was the hope of Brigham Young and others prior to the completion of the transcontinental railroad in 1869. In point of fact, of course, isolation was never complete. Even in the area of ideas the Saints in the West were aware of the main writings and intellectual fads of their time. It can be enlightening to examine the Mormon reaction to these. Elsewhere, in collaboration with the psychologist Gary L. Bunker, I have written about phrenology and mesmerism. Here I have considered nineteenth-century spiritualism, with which Mormonism was surprisingly consonant and yet in the final analysis importantly different at the core.

Among some, believe it or not, Mormons are known as dancers. Brigham Young University ballroom dancers win international awards. For many years, every congregation in the church had its training sessions in dancing as part of the weekly Mutual Improvement Association, and a great festival was held each June in the University of Utah stadium.

A dazzling spectacle, as I well remember. Here, as a historian, I have gone back into the nineteenth century to uncover the original attitude toward social dancing, ambivalent to say the least. The history of recreation thus reveals, at least in part, the Mormon stance toward the larger society.

Especially crucial in any movement, it seems to me, is the transition from the first to the second generation. Will the original impetus be maintained? The life of Brigham Young, Jr., is a case study of someone faced first of all with the challenge of living in the shadow of a larger than life father. Beyond that, we see in "Briggy" one of those who was forced to adjust to the fundamental fin de siècle transformations experienced by the church to which he had devoted his life. Since he kept a detailed diary, we are enabled to follow rather closely this poignant personal drama as it was experienced.

Part of Mormonism's great transition at the turn of the century—with the abandonment of polygamy and the achievement of statehood for Utah—was the arrival of the two major national political parties and subsequent elections. In 1903 a Republican, apostle Reed Smoot, was elected a U.S. senator. Accused of being a polygamist and of being part of a self-perpetuating group that dominated Utah, Smoot was subjected to a lengthy series of hearings before finally being seated. Less well known but equally interesting was the election of another Mormon general authority, the pugnacious B. H. Roberts, to the House of Representatives in 1898, which also led to a hearing and, in this instance, to his exclusion. In examining the Roberts case I have wished not only to introduce a colorful personality but also an episode in a period of difficult adjustment.

Finally, it has become inescapably obvious to me that most Mormons, like people generally, know little of their own history, and yet it is still important to them. This led me, in the spirit of a cultural anthropologist, to scrutinize the ritual forms by which the historical past was memorialized. Again, how the people understand or preserve their past, especially in public symbol, itself becomes part of group identity and part of history. Those unfamiliar with the Mormon obsession with pageant, parade, monument, and organizations paying tribute to ancestors will see Mormons in a new light. Descendants of the "pilgrim fathers," Daughters of the American Revolution, and even children of the Confederacy may discover a community of attitudes that transcends religious difference.

Much of what I present here is somewhat off the beaten path yet suggests the richness of the subject. Many facets of Mormon history have been treated in the past generation, but scores of others remain virgin territory. With the surviving documents—diaries, letters, newspapers, minute books, financial records, and so on—providing an unsurpassed hoard of primary source material, the historian of Mormonism has no reason to think that everything has been done. In the nineteenth century there are hundreds of separate community experiences, not to mention the thousands of individuals from different social and geographical backgrounds who gravitated to the faith.

In the twentieth century it is easy to assume that the subject loses its interest. No more polygamy, no more wagon trains crossing the plains, no more persecutions. Such can be the perception. Yet the subject remains challenging. There is the process of adaptation to a new social environment, experienced by Mormons, along with everyone else; each group at different paces and with different specific points of tension going through some form of modernization or of Toffler's "future shock." And with the expansive missionary programs of the past generation there is a separate Mormon history in many different settings—Chile, Korea, France, rural Utah, New York City—with both similarities and differences.

Mormons are not part of mainstream Christianity, this by apparent mutual agreement of the mainstream labelers and the Mormons themselves. In their own view, of course, they are Christians—believing as they do in the resurrection and atonement of Jesus Christ, following what they consider to be the Christian gospel in its original purity before the Constantinian age—but they have always known that they were different. If not different, Mormons from Joseph Smith to the present might well say, What is the point? What is our raison d'être? Some of these differences, along with experiences of common humanity that should resonate for all, are the subject of this book.

1

Early Mormon Lifestyles;
or, The Saints as Human Beings

TOO OFTEN history is studied in terms of kings and presidents, of wars and the large movements. These are important, of course, but at least since the famous third chapter in Macaulay's *History of England*, if not before, some historians have insisted that we should be equally interested in the life of the common people, in such undramatic but basic matters as diet and disease and family relationships. Only thus can we really begin to understand what life in the past was like. In trying to discover what life was like for ordinary members of the Church during the single lifespan extending from 1830 to about the end of the century, it will be worth our effort to consider such basic dimensions as place, shelter, food, and family. We should try to discover the patterns of work and recreation. Finally, since Mormonism was a religious movement, we should try to see what difference it made in the sense of time, of group consciousness, and religiosity as experienced by the Saints. In going over these matters we can scarcely avoid asking how, if at all, the basic lifestyle of Mormons was different from other people of the same period. For, as Maureen Whipple has justly observed, the Mormons were "human beings by birth and saints only by adoption."[1]

The Basic Framework of Mormon Life

Few things are so important to human life as the geographical setting in which it is lived. Most Mormons of the past century, like most Americans, lived in rural or semirural locations. Even when they lived in towns—Kirtland, Nauvoo, or later in Salt Lake City—they were much closer to farm life than to what we now think of as city life. Cattle and chickens were often kept in outbuildings, gardens were planted, and trips into the outlying countryside (or, in Utah, into the canyons) were frequent. The closeness to the country was due in part to the typical organization of "the Mormon village"—homes clustered together so as to make group life possible but with farmland surrounding the settlement. But in a general way the rural orientation was common in most American towns.[2]

It is often asserted that modern Americans move frequently, their geographical mobility contrasting with the relative stability of earlier generations. Recent work in demographic history may help to provide quantification of American patterns of moving. What can be said, even now, is that nineteenth-century Mormons were anything but geographically fixed.

At least three aspects of Mormon restlessness deserve comment. First, there was the "gathering." Conversion almost always meant a move to a new location, to Ohio or Missouri or Illinois or Utah. Even if the move was only a hundred miles, it could be a momentous event for those involved; and it is not hard to imagine the expectant joy and fearful wonder of those who gathered from far away.[3]

Second, the missionary activity expected of the Saints meant for many of them being on the road day after day, separated from their homes for weeks or months or years. The activity began even before the Church was officially organized, when Samuel Smith and others took to the road as itinerant book peddlers. Proselyting continued feverishly during the next several years. Young converts like Lorenzo Barnes went out from Kirtland to preach in the various Ohio settlements, stopped at home for rest and recuperation, and then started out once again, sometimes traveling many hundreds of miles. From 1837 on, there were Mormon missionaries in England and, soon after, on the Continent.[4]

The sending out of Mormon elders continued through the Nauvoo period and the latter half of the century. Missions became better organized, with such elements of stability as officers, headquarters, and records. The typical missionary "tour of duty" came to be two years, although longer and shorter missions were fairly common throughout the century. But the fact of traveling to distant locations to preach the gospel continued to mean, as it had from the first, that Mormons were less likely to put down permanent roots than others. Since the "call" often came without advance warning, and since it was not unusual for a man to be called on a second or a third mission, the hovering thought in the back of many minds must have been one of nervous uncertainty.

Third, even after gathering with the Saints, many people were greeted

not by a chance to settle down but by a call to go out into another settlement, with all that this meant in demands on supplies, physical energy,
and psychological resiliency. Occasionally such calls to go out from the
expected destination were received even in Missouri and Illinois. But
during the epic settlement of the Great Basin, extending as it did over
several decades, such relocations were frequent.[5]

When these practices were combined with the forced migrations
the result was a life of rootlessness for many early Mormons. Having
gathered to Ohio from New England, say, a family could have moved
on to Independence, Missouri, only to have to move out to Clay or
Caldwell county within a few months and from there make its way to
Nauvoo, Illinois. Forced to leave their "Kingdom on the Mississippi,"
this same family could be called upon to move westward, usually inter-
rupting the journey by stays of a few months or years in Kanesville,
Iowa, or elsewhere. Finally, after arriving in the Valley of the Great Salt
Lake, another series of moves might be set in motion. There were families who spent a year or two living in Salt Lake City, then moved out to
Bountiful, or Layton, or Ogden, only to be called to the Iron Mission or
the Cotton Mission or, later, to the Little Colorado in Arizona.

Quite aside from the gathering, missionary outreach, and calls to
settle specific areas already discussed, some people seemed to be home-
less wanderers, moving every two or three years. Here is Lorenzo Hill
Hatch, to cite one example, who had been born in Vermont. After going
to Nauvoo he made the great trek west to Utah and was then called
to England on a mission. But were his travels over? Hardly. For a few
years he had his family home in Lehi, but later we find that he moved
to Franklin, Idaho. Later he lived in Woodruff, Arizona. Toward the end
of the century, as his diaries recount, he was called as a missionary to
the Zuni Indians and spent several months moving from place to place
in New Mexico.[6] Examples could be multiplied of families that moved
six or eight or ten times. Many of them may have moved several times
even had they remained Gentiles, of course, but Mormonism provided
several specific stimuli to whatever migratory propensities may have
already existed. More than most people, therefore, Mormons lived in a
mood of uncertainty, pilgrims and strangers in the land.

Separate from the simple physical fact of moving from one location
to another was the tendency to see specific places within a religious
frame of reference. The places from which they gathered were seen as
"Babylon"; their destination was "Zion," a designation applied at first

to Jackson County, Missouri, but later extended to include the central gathering point of the moment, whether Nauvoo or Salt Lake City. In other words, there were sacred places and profane places. A heavenly aura seemed to surround the former, the earthly counterparts of the City of Enoch.

Let it be admitted that such considerations were easier in hope and expectation than in reality. The discrepancy between Zionic images and actuality was a source of frequent comment in the sermons. As Jedediah M. Grant said in 1851:

> I am aware that some Elders who go forth and preach long and pious sermons, frequently represent Zion as one of the most delightsome places in the world, as if the people in Salt Lake City were so pure and holy that the flame of sanctity would almost singe the hair off a common man's head. . . . The imaginations of some Saints have been so exalted by the Elders who preached to them, that they suppose that all our pigs come ready cooked, with knives and forks in them, and are running round squealing to be eaten; that every tray is filled with bread, every manger with potatoes, and every man's wagon with the choice fruits of the earth.[7]

Even so, some of those most disappointed upon their arrival at the Zion they had looked forward to were, soon after getting a stake in their new location, expounding the virtues of Zion to their old compatriots.

Shelter

If Mormons differed from their contemporaries with respect to the dwellings they lived in, it was primarily in the necessity of building so frequently—a function of the geographical mobility already discussed. Ohio, Missouri, Illinois—all were scenes of home building. The survival of several solid brick homes at Nauvoo suggests that the Saints there were surrounded by a good deal of comfort. Some were, but most Mormons, even there, lived in rather crowded quarters and shaky structures. For many of the Saints the exodus meant living in wagons, lean-tos, and huts. Others, in places like Kanesville, lived in more stable dwellings.

In the Great Basin the pattern of pioneering continued, with repeated moves meaning the construction of one house after another. Some of these were "dugouts," temporary shelters. Charles W. Nibley described such a dwelling at Wellsville in Cache Valley:

> It was probably the middle of November 1860 or a little later when we completed a little one room, part clay and part log house. We dug a square hole in the ground about three feet deep and then built logs around that hole 3 logs high. We built up to the gables with logs then put a center roof log and one on each side of that, halfway down to the wall. On top of these logs we laid small quaking aspen poles not larger than my wrist. On top of these we put straw and then covered that with a thick coat of dirt. My father built a cobble stone chimney in the opposite end from the entrance or door. The chimney was simply built of cobble stones and mud for plaster, as we had no lime or any other kind of plaster that would hold. The chimney never knew enough to draw the smoke up but spewed it out and filled the room. . . . There was no window of any kind whatever in our house. Neither was there a door. My mother hung up a quilt or piece of an old quilt which served as a door for the first winter. This was our bedroom, our parlor, our sitting room, our kitchen, everything in this room of about 12 × 16.[8]

Even homes intended to be permanent were often cramped and shaky. The diary of Joseph Beecroft tells of several catastrophes when the houses he had patiently built suddenly collapsed. It is clear enough that the pressure of time, lack of experience in building, and lack of resources combined to keep many Mormons living in confined, precarious quarters.

On the other hand, there were some Mormon homes of modest strength and elegance even from the beginning. In Kirtland there were signs of this improved building, and the same was true in Missouri—the home of Lyman Wight, for example. In Nauvoo, judging from the homes still standing and the known existence of many others, the achievement was considerably greater. In each of these early locations, it should be remembered, the time during which Mormon construction could take place was a half-dozen years or less.

In Utah came the chance of greater continuity and follow-through. In Salt Lake City and in settlement after settlement, the original shelters that were small, rudimentary, and inadequate were replaced or enlarged as quickly as possible. Utilizing materials appropriate to the environment, the pioneers built homes of adobe and stone as well as of wood. Austin E. Fife estimates that there may once have been as many as four hundred stone houses north of Salt Lake City, thirty-five in Willard alone. "The minimal housing needs of pioneers who earned their living by their own labors are satisfied therein with efficiency and a Spartan kind of elegance appropriate to the then prevailing economy of scarcity," Fife says. "Their every line bespeaks the will to survive with dignity and the rationale of a well-ordered household in a well-ordered society."[9]

When to these superb stone houses are added the hundreds of wood and adobe structures built during the first and especially the second generation after the arrival of the Saints in their western refuge, it becomes apparent that, even with the inevitable hardship and temporary shelters, they worked doggedly to establish shelters of comfort and strength. The tourist who visits Nauvoo will gain an appreciation for this central thrust of Mormon building, as will the visitor to the Beehive House in Salt Lake City or the house of Jacob Hamblin in Santa Clara. The Utah State Register of Historic Buildings provides additional examples.[10]

A factor that may have influenced the Mormons' building styles was polygamy, especially after the arrival in the Great Basin. With the exception of a few houses large enough to house two families or more, however, the pattern seems to have been one of separate households for the separate families. We shall see in a moment that polygamy had other kinds of impact on Mormon experiences, but on the physical construction of houses its influence was apparently slight.

Food

It seems doubtful that Mormon eating habits differed very much from those of other people of the past century. Converts from different parts of the United States and Europe brought some of their tastes with them, of course, but they were often limited by availability of the commodities they desired. However, two factors did influence Mormon attitudes in this area: the Word of Wisdom and the experience of scarcity.

The Word of Wisdom was a revelation received by Joseph Smith in 1833. In addition to a general injunction to eat meat sparingly and use fruits "in the season thereof" and to use wheat, the document admonishes the Saints not to partake of strong drink (alcohol), tobacco, or "hot drinks" (defined by Hyrum Smith as tea and coffee). It has been pointed out that most if not all the ideas contained in this health code could be found advocated by others in the early nineteenth century. But if not original in the strict sense, the Mormon Word of Wisdom was perhaps unique in its form of expression—as a revelation from God.

Since the Word of Wisdom was given "not by commandment or constraint," its effect on the actual practice of the Saints depended, in large measure, on the extent to which it was emphasized. Even during Joseph Smith's lifetime there were efforts to make it stick. In 1837, for example, a conference of the Church at Far West resolved unanimously "that we will not fellowship any ordained member who will not, or does not, observe the Word of Wisdom according to its literal reading." A year later, also at Far West, Joseph Smith spoke on the Word of Wisdom and said it "should be observed."[11]

Despite such urgings the Word of Wisdom was not observed with great strictness by many Saints throughout the nineteenth century. Tea and coffee were included in the lists of supplies brought west by the pioneers. Wine was manufactured in Utah's Dixie, and its use was not confined to the Gentiles. But the question of observance is one of degree. Perhaps Mormon families did make an unusual effort to avoid stimulants and narcotics. And there were, even in the nineteenth century, periods of revival or crusade.[12] To some extent at least, then, Mormon diets and habits were influenced by the code embodied in the Word of Wisdom.

One of the experiences of many early Mormons was that of scarcity or even near starvation. These experiences occurred at times of crisis: Nauvoo in 1839, or in the "wilderness" after 1845, or in the Valley during times of famine. Even after the original tenuous settlements were more firmly established, Mormons in the West realized how close they were to being left desolate by a drought or a grasshopper plague. It seems at least plausible that some of the recurring impulse to store food for the future—a theme heard even today—derived from the previous experience of scarcity.

It should not be thought that early Mormons were always on the verge of starvation. There were feasts even in Ohio and Missouri. The following statement from an 1855 sermon by Brigham Young reflects both a practice and a frustration:

Suppose I happen to say "Come, wife, let us have a good dinner today"; what does she get? Pork and beef boiled, stewed, roasted, and fried, potatoes, onions, cabbage, and turnips, custard, eggs, pies of all kinds, cheese, and sweet-meats. Now grant that I and my wife sit down and overload our stomachs, until we feel the deleterious effects of it from the crowns of our heads to the soles of our feet, the whole system is disturbed in its operations, and is ready to receive and impart disease. . . .

Will all the women hearken to this plain statement? No, you might as well talk to the wild geese that fly over us.[13]

Perhaps this is a good example of the fact that pleas from the pulpit are not necessarily accurate descriptions of practice.

Family

Nothing is more basic to the existence of any people than the nature of family life, including courtships, marriage, size of family, and relationships between children. Closely related are those experiences of life that normally take place in the family setting: birth, sickness, and death.

There are few examples of Mormon courtships from the 1830s and early 1840s. Presumably they occurred, but few of the details have survived. Wilford Woodruff's marriage to Phebe Carter was tenderly recorded in his journal, but there are practically no details. Examples become more numerous in the western phase of Church history.[14] "Sparking" or "keeping company" were the terms used to describe what we call flirting, dating, going steady, and getting "pinned" or engaged. Engagement rings were uncommon, we are told, because of the expense.

Interesting situations were created by the necessity of carrying on this basic activity of life during times of hardship and travel. Converts sometimes found the question of religious loyalty a complicating factor if the sweetheart was a lukewarm Mormon or a Gentile with no interest in converting and emigrating. Problems of language could be obstacles for Scandinavian and other foreign converts, and polygamy, when it was involved, introduced complications that were highly abnormal. Two or three examples can suggest the variety of situations that could arise.

An issue of the *Utah Historical Quarterly* devoted to Utah's Dixie (July 1961) tells of the frustration of the women employed at the Cotton Factory at Washington. They worked long hours and had little opportunity for contact with young men. One day C. L. Christensen came in search of a second wife. The account continued:

He arrived at the factory just at noon, as the girls were coming out of doors to eat their lunch, buxom, healthy girls eager to get

out into the spring air. Quickly he formulated a plan. Mounting
a large rock near the place where the girls had spread out their
food, he took off his hat—conscious, perhaps, that his six-foot-
two height, curly blond hair, and fine set of teeth made him not
hard to look at—and called out in the manner of a Mormon missionary at a street meeting:

"Give me your attention, please! I am Chris Christensen of San
Pete County, commonly called Chris Lingo. I have come to Dixie
on business and will be here only a short time. One of my hopes
is that I may be able to find for myself a second wife, that I may
please my first and fulfill the celestial law. Look me over, girls,
and if any of you would like to get better acquainted, I'd be very
glad to visit with you after dinner."

The girls giggled and whispered and dared each other, until
finally a group of a half-dozen or more went to talk with him. He
found his wife Serenie [?] there, married her and took her back
with him.

In his journal, John Pulsipher told of his marriage in 1853 to Rozilla
Huffaker: "When I had sufficiently learned to govern myself as to be
worthy of a wife the Lord sent me one—not a wife—but a good pattern to make one of—a young woman aged about 17." After a happy
relationship that lasted eighteen years Rozilla died. The following year,
in 1872, Pulsipher traveled from Dixie to Salt Lake City "to get me a
wife & some other supplies." He met a woman who struck his fancy but
he was forced to return home. From there he carried on his successful
courtship by letters, one of which came right to the point: "As we live
in the days of short prayers, short sermons, & short courtships, I would
like you to write me a plain, mountain-English letter & tell me truly,
if you think it would be best & proper for us to be joined in marriage."
She did and they were.

The trials of Mormon polygamous marriages have been summarized in Kimball Young, *Isn't One Wife Enough?: The Story of Mormon
Polygamy* (1954). The main thing to remember is that there were two
sides, examples of cooperation as well as competition, of sisterly relationships between the wives as well as animosities, of satisfying experiences as well as frustration and tragedy.

Polygamy was limited to relatively few families before the exodus to
Utah. Even at its height, according to Stanley S. Ivins, not more than 15
or 20 percent of the families in the Church were polygamous. He con-

cluded that "far from looking upon plural marriage as a privilege to be made the most of, the rank and file Mormons accepted it as one of the onerous obligations of Church membership. Left alone, they were prone to neglect it, and it always took some form of pressure to stir them to renewed zeal."[15] When the Woodruff Manifesto brought a formal end to polygamous marriages in 1890, although there were some complaints and recurring problems of enforcement, the majority of Mormons apparently sighed with relief.

Families were larger than they are now, but not, if we count each mother with her children as a family unit, as large as might be expected. According to Stanley Ivins, "3,355 wives of polygamists bore 19,806 children, for an average of 5.9 per woman. An equal number of wives of monogamists, taken from the same general group, bore 26,780 for an average of eight."[16] Living in a polygamous family could, if the mother had a separate house, mean the child was surrounded by fewer siblings. Father might be less in evidence, especially if the families were in separate towns or states. On the other hand, since most polygamists had only two wives living in the same house or houses close together, the husband could very probably, if he farmed for a living, be seen by his wives and children more than the average father today.

The diaries contain examples of marital tensions and of quarrels between parents and children—generation gaps were known to exist. But there are also numerous examples of close relationships, of girls working in the home, of boys working in the field with their fathers.

One family at least held regular family meetings. This was the family of Daniel Wood, whose meetings began in 1863 and continued into the early 1870s. Some of these meetings included other young people from the locality, thus adumbrating the later Mutual Improvement Association. Charles E. Pearson, adopted son, kept the minutes and wrote several homely poems and songs for use in these meetings, including the following, sung to the tune of "Marching to Georgia":

> Come all my young companions, let's go to Brother Wood's,
> For he's going to have a meeting to teach us what is good,
> And we'll be sure to hear what'll make us all rejoice
> And be learned to make our lives useful.
>
> CHORUS:
> Hurrah, Hurrah, come let us all be going.
> Hurrah, Hurrah, for meeting time is coming.

And we will always go when we can get the chance.
God bless Brother Wood forever.[17]

And so on through seven verses. Not great poetry perhaps, but there
seems little doubt that this effort of a single family was generally constructive and well received.

Sickness and death were common experiences in the setting of home
and family. But were the Mormons any different from other families?
Probably not in the basic pain and suffering or in the grief following
death: "If you prick us, do we not bleed? If you tickle us, do we not
laugh? If you poison us, do we not die?" But in both sickness and death
there were special Mormon values that came into play.

Sickness among the Mormons was seen within a religious context.
Referring to the New Testament injunction to pray for the sick, Mor-
mons often showed a strong bias against professional medical doctors.
The diaries are full of accounts of praying for the sick, calling in the
Elders to administer, and then waiting for the healing or the expiration
of the patient.

The bias against medical doctors did not mean omitting all treatment of the patient. But many early Mormons, influenced by the ideas
of Thomsonianism, favored rest and simple, natural remedies. Here, for
example, is one among several statements by Joseph Smith: "I preached
to a large congregation at the stand, on the science and practice of medicine, desiring to persuade the Saints to trust in God when sick, and not
in an arm of flesh, and live by faith and not by medicine, or poison; and
when they were sick, and had called for the Elders to pray for them, and
they were not healed, to use herbs and mild food."[18] Given the deplorable state of medical practice at the time, this may have been a sensible
approach.

Willard Richards was one of the Thomsonian doctors who joined the
Church. Another, who joined in 1840 and continued practicing medicine until his death in 1886, was Priddy Meeks. His journal is a chronicle
of the aches and diseases of early Mormons.[19] Treatments consisted
mainly of the use of roots and herbs. The two favorites were lobelia and
cayenne pepper. Although many of his medicaments and cures would
be scoffed at by the modern medical profession, Meeks did have remark-
able success in treating patients. He lived to the age of ninety-two, his
wife Sarah to the age of ninety-nine, and his wife Mary Jane to the age of
ninety-three. "It would seem," J. Cecil Alter has noted, "that Dr. Meeks'

views on living and his theories and practice of medicine were not unfavorable to longevity."[20]

During the first two generations of Mormon history most babies were delivered by midwives. It must be admitted that they included in their bag of tricks a few practices that were superstitious. Yet they did much good work, administering comfort where it was needed.[21]

The movement of modernizing medical practices coincided roughly with the same movement on the national level. In 1863, Wilford Woodruff, speaking as chairman of the Board of Examination of Physicians, said: "We have been imposed upon by pretensions of all species of quacks, Allopathic, Homeopathic, Old School, New School, Electrobiological, Astrological, Hydropathic, Thomsonian, semi-Thomsonian, and simmered down Botanic."[22] Gradually doctors became common and were sought for all serious illnesses. If medicine retained anything special among the Mormons, it was probably the continued willingness to "call in the Elders," but usually this was done only after first calling the doctor.

If death is death, then perhaps Mormon experience here was substantially the same as that of other people. But death is surrounded by a mood and memorialized by societal forms. Mormons at the time of approaching death sought comfort in their belief in the hereafter. References were made to "going home" and rejoining loved ones. There were frequent references, especially during the middle decades of the century, to Joseph and Hyrum, who were seen as friends on the other side. Funeral sermons explained the death, especially if the deceased was a child or a young adult, in terms of a more exalted "calling" or mission. God had a better work for the person to do on the other side of the vale. And in family tradition and folklore, all of this was given additional compelling authority by testimonies of dreams, visions, and "returns" from the dead.[23] It should be obvious that the structure of Mormon theology left room for, and even encouraged, such beliefs.

The Saints at Work and Play

From the early gathering to Kirtland on through the Missouri and Illinois periods, some Mormons stand forth as printers, builders, and merchants. In Nauvoo and later in Salt Lake City, such specialization, an earmark of urbanization, became more common. But most Mormons of the time were called upon to perform a variety of tasks.

Work

Farming perhaps for a living, or at least gardening and raising a few domestic animals, men were close to the soil. And they were called upon to perform the various tasks that could not be escaped: repairing, building, masonry, butchering, leatherwork, freighting, marketing, and work on railroads, canals, and dams.

The versatility of some of these early Mormons was incredible. In 1853 Andrew Love had just moved to Nephi, Utah, where the Indians were enough of a threat that the settlers organized a militia. He wrote in his diary: "So here we are at Nephi City soldiering drilling harvesting haying and acting in my office as commissary which consists in butchering & dealing out a few pounds of beef in part, & sending off our cattle to be herded at the city to keep the Indians from stealing them, with various other labors & duties turning & overturning mixing & intermixing."[24]

One of the best examples of versatility is John McLaws, one of those called to settle in Arizona along the Little Colorado. At different times he could be classed a carpenter, wheelwright, blacksmith, painter, musician, teacher, hunter, butcher, sheep-shearer, shoemaker, watch-maker, student, civil servant, churchman, secretary, farmer, mechanic, handyman, and entertainer. George S. Tanner and J. Morris Richards, who closely studied the McLaws diaries, have analyzed the incredible diversity of his activities.[25]

Much more common among most people in the past century than it is today, such versatility was stimulated among the Mormons by the repeated challenges connected with pioneering new communities.

Noticeable throughout Mormon life during the first couple of generations, at least until nearly the end of the century, was a pronounced antiprofessionalism—that is a bias against the traditional professions of the ministry, law, and medicine. The antagonism toward the Christian clergy is not surprising in view of the lay organization that prevailed in Mormonism. From the beginning the clergy had been denounced by Mormon missionaries, some few of whom had been ministers of other denominations before their conversion, as "priestcraft." The ill will was intensified by the fact that clergymen had, from the beginning, been in the forefront of the efforts to suppress Mormonism. Their leadership of the mob activity in Ohio, Missouri, and Illinois, though less than alleged at the time, makes the Mormon attitudes understandable. In Utah, the leadership of Christian clergy in the various national campaigns against Mormon polygamy again did not endear them to Mormons. Thus the natural suspicion inherent in a lay church was intensified by specific experiences.

Lawyers in the nineteenth century had a "bad press," and Mormons carried on the image of the pettifogging attorney who profited from the miseries of others, who stirred up trouble, and who was anything but honest. But, again, there were specific reasons within the Mormon experience that enhanced an existing bias. Joseph Smith's repeated encounters with the law—"vexatious lawsuits," as he called them—helped to establish his low opinion of lawyers, although he did benefit from the advice of friendly attorneys and did show an interest in the personal study of the law.

In the West there was an effort to operate a society without lawyers as usually understood. Here, perhaps, was a major difference from the mainstream of American society: Mormons attempted to solve many if not all of their disputes without going to the courts. Ward teachers tried to bring about amicable settlements; bishops' courts rendered decisions; high councils did the same—a whole series of church courts, in other words, attempted to deal with the inevitable human clashes that occurred.[26]

Gradually, the bias began to break down, and by the closing decades of the century young Mormons were being encouraged to go to law school. With such training, it was argued, they could help to defend their people.

We have already noticed the bias against medical doctors. As a further example of antiprofessionalism, here is a statement from Brigham Young: "I am happy to say I have never been under the necessity of calling a doctor to my family for forty years. I have had them in my family, but not from necessity. I like them when they are gentlemen; when they are wise and full of intelligence I am very fond of them; but I do not ask them to doctor my family in any case; and there are no circumstances under which I think them necessary."[27] Gradually, with the improvement of medicine and with the increased contacts of Latter-day Saint society and the "outside world," the medical profession became established in Utah much as it exists anywhere else.[28]

Mormons started with a "work ethic"—perhaps inherited from their New England forebears, perhaps simply part of the general American attitude—and continued to manifest incredible determination and diligence through the thick and thin of successive settlements. If they were different in this respect, it was mainly in degree, for they did have the "opportunity" to pull up stakes and start again more frequently than most people, and the natural environment in the arid west was extraordinarily foreboding. Because of their isolation, at least after the move west, and as part of the frontier or agricultural emphasis, great versatility was required, or at least stimulated. Finally, starting with ordinary biases against the ministry, law, and medicine, the Mormons had special experiences or beliefs that stimulated hostility toward the professions during the first generation or two of church history.

Play

Mormons, like other people, experienced the need for diversion from the intensity of work and the drudgery of routine. Since the past century did not have the mass media or commercialized sports, recreational patterns among the Mormons may not have been much different from those elsewhere. Still, there were special emphases and problems that deserve comment.

First, one of the popular activities from the 1840s on was dancing. There were dances in Nauvoo, and it was common in crossing the plains to seek rejuvenation in dancing during the evening hours. Probably no other single form of recreation was so common in the Mormon communities that sprang up in the Great Basin. As a group activity these square dances were obviously fun, appealing to all ages, and requiring a minimum of musical talent. Sometimes several musicians would perform, but one or two could suffice. In 1859, according to the diary of Charles R. Bailey, the settlers of Wellsville got along on even less: "We had a dance on Christmas Night and New Years also our meeting house was very small 14 × 16 and our music was very scarce only one violin and there was too many for the house so we divided up and one part went to Brother John Maughan's house but when we got there we had no music so I was called to make music for the dance being a good whistler. I had to do my best John Maughan and Brother Frank Gunnell did the calling we had a good time all the same but in those days I could make as good music as a flute or pickalo."[29]

Polygamy presented some problems in the area of dance. It was customary, one gathers, for men to take only one companion. If two wives were escorted to a dance, it must have been understood that there would be some "taking turns." Some hilarity can still be sensed in reading an invitation to a "weight ball" in St. George:

On entering . . . each lady will be given a number and a corresponding number will be deposited in a box. At 10 o'clock the gentlemen will each draw a number from the box, and the lady holding the corresponding number will be weighed and presented to the gentleman as his partner for the evening.

The admission will be free, but on receiving their partners, the gentlemen will be expected to pay three quarters of a cent per pound for the full weight of the lady.

No gentleman will be admitted without a lady and any gentleman bringing more than one will be expected to buy ladies proportionately.

Any gentleman coming after 10 o'clock will be required to pay for the weight of the heaviest lady in the house.[30]

Despite the popularity of dancing, it suffered from two inhibitions. First, there were some who viewed dancing with disfavor, perhaps a remnant of their previous religious backgrounds. Second, there was strong opposition to new dance forms when they were introduced. The "round dance" apparently seemed less wholesome than the square dance, and Church leaders inveighed against it with only partial success. The effort to continue dancing as a proper form of recreation but prevent it from deteriorating was reflected in rules passed by the St. George Stake High Council in 1887, two of which stated:

Loud or boisterous talking, stamping, or other unseemly noises should be avoided; and all double, or excessive swinging in cotillions, quadrilles, or contradances are hereby disapproved; as gentlemanly and lady-like deportment, should be observed by all; in the ball-room or elsewhere.

We are opposed to round dancing, and in regard to waltz, schottische, or polka, or any other dance embracing the features of these dances, we quote the words of the Epistle of the Apostles signed by President John Taylor, 1877. "We do not wish to be too restrictive in relation to these matters, but would recommend that there be not more than one or two [round dances] permitted in an evening."[31]

Mormons of different ages also found enjoyment in corn husking parties, candy pulls, quilting parties, competitive pest hunts, fishing trips, ice skating, sleigh rides, summer hay rides, picnics, swimming parties, and races. Nor should it be forgotten that there was a social aspect to church meetings and attendance at stake and general conferences. These were times to visit with friends and relatives and, for people who came from a distance, to do shopping and sight-seeing and perhaps visit the territorial fair.

One form of entertainment that aroused enthusiasm, starting at least as early as Nauvoo, was drama.[32] Especially after the conversion in 1841 of Thomas A. Lyne, a prominent tragedian from Philadelphia, the quality of theater in Nauvoo was improved. Lyne's company produced such plays as *William Tell, Virginius, The Iron Chest, Damon and Pythias,* and *Pizarro.* After the arrival of the Saints in the Salt Lake Valley, theatricals were produced in the Bowery as early as 1850. The Salt Lake Theatre, destined to become one of the well-known theaters in America, was dedicated in 1862. Moreover, there were numerous dramatic societies even in small, recently founded settlements. Anyone who wished could probably have the opportunity of acting, and of course attending such plays was one popular form of diversion.

Not all of these productions were of high quality. The existence of critical standards is indicated by an August 13, 1879, editorial in the Provo *Semi-Weekly Enquirer:* "The performances given during the last month or two by our local companies may be regarded, on the average, as meritorious successes. All our actors have their peculiar faults, however; and although an indulgent audience may choose, for the time being at least, to overlook them, they ought not to be lost sight of by the parties possessing them." A few days later, on August 20, 1879, the reviewer for the Provo newspaper commented favorably on the farce *Rent Day,* adding: "We have had too many dime novel productions in the past, too many of the Indian warwhoop and blood and thunder kind, and the Home Company deserves commendation for inaugurating a new era in this respect."[33]

It is important, in trying to capture the flavor of life among Mormons of the past century, to realize the pattern of their year. What occasions were there, in an average year, for celebration and festivity? Aside from the regular Sunday church service and for many years the Thursday night fast meeting, what occasions brought them together? Some of the common occasions were:

—Conferences, held quarterly on the stake level and semi-annually on the general church level.
—Family reunions, birthdays, and anniversaries, often used as occasions for inviting friends and relatives.

—National holidays: Christmas, New Years Day, Independence Day, and others.
—Pioneer Day (July 24), celebrating the 1847 arrival of the pioneers in the Salt Lake Valley, perhaps the biggest single annual celebration.
—Jubilees, the biggest of which were in 1880 (fifty years after the organization of the Church) and 1897 (fifty years after the arrival in the Valley).
—Dedications of new buildings: ward houses, civic buildings, and temples.
—Reunions of specific groups, such as the survivors of the Mormon Battalion, of Zion's Camp, of the original pioneer company.

Any or all of these celebrations could be occasion for dances, speeches, parades, pageants, concerts. Frequently there were toasts, as the following given on different occasions by Charles L. Walker:

The Mayor of St. George. May he never be hobbled.
The Pioneers of forty-seven. May every last one go to heaven.
God bless the old Battalion boys. May God increase their peace
    and joys.[34]

Walker lived in a small settlement, far from Salt Lake City, beset by many trials of climate and nature. One example among many of a celebration that must have meant much to these people is found in this diary entry for June 14, 1867: "Hot. With quite a goodly number of—citizens I went 9 miles up the Santa Clara River & spent the day in recreation: eating drinking singing swinging dancing romping & shouting in short casting off all but to make merry a good feeling prevaild no intoxicating drinks were used no tobacco smokeing (and very little chewing) all happy sober lighthearted enjoying themselves as Saints only can."

Closely connected with play and recreation were the numerous avenues of self-improvement used by the Mormons. There were schools, lyceums, debating societies, and all kinds of special-interest organizations. Even in Kirtland and Nauvoo debating was often used as a means of entertainment and instruction.[35] In 1874 Brigham Woodruff told of his attendance at the Young Men's Literary Temperance Society: "they had a question for debate it was which is the most useful the huny bee or the silk worm. I was chosen captain on the bee. my side beat the worm."

In the diary of Charles Lambert several pages are filled with notes he kept as a secretary for the Seventh Ward Polysophical Society, organized in 1855. The main purpose of the organization was "that this society be entertained by members and visitors with Essays Poetry Anecdotes speeches singing music &c &c and that no speech or oration exceed 15 minutes without permission from the President."

Such societies were numerous in Utah from the 1850s on and included such varied organizations as the Deseret Typographical Society, the Deseret Philharmonic Society, the Polysophical Association, the Deseret Theological Institute, and the Ladies' Literary Club. Differing in some respects, these all had in common the pursuit of education and recreation by relatively small groups in a nonacademic setting.[36]

Similar in some ways, although more closely sponsored by the Church, were the Female Relief Society, first organized by Joseph Smith in 1842, and the Young Women's (1869) and Young Men's (1875) Mutual Improvement Associations. The drive for self-improvement coupled with moral fervor can be sensed by reading the following resolutions adopted by the young ladies of Logan in 1875:

1. *Resolved,* That we will always try to do unto others as we would have others do unto us.

2. *Resolved,* That we cease from all loud laughter, light speeches, light mindedness and pride and all evil doings.

3. *Resolved,* That we always cultivate a kind, pleasant and cheerful disposition towards all, and always act charitably towards the poor.

4. *Resolved,* That we observe strictly the principles of virtue, modesty, sincerity and truth, in our conversation and deportment towards all with whom we are associated.

5. *Resolved,* That we cease to be covetous, cease to be idle, cease to be unclean, and cease to find fault with each other.

6. *Resolved,* That we cease to follow or pattern after foolish and extravagant fashions, but will be plain and simple in our manner of dress.

7. *Resolved,* That we will not keep the company of nor associate with persons who are not of this Church.

8. *Resolved,* That we strictly obey the counsels of our parents and also the authorities who are placed over us.

9. *Resolved,* That we pray to God, our Heavenly Father, for His care and protection, that we may endure unto the end.

10. *Resolved,* That we will not associate with nor keep the company of young men who will indulge in the use of intoxicating liquors or tobacco.

11. *Resolved,* That we will cease from what is termed "round dancing."[37]

The powerful motivation for education and self-improvement was at its strongest when coupled with recreational and religious values. There is no need to say that the Mormons were unique in such activities; after all, a debating society existed in Commerce, Illinois, before the Mormons ever arrived, and lyceums and literary societies were common.[38] If it can be noted that Mormon theology encouraged education and individual progress, it should also be noted that the schools were noticeably deficient throughout the past century—in Ohio, Missouri, Illinois, and Utah.[39] Thus the proliferation of clubs and societies showed extraordinary zeal but also reflected the inadequacy of the system.

The Religious Dimension: Time, Distinctiveness, and Worship

All of Mormon life was permeated with religion. Both Joseph Smith and Brigham Young insisted that the traditional dichotomy of spiritual and temporal was false; religion was not a special compartment of life but was, rather, a set of attitudes and values that influenced everything one did. Already we have noticed that in many areas of living, from food and shelter to work and recreation, Mormons were influenced by their religious beliefs. Yet there were some facets of experience even more obviously molded by their religion. It is time to consider these, starting with their extraordinary sense of time.

Mormons of the past century were indeed Latter-day Saints, believing themselves to be literally in the "last days." The Book of Mormon contained numerous passages describing dramatic events by which God would gather his sheep out from the world, the Indians would enlist in the cause of God, and the divine wrath would be poured out on the ungodly.[40]

Even if expectations that the whole sequence of events would take place in the 1830s or 1840s turned out to be wrong, the eschatological frame of reference was not allowed to fade from the Mormon consciousness. Both in patriarchal blessings to individuals and sermons to groups, assurances were given that people then living would participate in these events. Confirmation was provided by the "signs of the times." Natural disasters, shipwrecks, fires, earthquakes—all were seen as such signs. Revolutionary activity and wars throughout the world were signs. So too was the persecution experienced by the Saints. When the Civil War broke out, many Mormons saw it not only as a fulfillment of one of Joseph Smith's prophecies but also as a judgment on the nation for persecuting the Saints.[41]

Some Mormons were more closely tuned in on these apocalyptic wavelengths than were others. Wilford Woodruff thought of himself as a participant in a cosmic drama; his journal records his notice of different signs, his expectations, his sense of haste. A similar time-sense is revealed in the following excerpts from the diary of Andrew Love:

> *1856.* It appears at this time there is as much animosity as ever existed against this people, the adversary knows his time is short so mote it be.

> *1858.* Our enemies will injure us all they are permitted to do, but the Lord is able to fight the battles of the saints and he has promised he will, and if he uses us as instruments to kick up a little dust who cares.

> *1861.* Civil war is raging in the States preparatory for the return of the saints to the land of Missouri. . . .

The theme persisted, with every renewed assault on the Mormon institutions, especially in the 1870s and 1880s, providing further evidence that the time was short. One year that was seen by at least some Mormons as the annus mirabilis was 1891, because Joseph Smith had once written the following:

> Joseph, my son, if thou livest until thou art eighty-five years old, thou shalt see the face of the Son of Man; therefore let this suffice, and trouble me no more on this matter.

> I was left thus, without being able to decide whether this coming referred to the beginning of the millennium or to some previous appearing, or whether I should die and thus see his face.[42]

Some concluded that the Second Coming would occur sometime between December 23, 1890, and December 23, 1891. At the beginning of 1891, Charles L. Walker wrote in his diary: "Some say and have written that great things are to happen this year and the fulfillment of Daniels prophecies as to the prophetic numbers will be plainly Manifested this year 1891. Yea dire and dreadful things are to transpire. Some even declare that Christ will come and the Millennial Reign inaugerated. I think some of these things will not happen as stated but God holds all these things in his hands and at the close of 91, we shall tell more than now." At the end of the year Walker noted that the year had passed without fulfilling the expectations of "some wiseacres." But his own millennial hope was still intact: "the End is not yet and still Satan holds immence power on this Earth. But his power is being curtailed and methinks the faint streaks of the Millenial Morn are discernable on the Horizon. God speed the Day for the sake of the Righteous and the Poor and Meek of the Earth."

The theme of the Second Coming continued. Walker in 1894 composed a poem, "As It Is," dealing with the apocalyptic events and their significance. Here are the first two and the last verses:

> What mean these strange sounds of riots we hear,
> Of bloodshed and murder, men's hearts fill'd with fear,
> Of floods, fires and cyclones that sweep o'er the land?
> 'Tis but a beginning of those close at hand.

> What mean these strange feelings of distrust and dread
> From the tramp on the road to our nation's great head,
> These omens of evil, this bloodshed and war?
> They're but a small preface of those yet in store
> . . . .

> Rejoice all ye Saints for the favors of God,
> The blessings of peace, and your own quiet abode.
> While death and destruction are sweeping the land,
> Ye are kept and preserved by the might of his hand.[43]

At the end of the century Lorenzo Snow, then president of the Church, was assuring congregations that persons sitting in the congregation would witness the Second Coming. And, of course, the belief has persisted although necessitating readjustments in the supposed timetable.

While recognizing that the eschatological frame of reverence was part of the atmosphere in which nineteenth-century Mormons lived, breathed, and had their being, it should be acknowledged that some were more uptight about the doctrine than others. By and large, the decisions of the Church leadership were eminently practical, and many, perhaps most, Mormons went for years, even their entire lives, without paying much attention to the subject. The whole associated mentality did help, to an extent, to explain events of the day, especially the sufferings of the Saints, and to give them a larger, eternal significance. It was a doctrine that could be brought out of the knapsack on specific occasions.

Closely related to the sense of time was the experience of persecution. The original emigration to join the Mormons in Ohio or Missouri, the loss of family and friends, the successive driving, and finally the experience of invasion by federal troops in the Utah War and later by Gentile commissioners, judges, and governors whose lack of sympathy for Mormon institutions was no secret—all this was not mere imagination. It is worth noticing, however, that the whole experience, including of course the Mormon reaction, froze the Saints into a strong suspicion of "outsiders." It was in-group versus out-group, we versus they. Outsiders were associated with threats to the Mormon values—in Salt Lake City, in St. George (as they looked toward the mining town of Silver Reef), in Orderville (as the young people went off to the big city). The defensiveness of the Mormon leaders was perfectly understandable. They were not making up the experiences they had had; their fears were real and were often perfectly justified. But the result was a "garrison mentality" that could also include self-righteousness and parochialism.

It is easy to assume—and some insensitive observers have assumed—that rejecting the spiritual-temporal dichotomy was tantamount to a secularization of all of life. The possibility was a real one, and some Mormons undoubtedly succumbed to temptation. But the lives of devout Mormons were not so experienced; rather, they sought the Spirit of God in all thoughts and actions. Personal prayers started and ended the day. There were family prayers and special prayers for the dedication of flocks and fields, chapels and temples, and private houses. Grace was said at the table. At least this was the ideal, and it is not hard to find diary accounts showing the prevalence of such practices.

Such external utterances could conceivably have been merely pretense, a sham. Who is to say that some individuals may not have been cynically motivated? But on the whole a close reading of the personal diaries removes such suspicions. The spontaneous utterances to God found in the diaries of Joseph Smith, Heber C. Kimball, Franklin D. Richards, William H. Smart, and many others are compelling evidence of the sincerity of their writers and their close relationship to God. Personal letters give further evidence of sincere dedication. Here, a single example among many, is Brigham Young writing to his son Alfales in 1875: "It affords me great joy to know that you are realizing some of the powers of the Gospel and the knowledge of its Truth. Give your heart to God and your life to his service and this testimony will continually increase with you and will never grow dim, and your strength will increase with your increasing years until you will have passed away and your faith in the Lord and in His work will be undivided."[44]

Grasping the nature of Mormon spirituality is not easy, especially for one not of the tradition. We are close to dealing with the "unutterable things of the spirit." Nevertheless we can recognize certain characteristic forms of Mormon religiosity. In some respects, of course, Mormons were not greatly different from Protestants; the similarities should not be forgotten. But there were still some special Mormon emphases and styles.

Mormon worship services basically consisted of prayers, songs, the sacrament, and one or more sermons. Prayers were given by different members of the ward on a kind of rotating basis. Singing was congregational, using one of the different hymnals that were published starting with Emma Smith's in 1835. (Before 1835, naturally, there was singing as well, based on words published in the early church periodicals.) Occasionally choirs were heard, but these were usually organized for special occasions.

At Kirtland and Nauvoo the worship services must have been dominated largely by Joseph Smith and some of the other leaders. Some visitors to Nauvoo commented negatively on Joseph's sermons, but scores of diaries attest to his success in reaching his followers. "I never heard such good preaching in my life as I have since I came here," wrote Martha Haven to her parents in 1843. "We have some *very* smart men."[45] On the basis of reports in the *Journal of Discourses*, the newspapers, and some diary summaries, it appears that the Mormon leaders were remarkably successful in communicating messages of relevance. Here is a brief sermon of Heber C. Kimball's, given on the plains, June 1847, as summarized in the diary of Norton Jacob:

> Tuesday, 1st day of June 1847—A warm, pleasant morning. all seem to be under the influence of the good Spirit. Brother Heber was speaking of selfishness; that everyone should feel as though they could take hold and assist one another just as quick as they

would themselves; that when we would feel an interest in all our brethren's welfare we would be filled with light and life; while selfishness tends to death; it kills the soul. One who acts for the good of the whole acts like a god, while he that coils himself up in himself and only strives to advance his own affairs will sink down to nothing.[46]

Whether in the "grove" at Nauvoo, in a circle of covered wagons on the plains, at the log tabernacle at Kanesville, in the temporary Bowery at Salt Lake City, or in one of the more solid tabernacles and ward houses that were erected from the 1850s on, sermons of General Authorities were practical, commonsensical, and directed to needs of the moment.

It is interesting to see how Mormon services impressed various travelers and reporters. During their 1855 journey, Jules Remy and Julius Brenchley heard few preachers who "can be considered accomplished speakers." Orson and Parley P. Pratt were worthy of praise. And Brigham Young had "a certain kind of natural eloquence which is very pleasing to his people." But most preachers indulged in "strange ramblings."[47]

In 1860 came Richard Burton, who attended a meeting in the Bowery. He heard an address by Abraham O. Smoot, who "appeared to speak excellent sense in execrable English." Burton had heard reports that Brigham Young and others often lapsed into profanity and vulgarity in their sermons but he failed to confirm the rumor. "I never heard, nor heard of, any such indelicacy, during my stay at Gt. S. L. City. The Saints abjured all knowledge of the 'fact,' and—in this case, *nefas ab hoste doceri*—so gross a scandal should not be adopted from Gentile mouths."[48]

In 1861 U.S. mail agent H. S. Rumfield attended a meeting in the "old" Tabernacle. Describing the congregation, he betrayed more than a little snobbishness: "The assembly presented the anomalous spectacle of a vast Museum in which was collected all that is eccentric, misshapen, and curious in the human family. Deformity in all its varied aspects was visible on every hand, and the mass together exhibited a picture of idiocy and sensuality, stupidity and ignorance, credulity and fanaticism which no generous soul could contemplate except with feeling of mingled sorrow and disgust." He did concede that the leaders included "many men of fine appearance and undoubted intellectual vigor." The music by the choir he considered "very well performed." There was a prayer by one of the Apostles. Then there was a sermon by Bishop Leonard Harrington, which could not be heard. Lack of reverence was noticeable. Rumfield remarked that coughing, hawking, and spitting were "so general and incessant, as to have the painful impression upon the mind of a stranger that the Saints were all afflicted with pulmonary disease." He gave quite a detailed summary, almost a transcription of Brigham Young's sermon, remarking that it "abounded in the most profane and filthy expressions."[49]

When W. F. Rae visited Utah in 1870 he observed that with the Mormons "Sunday is emphatically a day of rest." There were morning and afternoon services at the Tabernacle. Rae noticed the barrels of water in front of the hall. This, of course, was for the sacrament, which was "handed about in tin cans to every person in the congregation." In the evening each ward had its meeting. There he heard singing by a choir, prayers, and two sermons, which impressed him as "harangues about things in general."[50]

In 1872 Mrs. Thomas L. Kane attended a sacrament meeting at Nephi. Music was provided by a choir of fourteen voices. She noticed differences between the two speakers, one using the Scriptures but not bothering to give a "literal reading," the other giving a very emotional testimony of his conversion. The sacrament was passed during the sermon (which was interrupted for the sacramental prayer). Since Mrs. Kane proved to be a perceptive observer in other respects during this same trip, her summary evaluation of the meeting rings true: it was characterized, she said, by "a certain unceremonious manner, not irreverent, but which somehow seemed to be protesting against formalism."[51]

In 1884 Emily Faithful attended a service in the Assembly Hall, where the crowds were so large that she had a hard time finding a seat. She described the administration of the sacrament: twelve elders standing behind a long table to break the bread; the passing to the congregation by "young men," who "followed with silver flagons containing water." She noticed the "shrill screams" of babies and the fact that the preacher broke off his discourse in order to partake. The overall impression was decidedly negative, but at least Miss Faithful recognized the importance of her own frame of reference: "As an Episcopalian, I must certainly say that the administration of the Holy Communion on the Sunday afternoon I attended the service there struck me as most painfully, though doubtless it was unintentionally, irreverent."[52]

A few years later Alexandra Gripenberg noticed the table covered with a white cloth, the nine men who broke the bread, the young men dressed in black who distributed the bread in baskets, and the water in "small glass jars." The young gentlemen she saw as discharging their duties "quite frivolously, for they seemed to have plenty of time for small, pleasant flirtations with the younger and prettier communicants of the opposite sex." She heard two sermons, one of which seemed quite "Unitarian," containing "only sound and humane morality." The other "breathed more of pure Mormonism."[53]

These different descriptions by non-Mormon travelers often appear superficial, but much of what they say can be amply documented from the minutes and diaries of Mormons. There does seem to be agreement that the audiences were varied, including some children, that there was a tendency toward noise and lack of reverence, and that the sermons, even at best, tended to ramble and to be delivered in an informal, colloquial style.

Many Mormons would agree with the basic description and would deplore the lapses in quality and lack of reverence. But some of what offended their visitors derived from a different conception of the aims of the meeting. With respect to preaching it was a long-standing tradition in Mormonism that the Spirit of God was the essential ingredient; this meant in practice that carefully written and delivered homilies were not likely to be well received. If given sincerely, as the Spirit directed, a sermon could benefit the congregation even if it failed to measure up to the homiletic standards of the seminaries. Not that the speakers were entitled to say nothing. In 1860 Brigham Young said:

When the preaching is very dry, the Bowery is generally thinly attended; but when the preaching is full of marrow and good things, the Bowery will be full of people. This reminds me of an anecdote. A Presbyterian priest invited an Indian preacher to occupy his pulpit; and when the Indian was through preaching, the priest asked him why the people kept awake during his preaching, remarking that they invariably fell asleep while he was preaching. "I will tell you," said the Indian: "you feed them with a silver dish and silver spoon; you rap the dish with the spoon, and the ringing sounds put the people to sleep. But the Indian takes his wooden bowl and ladle, and lades out the rich, nourishing succotash to the people, which makes them wide awake, and they want a little more."[54]

It seems safe to say that large quantities of "succotash" were dispensed in Mormon meetings. For those participating it was not a highly structured, liturgical experience but rather an assembly for fellowship, entertainment, instruction, and renewal of inspiration and determination. Judged in these terms, the Mormon sacrament services, even with their deficiencies, were not altogether failures.

Since visitors often attended only a single service, usually in the Bowery or the Tabernacle, their view of the Mormon pattern of worship was quite incomplete. For one thing, there were other meetings besides sacrament meetings, each with slightly different emphasis or purposes as well as some overlapping: priesthood quorum meetings (usually held on week nights), Sunday Schools (from about 1850), primaries for children (from 1878), and others.

Three kinds of meetings offered a worship experience of genuine profundity. First, the fast and testimony meeting—held on the first Thursday night of each month from its beginning in Kirtland to 1896, and thereafter on the first Sunday—offered possibilities, in a setting of gratitude and rededication, for intense spiritual experiences. Somewhat akin to Quaker meetings in their personal testifying or to Pentecostal meetings in their occasional manifestations of glossolalia, the Mormon testimony meeting served an obvious purpose and for many was unquestionably a religious occasion of high value.

Second, there were in Utah, if not even to some extent in Nauvoo, "circles" of adult Saints who gathered every few weeks. The history of these groups, somewhat outside of the main, formal pattern of the Church, remains to be written but it is clear enough that they included prayers and were a source of mutual spiritual reinforcement.

Finally, there were the temples. Some of the more acute observers recognized that they were in fact the setting for the most exalted Mormon worship experience. Others were condescending toward the whole temple idea, including the various ordinances performed there; these were described in considerable detail by a half-dozen Gentile writers before the century was over, seldom with total accuracy, usually with an attitude of cynical ridicule. The temples were not, in fact, places of public assembly. They were entered only by Saints who had obtained a "recommend" certifying their worthiness. The ordinances performed there included baptism for the dead, endowments, marriage for time and eternity, and sealings. In the endowment a highly structured, almost liturgical sequence gave instruction in basic gospel principles and required the taking of specific covenants and obligations. The temple ordinances undoubtedly provided rich spiritual experiences for thousands of Saints in the past century, some of whom might well have agreed with these more recent words from a former Protestant minister who converted to Mormonism: "Latter-day Saint worship reaches its highest fulfillment in doing temple work. . . . Nowhere has the writer been more aware of God, felt a more penetrating sorrow for his sins, received greater inspiration to restructure his life, and been able to render a more unselfish service than in the temple of the Lord. . . . Those who have no knowledge of the temple endowments cannot realize the joy and blessing available in this unique experience."[55] Mormon worship had its problems: lack of reverence, low attendance, inferior sermons and music. But for many it also had its depths.

Many facets of Mormon life have had to be omitted from this brief survey: immigration, encounters with Indians, the development of schools, music, art, journalism, book publication, and many others. Within Mormon life, however simple it might appear in broad outline, there were very diverse experiences. Quite aside from the chronological developments over several decades, there were geographical differences: Mormons who never emigrated, special colonies such as the Hawaiians at Iosepa, settlers at Mesquite or Bunkerville or Bluff who were far from "civilization," as well as those at Salt Lake City who moved in the upper circles of the hierarchy, and so on. Even within the same setting individuals could react differently.

With all of these obvious limitations, the present study has given some idea of what life was like for Mormons before 1900. They ate, wore clothes, built houses, married, had children, worshiped, worked, played, got sick, and died. In many respects they were much like other Americans of the same period, whether native-born or immigrants in the process of becoming Americanized. But in their own eyes—and of course in the eyes of their detractors—Mormons were Americans with a difference. This was true not only in the theological sense. In one after another of the activities of life there was rhythm or tone to the Mormon lifestyle, sometimes slight, sometimes more noticeable, that enhanced their sense of being a "peculiar" people.

It was not always easy to maintain this sense of separateness, of being a people with a special mission, set apart from the world. In 1870 Eliza R. Snow, speaking to the women of the newly formed Retrenchment Association, said, "If the angels were to come in our midst, how would they be able to distinguish us from the Gentiles? We dress the same, and too often act the same."[56] This in essence was the problem that would increasingly plague the Saints as they moved into the twentieth century—how to be in the world but not of the world.

Notes

An earlier version of this chapter appeared in *The Restoration Movement: Essays in Mormon History* (Lawrence, Kans.: Coronado Press, 1973), 273–306.

1. Maureen Whipple, *The Giant Joshua* (Boston: Houghton Mifflin, 1941), preface.

2. The rural orientation of American towns is suggested by census figures indicating a number of "farmers" and by indication of horses and cattle kept in the towns. City directories of the past century provide some of these glimpses.

3. On some aspects of the gathering, see William Mulder, *Homeward to Zion: The Mormon Migration from Scandinavia* (Minneapolis: University of Minnesota Press, 1957); and Philip A. M. Taylor, *Expectations Westward: The Mormons and the Emigration of Their British Converts in the Nineteenth Century* (Edinburgh and London: Oliver and Boyd, 1965).

4. See Davis Bitton, "Kirtland as a Center of Missionary Activity, 1830–1838," *BYU Studies* 11 (Summer 1971): 497–516.

5. Examples of what is meant to be called to help establish a new settlement are Andrew Karl Larson, *I Was Called to Dixie* (Salt Lake City: Deseret News Press, 1961); David E. Miller, *Hole-in-the-Rock: An Epic in the Colonization of the Great American West* (Salt Lake City: University of Utah Press, 1966); and Charles S. Peterson, *Take Up Your Mission: Mormon Colonizing along the Little Colorado River, 1870–1900* (Tucson: University of Arizona Press, 1993).

6. Lorenzo Hill Hatch, Diaries, Historical Department of the Church of Jesus Christ of Latter-day Saints (hereinafter cited as HDC). Unless otherwise noted, all diaries and journals mentioned in the text are in the HDC.

7. *Journal of Discourses*, 26 vols. (London: Latter-day Saints Book Depot, 1854–86), 3:65–66.

8. Charles W. Nibley, *Reminiscences*, as quoted in Joel E. Ricks and Everett L. Cooley, eds., *The History of a Valley: Cache Valley* (Logan, 1956), 47.

9. Austin E. Fife, "Stone Houses of Northern Utah," *Utah Historical Quarterly* 40 (Winter 1972): 19.

10. See Paul Goeldner, *Utah Catalog: Historic American Buildings Survey* (Salt Lake City: Utah Heritage Foundation, 1969).

11. Joseph Smith, *History of the Church of Jesus Christ of Latter-day Saints*, 7 vols., 2d ed. rev. (Salt Lake City, 1948), 2:482, 3:15.

12. Leonard J. Arrington, "An Economic Interpretation of 'The Word of Wisdom,'" *BYU Studies* 1 (Winter 1959): 37–49.

13. *Journal of Discourses* 2:269–70.

14. See "Pioneer Courtships," *Heart Throbs of the West*, 12 vols. (Salt Lake City: Daughters of Utah Pioneers, 1939–51), 2:429–32.

15. Stanley S. Ivins, "Notes on Mormon Polygamy," *Western Humanities Review* 10 (Summer 1956); reprinted in *Utah Historical Quarterly* 35 (Fall 1967): 313.

16. Ibid., 318–19.

17. Daniel Wood, Journals, vol. 3, Church Archives, Salt Lake City.

18. Joseph Smith, *History of the Church* 4:414.

19. Priddy Meeks, "Journal," *Utah Historical Quarterly* 10 (1942): 145–223.

20. Ibid.

21. Juanita Brooks, "Mariah Huntsman Leavitt: Midwife of the Desert Frontier," in Austin Fife, Alta Fife, and H. H. Glassie, eds., *Forms upon the Frontier* (Logan: Utah State University Press, 1969); Claire Noall, "Mormon Midwives," *Utah Historical Quarterly* 10 (1942): 84–144; and Claire Noall, "Superstitions, Customs, and Prescriptions of Mormon Midwives," *California Folklore Quarterly* 3 (1944): 102–14.

22. As quoted in Robert E. Reese and George E. Osborne, "Early Utah Materia Medica: Priddy Meeks," *American Journal of Pharmaceutical Education* (July 1954): 401–9.

23. See Ray R. Canning, "Mormon Return-from-the-Dead Stories," *Proceedings of the Utah Academy* 42 (1965): 29–37; J. H. Adamson, "Tales of the Supernatural," in Thomas E. Cheney, ed., *Lore of Faith and Folly* (Salt Lake City: University of Utah Press, 1971), 251–60.

24. Andrew Love Journal, 1853, Church Archives, Salt Lake City.

25. George S. Tanner and J. Morris Richards, *Colonization on the Little Colorado* (Flagstaff, Ariz.: Northland Press, 1977).

26. See Nels Anderson, *Desert Saints: The Mormon Frontier in Utah* (Chicago: University of Chicago Press, 1942) for interesting references to material from the ecclesiastical courts.

27. *Journal of Discourses* 13:142.

28. Ralph T. Richards, *Of Medicine, Hospitals, and Doctors* (Salt Lake City: University of Utah Press, 1953).

29. Ricks and Cooley, eds., *History of a Valley*, 414–15.

30. Larson, *I Was Called to Dixie*, 426–63.

31. As quoted in ibid., 461.

32. George D. Pyper, *The Romance of an Old Playhouse,* rev. ed. (Salt Lake City: Deseret News Press, 1937).

33. Burnett Ferguson, "History of Drama in Provo, 1853–1897" (M.A. thesis, Brigham Young University, 1952).

34. *Diary of Charles Lowell Walker,* ed. A. Karl Larson and Katharine Miles Larson, 2 vols. (Logan: Utah State University Press, 1980), 1:248, 375.

35. A debating society, which cannot have been very large, existed at Commerce, Illinois, as early as 1836. Letter of Daniel H. Wells, dated 12 March 1836.

36. See "Men's and Women's Societies, Clubs and Associations," *Heart Throbs of the West* 11:209–52.

37. Ricks and Cooley, eds., *History of a Valley,* 299–300.

38. Letter of Daniel H. Wells, dated 13 March 1836, HDC.

39. The glaring deficiencies of Utah schools in the 1870s and 1880s are clearly set forth in the biennial reports of the Territorial Superintendent of Common Schools.

40. Klaus J. Hansen, *Quest for Empire: The Political Kingdom of God and the Council of Fifty in Mormon History* (East Lansing: Michigan State University Press, 1967), chaps. 1–2.

41. Boyd L. Eddins, "The Mormons and the Civil War" (M.S. thesis, Utah State University, 1966).

42. Smith, *History of the Church* 5:324. A comparison of other passages on the same subject is found in Richard Lloyd Anderson, "Joseph Smith and the Millenarian Time Table," *BYU Studies* 3 (1961): 55–56.

43. *Diary of Charles Lowell Walker,* ed. Larson and Larson, 776–77.

44. Brigham Young to Alfales Young, 2 September 1875, Brigham Young Letterbooks, HDC.

45. As quoted in William Mulder and A. Russell Mortensen, *Among the Mormons* (New York: Alfred A. Knopf, 1967), 129.

46. *The Record of Norton Jacob* (Salt Lake City: Norton Jacob Family Association, 1949).

47. Mulder and Mortensen, *Among the Mormons,* 280.

48. Richard F. Burton, *The City of the Saints and Across the Rocky Mountains to California* (New York: Alfred A. Knopf, 1963), 290. Burton's book was first published in 1861.

49. Archer Butler Hulbert, ed., *Letters of an Overland Mail Agent in Utah* (Worcester, Mass.: American Antiquarian Society, 1929), 32–41.

50. W. F. Rae, *Westward by Rail: The New Route to the East* (New York, 1871), 106–7, 123–24.

51. Elizabeth Wood Kane, *Twelve Mormon Homes* (Salt Lake City: Tanner Trust Fund, University of Utah Library, 1974), 43.

52. Emily Faithful, *Three Visits to America* (New York, 1884), 171–80.

53. Alexandra Gripenberg, *A Half Year in the New World: Miscellaneous Sketches of Travel in the United States*, trans. and ed. Ernest J. Moyne (Newark: University of Delaware Press, 1954), 175–87.

54. *Journal of Discourses* 8:144.

55. John Franklin Heidenreich, "An Analysis of the Theory and Practice of Worship in the Church of Jesus Christ of Latter-day Saints" (M.R.E. thesis, Brigham Young University, 1963), 195–96.

56. Susa Young Gates, *History of the Young Ladies' Mutual Improvement Association* (Salt Lake City: Deseret News Press, 1911), 34–35.

2

Polygamy Defended: One Side
of a Nineteenth-Century Polemic

POLYGAMY (or polygyny or plural marriage) was introduced privately among a few Mormons before the death of Joseph Smith in 1844, but it was not publicly acknowledged until 1852.[1] Thus it was during the Utah Territorial period that the issue really came onto the public stage, especially after the Morrill Act of 1862, the first national legislation forbidding the practice in the territories. For nearly four decades the Mormons' plural marriage system—which at times may have included some 25 percent of their families[2]—was the object of a national campaign of denunciation. Although it was not the only practice that aroused opposition to the Latter-day Saints, it served as a moral question with which to attack this curious group in the West.[3] In 1890 the Church officially renounced the practice by a manifesto of President Wilford Woodruff. The practice rapidly dwindled among the Mormons until today anyone found guilty of advocating or practicing plural marriage is excommunicated.

In the sense that it had virtually no genuine defenders except the Mormons themselves, it may seem that little could be said in its favor. But the Mormons did offer a defense of their system. Through friends in Congress and the courts they fought on legal and political grounds. They carried their arguments to the public platform in newspapers, pamphlets, legal briefs, poetry, song, and sermons. On several occasions large assemblies of Mormon women—as in the "indignation meetings" of the 1870s and 1880s—gave speech after speech in defense of their virtue and honor against what they saw as the self-righteous attacks of their opponents.[4] "The Tabernacle in winter and the Bowery in summer," said T. B. H. Stenhouse, resounded "with arguments in favor of polygamy."[5]

An examination of these arguments in defense of Mormon polygamy tells much not only about the Mormon values but also, as we shall see, about the mindset of nineteenth-century America.

Here are the main arguments advanced in defense of Mormon polygamy between 1852 and 1890:[6]

1. *There was nothing inherently evil about polygamy; prejudice against it was the result of tradition.* The fact that the Christian nations constituted a minority of the world's population was asserted to break down the assumption that monogamy was inevitable or obviously superior. The influence of tradition in inculcating world values contradictory to the higher standard of the restored gospel was a recurring theme in Mormon sermons.[7]

2. *Plural marriage was the simplest, most realistic way of providing fulfillment of man's natural instincts within proper bounds.* Sometimes the Mormon leaders made interesting claims for the rejuvenating effects of plurality, as, for example, Heber C. Kimball, who said: "I would not be afraid to promise a man who is sixty years of age, if he will take the counsel of brother Brigham and his brethren, that he will renew his age. I have noticed that a man who has but one wife, and is inclined to that doctrine, soon begins to wither and dry up, while a man who goes into plurality looks fresh, young, and sprightly. . . . For a man of God to be confined to one woman is small business."[8] A more interesting elaboration was based on man's sexual propensities. In the papers of George Q. Cannon there is a memorandum that compares the principles of "amativeness" (what we would call the sex drive) to the appetite for food and sleep, noting that there are individual differences among people:

> The principle is stronger in man than in woman, and sometimes when there is an excess of this passion it becomes almost uncontrollable and leads in many instances to those disgraceful and indecent developments that are so common among mankind . . . as it is not a crime in any man to possess this exuberance and unnatural desire for sexual association God provided a system of polygamy that where this excess prevailed it might be met on a legitimate principle, and thus while the demands of nature might be met, decency and propriety might be exhibited in all the relations of life.[9]

Although modern sexologists would certainly regard this view of male-female differences as oversimplified, to see the sexual drive as natural and healthy was in some ways quite advanced for the time.

3. *Plural marriage was a practical, honorable means of providing marriage and motherhood for thousands of deserving women who would otherwise be condemned to a life of spinsterhood.* Occasionally

it was said (and continues to be repeated to the present) that there was a surplus of women in territorial Utah. Actually, the most reliable census data indicate no preponderance of females in early Utah although it did lack the large surplus of males typical of the frontier. What the Mormon writers said can be summarized as follows: (a) the number of males and females must be approximately equal at birth; (b) a certain number of males were killed in war; (c) a certain number of males (more than the few females in the same category) chose not to marry; (d) males were more given to vice and worldliness than were females.[10] Even if the adult population seemed to be divided approximately 50–50, therefore, the number of worthy, marriageable females exceeded the number of worthy, marrying males. The solution seemed obvious. As Orson Spencer asked, "How many virtuous females would [not] infinitely prefer to unite their destinies to one and the same honorable, virtuous, and high-minded man than to separate their destinies each to an inferior, unvirtuous, and vicious man."[11] The Mormon leaders saw plurality as a natural, honorable solution to spinsterhood. Incidentally, to reconcile oneself to an unmarried existence, not easy for anyone in the nineteenth century, was doubly hard for the Mormons, who saw marriage as essential to salvation in the highest heaven.[12]

4. *Plural marriage was an excellent means of improving the race, a program of practical eugenics.* This was mainly a counter-argument, attempting to answer those who claimed to see polygamous children as suffering physical and mental handicaps. Such charges ranged from Horace Greeley's claim that the average "phrenological development" of Mormon children was bad to supposedly scientific studies near the end of the century.[13] The Mormons contended that the superior attributes of the polygamous males (superior by reason of the qualifications they had to possess) would redound to the benefit of the offspring.[14]

5. *Plural marriage led to larger families.* Nineteenth-century Mormons were conscious of no population explosion. What they were acutely aware of was the need to people a wide, empty land and to increase geometrically so as to raise up a real Kingdom in the tops of the mountains. The polygamous family was described with terms such as "expansive," "generous," "natural," "vigorous," while the monogamous family of one child or two children was deprecated as "narrow," "constricted," "restricted," "pinched," and "selfish." In this spirit George A. Smith could proclaim: "We breathe free air, we have the best looking men and the handsomest women, and if they envy us our position, well

they may, for they are a poor, narrow-minded, pinch-backed race of men, who chain themselves down to the law of monogamy."[15] If William Appleman Williams is right about the prominence of the vocabulary of expansion in nineteenth-century America, then the Mormons were in tune with the spirit of their times in ways they could not recognize.[16]

6. *Plural marriage harmed no one.* In this respect it was unlike suttee and thuggism, with which it was frequently compared. "In the name of common sense," asked George Q. Cannon, "what possible analogy can there be between the destruction of life and the solemnization of marriage, between practices which extinguish life and an ordinance which prepared the way for life to be kindled and perpetuated?" Cannon did not deny the right of the government to outlaw acts that were *mala in se,* as, for example, human sacrifice. But because human sacrifice is wrong, he asked, "does it necessarily follow that human propagation is wrong?" Likewise, the crime of bigamy and polygamy as practiced in oriental countries was radically different from the "patriarchal marriage of the Latter-day Saints":

> The crime of bigamy, as usually committed, is a wrong of the most grave and damning character. A man marries a woman; he afterwards deserts her and marries another. From the first woman he conceals his intention to marry again. From the second he conceals the fact that he already has a wife. Both are wronged, both are deceived, and society is outraged. Such a man is a base wretch. He imposes upon female innocence, breaks the hearts and destroys the happiness of his victims, and inflicts upon them cruel and in many cases, irreparable wrongs. Such a man deserves punishment.
>
> But this is not the patriarchal marriage of the Latter-day Saints. There is not a single point of similarity between them, except that the ceremony of marriage is observed in both cases. In every other feature they are as far apart as the antipodes.[17]

The national legislators and judges were assuming what needed to be proved, namely, that polygamy as practiced by the Mormons was in fact an evil. Who was wronged by the practice, the Mormons wanted to know? It was entered into knowingly by consenting adults. The woman was free to get a divorce or separation at any time. As for the fear that polygamy was sweeping the nation and thus would undermine the entire national marriage system, the Mormons maintained simply that they were practicing it off by themselves, that they did not wish to force the practice on anyone else, that the divine authorization was given to them and doubtless would not even be claimed by any other group, and, in more practical terms, that there were not enough women for the system to spread far under any circumstances.[18]

7. *Plural marriage was an alternative to prostitution and other social evils.* Weary of being lectured on their morals, the Mormons lashed back at the system of monogamy and what they saw as its attendant evils. The most basic "social evil" was prostitution. As Heber C. Kimball describes the problem, "The cities of Christendom are crowded with prostitution; their young men are destroyed in the dawn of their days by the terrible crime of prostitution. How shall these fearful evils be cured? Has there been sufficient wisdom found among men to do it? No; they have confessed their utter inability to cope with it. It is overwhelming them and sweeping them off like a flood throughout the length and breadth of the land, until physicians say that half the diseases that prevail among mankind in Christendom are directly traceable to this devouring evil."[19]

Up to a point the Mormons were simply and understandably carrying the attack to their opponents, hoping to puncture some of the pompous moralizing of the crusaders. It was the "men who live in glass houses" response. In describing the whoredoms and abominations of the civilized world, the Mormon preachers spared no details before their horrified congregations. The system of monogamy, it appeared, had created one huge iniquitous cesspool of filth and corruption.[20] Occasionally the Mormon leaders went one step further to argue that polygamy was the only ultimate cure for the social evils.[21]

8. *Plural marriage was part of Mormon religious belief.* Throughout the period the Mormons insisted on the religious basis of their system of plural marriage. That it was part of their religion could be demonstrated in relation to the Bible, Mormon cosmology, and modern revelation. We are of course separating out for purposes of discussion ideas that were seldom so clearly differentiated in the original statements, where the arguments tumbled over each other pell-mell.

a. *Polygamy was sanctioned by the Bible.* In essence the Mormon speakers and writers argued that plural marriage as practiced by the Old Testament patriarchs had the approbation of God. When it came to the New Testament they had a harder time, for the ammunition was scarce. One example of a passage around which arguments could continue was St. Paul's injunction to Timothy

that a bishop should be "the husband of one wife." Whereas Rev.
Newman and others considered this to mean that a bishop should
be the husband of *no more than* one wife, the Mormon pamphle-
teers and preachers insisted that it was simply a rejection of celi-
bacy and meant that a bishop should be the husband of *at least*
one wife. Actually, the Mormons did not typically claim the Bible
as the sole basis for their practice but simply maintained that it
presented no obstacle.[22]

b. *Plural marriage was authorized by a divine revelation to
Joseph Smith.* It is significant that when plural marriage was first
publicly acknowledged, in 1852, the revelation on celestial marriage was carefully read and published. Such an authorization was
necessary if for no other reason than the fact that the Book of
Mormon itself contained what appeared to be a condemnation of
polygamy: "Wherefore, my brethren, hear me, and hearken to the
word of the Lord: For there shall not any man among you have save
it be one wife; and concubines he shall have none; . . . For if I will,
saith the Lord of Hosts, raise up seed unto me, I will command my
people; otherwise they shall hearken unto these things." The last
clause, as it turned out, provided the necessary loophole by imply-
ing that there might be circumstances under which more than one
wife would be allowed if specifically commanded.[23] The claim of
a special modern revelation was not likely to influence congressmen or judges or the Protestant clergy. However, it was particularly important within the Mormon population. It is significant
that the rise of the Reorganized Church of Jesus Christ of Latter
Day Saints coincided with the outbreak of antipolygamy legislation after the Civil War and the active prosecution of the 1880s.
Not the least of the threats posed by the Reorganized Church
was its claim that the revelation on Celestial Marriage was an invention of Brigham Young. The repeated testimonies of the Utah
leaders regarding the origin of the practice during Smith's lifetime, strengthened by the firsthand testimony of women who had
been Smith's wives, must be understood in this context.[24]

c. *Plural marriage was consistent with if not implied by Mormon theology.* It would not have been sufficient to bring forth a
simple command as authorization of the plural marriage system.
It had to be seen in relation to God and humans and their eternal
relationship. Mormon theology did in fact provide such a support,

although it must have seemed far-fetched to even sympathetic
Gentile observers. Mormons believed that the spirits of human
beings exist with God prior to their birth into mortality, that a
given number of such spirits have been designated to undergo a
mortal probation, that it is the privilege and responsibility of the
Saints to provide earthly tabernacles for as many of these spirits
as possible, that salvation in the Celestial Kingdom is impossible
to a single person, that family interconnections and offspring are
important to present happiness and as an initial phase of eternal
life, that marriage and family relationships can be eternal, continuing beyond the grave, and that the highest level of salvation
in the hereafter is an active, continuing progress, creating and
peopling worlds, as God has done here.[25] To those accepting such
a congeries of beliefs, polygamy might have seemed natural.

Why, if there were sound practical and naturalistic reasons for the
system, were the Mormons so anxious to establish the religious basis of
plural marriage? First, only by constantly reminding themselves of the
divine sanction could they overcome their own inherited bias against
such a system. Second, insisting upon the religious motives enabled
them to resist the portrayals of themselves as rakes and debauchees.
George Q. Cannon, who as delegate to Congress felt particularly sensitive about the leers, the knowing winks, and open allegations, said in
1881: "Why should I stand here and be assailed, abused, and denounced
as I have for lechery, because of marrying wives? Was it necessary that
wives should be taken to gratify sensuality? I have no need to take any
wife to accomplish that. I have no need to take to myself the burden and
responsibility of a family for that purpose."[26] Third, it was as a religious
practice that the Mormons thought polygamy stood the best chance of
escaping legislative and judicial sanctions.

Opponents of the system were not comfortable with the idea of opposing religious belief and practices and tried to make a distinction.
Here, for example, is vice-president Schuyler Colfax: "I do not concede
that the institution you have established here, and which is condemned
by law, is a question of religion." To which Apostle John Taylor gave a
decisive answer:

> Now, with all due deference, I do think that if Mr. Colfax had
> carefully examined our religious faith he would have arrived at

other conclusions. In the absence of this I might ask, who constituted Mr. Colfax a judge of my religious faith? . . .

Mr. Colfax has a perfect right to state and feel that he does
not believe in the revelation on which my religious faith is based,
nor in my faith at all; but has he the right to *dictate* my religious
faith? I think not; he does not consider it religion, but [it] is nevertheless mine.[27]

In the crucial Reynolds decision (1879) the Supreme Court did not deny
that plural marriage was part of the Mormon religion but maintained
that, even so, society had a right to forbid such antisocial practices.
The decision did not silence the Mormons, who continued to insist
that plural marriage, for them, was due not to lust or whim but to a
solemn religious obligation.[28] Obviously they also denied its negative
social consequences when properly practiced.

We have not considered here the legal and constitutional bases by
which the Mormons sought to defend their peculiar institution. These
were not really arguments *for* polygamy but were rather claims that,
whether otherwise defensible or not, polygamy was beyond the reach of
constitutional laws. The Mormons were sure of their constitutional im-
pregnability on two grounds: first, as just indicated, they insisted that
with them plural marriage was a religious practice and was therefore
protected by the First Amendment; second, following the "popular sovereignty" doctrine, they considered marriage to be beyond the jurisdiction of the national Congress.[29] The Reynolds decision of 1879 struck
down both of these constitutional defenses. (Ironically, a more recent
decision seems to reverse the 1879 Reynolds decision, at least in part,
but by now the Mormons have no interest in restoring polygamy.)[30]

It will have been recognized that the Mormon defense of polygamy
was similar in many respects to the defense of slavery as expounded by
southerners during the generation leading up to the Civil War.[31] Both
Mormons and southerners appealed to the idea of popular sovereignty. If
the southern spokesmen did not attempt to claim slavery as part of their
religion, they did construct an elaborate biblical justification and did
attempt to show its consistency with Christian morality. The southern
assertion that the Negro was by nature servile and in need of paternal-
istic protection is in some ways comparable to the Mormon belief that
a husband was necessary to protect women from spinsterhood, sexual

exploitation as prostitutes, or the sorrow of being consigned to life with a callous, inferior, brutish man. Both the defenders of slavery and the defenders of polygamy argued that certain practical considerations justified their systems. The condition of the labor market, the kind of labor that needed to be performed, and the necessity of the plantation system to the southern economy were said to require slavery as a labor system. For the Mormons it was the surplus of females that required polygamy. When considering the "fruits" or results of their system, both called attention to presumed improvements and benefits. Negroes were said to be better off than they had been in their savage state in that they were provided with the necessities of life, the benefits of Christian religion, and at least some education. The children of plural marriages were said to be healthier, stronger, and of course more numerous than those of artificially constricted monogamous families.

Both groups looked upon their practice as their own business, a custom of their own home area. As they were not attempting to force their custom on others, they did not need "outside agitators" to tell them what to do. And both the southerners and the Mormons, disgusted with what they considered the hypocrisy of their critics, launched a counterattack against the corrupt institutions of the Northeast. The evils of capitalism and its "wage slavery" were denounced by the defenders of slavery, just as the deterioration of family life, infanticide, and prostitution were grist for the mills of the Mormon spokesmen.

Such parallels are not surprising. Recognizing important differences between polygamy and slavery, one is struck by repeated similarities in the two situations. Both peculiar institutions affronted the moral sensibilities of the great majority of American people, both were associated with more primitive or non-Western societies, and both were practiced in an isolated region of the country that made it possible to think in terms of "we" and "they." Both presented the same constitutional dilemma.[32] Both were exacerbated by travelers' accounts, results of brief, inadequate visits, often with opinion already firmly established; and by the harrowing testimony of escaped "victims," slaves or wives, whose lurid stories were not meant to provide a sympathetic or objective picture. The flames of passion in both cases were fanned by organizations and vested interests who planted informants, helped escapees, organized lecture tours, and helped to write and publish denunciatory pamphlets and tear-jerking novels.

One of the most significant characteristics of the polygamy controversy as well as the conflict over slavery is what Richard Hofstadter called the "paranoid style."[33] Those living in such a frame of reference saw a world of black and white, good versus evil, with no possible compromise and little if any concession to the motives of the opponents, who were seen as the embodiment of evil engaged in a sinister conspiracy. It was a doom-shaped world, to use Harry Overstreet's phrase, in which a giant, apocalyptic conflagration was anticipated, a kind of Armageddon that would find the forces of good pitted against the forces of evil.[34]

The paranoid tendencies in the attacks on Mormon polygamy are unmistakable in a sermon delivered in 1880 by the Reverend T. De Witt Talmage. After denouncing Mormonism as "an organized filth built on polygamy," Talmage went on to say:

> I tell you Mormonism is one great surge of licentiousness; it is the seraglio of the Republic, it is the concentrated corruption of this land, it is the brothel of the nation, it is hell enthroned.
>
> This miserable corpse of Mormonism has been rotting in the sun, and rotting and rotting for forty years, and the United States Government has not had the courage to bury it.
>
> . . . I tell you that Mormonism will never be destroyed until it is destroyed by the guns of the United States Government. . . . What grave [is] deep enough for this stout, thousand-armed, thousand-footed, thousand-headed, thousand-horned, thousand-fanged corpse? . . .
>
> Oh! good people of the United States, . . . I will have to tell you that, unless we destroy Mormonism, Mormonism will destroy us.[35]

Or consider the diatribe of Judge Cradelbaugh, who had unpleasant experiences in Utah as territorial judge following the Utah War: "I have said that their doctrines were repulsive to every refined mind. Every other false faith which has resigned its evil time upon this goodly world of ours has had some kindly and redeeming features. . . . It was reserved for Mormonism, far off in the bosom of our beloved land, to rear its head, naked in all its hideous deformity, and unblushingly, yes, definitely, proclaim a creed without the least redeeming feature."[36]

No redeeming virtues; totally evil; destroy it before it destroys us— this was not the language of friendly communication and was not calculated to stimulate a spirit of mutual trust. There is the assumption in such statements, sometimes implicit and sometimes explicit, that the time was short, that unless something was done quickly a national catastrophe was unavoidable.

What must also be recognized (and has not, I think, always been noticed by students of anti-Masonry and anti-Catholicism) is that the defenders could be equally absolutist, paranoid and apocalyptic, equally unable to think in terms of compromise, equally unable to see anything but evil and hypocrisy in their critics. When vice-president Schuyler Colfax ventured to defend the morality of the great majority of Americans, he left a perfect opening for the Mormon apostle John Taylor to make a concession in the interest of fairness.

But Taylor insisted that social crimes "run riot in the land, a withering cursing blight."[37] Similarly, Eliza R. Snow, when she heard polygamy described as an "ulcer," responded in kind:

> How preposterous the hue and cry of this adulterous generation about purifying Utah. The purity of the latter-day Saints is what our persecutors fear. Were the Mormons a people of whoredoms—were plural marriage an institution of debauchery—were the Mormon women prostitutes, there would be no trouble—no "loathsome ulcer" to eradicate. Were plural marriage a corrupt institution, those now most blatant against it would hail with delight and hold it in fond fellowship. . . . Their hellish warfare is entirely aimed against sexual purity—to so clear the way that unbridled adultery with its attendant evils may ride rampant and unrestrained on the pampered steed of popularity.[38]

Refusing to bow to the decisions of the Supreme Court, the Mormons saw themselves as the Saints of God persecuted by the wicked world. Duplicating an attitude toward the past found in earlier radical literalists, they saw themselves as the true defenders of the Constitution. In this spirit polygamists sentenced to a term in the territorial penitentiary were hailed as the true defenders of constitutional rights, as prisoners "for conscience' sake."

There was a constantly reiterated refrain contrasting the ways of Zion and those of the world. A characteristic statement, one example among many, was the following by Mormon Apostle Parley P. Pratt: "Let the monogamic law, restricting a man to one wife, with all of its attendant train of whoredoms, intrigues, seductions, wretched and lonely single life, hatred, envy, jealousy, infanticide, illegitimacy, disease and death, like the millstone cast into the depths of the sea—sink with Great Babylon to rise no more."[39]

The Mormon position, when reduced to its barest essentials, was that plural marriage was commanded by God. God was more powerful than human legislators and judges; he would overrule the government decisions for good. There seem to have been two or three ways in which different Mormons expected this divine "overruling" to occur. It was pointed out by some that the continued litigation, the debates in Congress, and the antipolygamy crusades organized by protestant clergy and other reformers all helped to disseminate knowledge of Mormonism. It was a kind of free publicity that, some said, would leave the world without excuse for rejecting the message of the Restored gospel.[40] Others were thinking more in terms of a reversal of the Supreme Court's unfair decision and perhaps the rise of a Mormon to national political power. In either case the Mormon Elders would then be seen to be the true defenders of the Constitution.[41] Finally, there is no doubt that some Mormons expected divine intervention in the sign of a Second Coming of Christ. Such an apocalyptic solution must have seemed the only way out as prosecutions continued unabated and as efforts to salvage part of the system failed.[42]

The Mormon defense of polygamy was blasted by the Manifesto of 1890 and the antipolygamy plank of the first state constitution. In many respects Mormonism now began a series of accommodations with national economic, political, and social norms. The expectation of an impending apocalypse faded away. The Church at first continued to defend polygamy in theory while recognizing that it could not be practiced. Then even the theoretical advantages gradually faded from view. The pro-polygamy argument is as unknown to modern Mormons as to anyone else. The ideas reviewed in this essay seem to come from another age, another planet. They are from the "lost world" of Brigham Young and the other outspoken Mormon defenders. But if the present analysis is correct, both militant anti-Mormons and Mormon apologists shared a common mindset, which saw the world as the scene of a Manichean struggle between light and darkness.

Notes

1. The best summary of the religious doctrine of plural marriage is Richard D. Poll, "The Twin Relic: A Study of Mormon Polygamy and the

Campaign by the Government of the United States for its Abolition, 1852–1890" (M.A. thesis, Texas Christian University, 1939), chap. 2. See also Kimball Young, *Isn't One Wife Enough?: The Story of Mormon Polygamy* (New York: Henry Holt, 1954), chap. 2; and Hubert Howe Bancroft, *History of Utah* (San Francisco, 1889), 338–95. One of the best monographs on the subject is Lawrence Foster, *Religion and Sexuality: Three American Communal Experiments of the Nineteenth Century* (New York: Oxford University Press, 1981; University of Illinois Press, 1984). An overview is Richard S. Van Wagoner, *Mormon Polygamy: A History*, 2d ed. (Salt Lake City: Signature Books, 1989).

2. Stanley S. Ivins, "Notes on Mormon Polygamy," *Western Humanities Review* 10 (Summer 1956): 229–39; Leonard J. Arrington and Davis Bitton, *The Mormon Experience: A History of the Latter-day Saints* (New York: Knopf, 1979), 199. For one estimate of the incidence of polygamy among the Mormons that ranges upward of 25 percent, see Larry M. Logue, *A Sermon in the Desert: Belief and Behavior in Early St. George, Utah* (Urbana: University of Illinois Press, 1988). The problem of such estimates is that there were differences from community to community and from year to year.

3. A good analysis of antipolygamy arguments is Charles A. Cannon, "The Awesome Power of Sex: The Polemical Campaign against Mormon Polygamy," *Pacific Historical Review* 43 (Feb. 1974): 61–82.

4. For example, a "great indignation meeting" held on 13 January 1870, is described in the *Latter-day Saints Millennial Star* 32 (1870): 132. An 1878 meeting is described in *"Mormon" Women on Plural Marriage: Fifteen Hundred "Mormon" Ladies Convene in the Salt Lake Theatre to Protest against the Misrepresentations of the Ladies Engaged in the Anti-polygamy Crusade* (Salt Lake City, 1878?).

5. T. B. H. Stenhouse, *Rocky Mountain Saints* (New York, 1873), 582.

6. These arguments are repeated endlessly in the sermons, pamphlets, and articles published by Mormon defenders in the second half of the nineteenth century. They are presented here in summary fashion in order that modern readers might readily see of what the Mormon defense consisted. For a more historical presentation, grounding the arguments in specific works, see David J. Whittaker, "Early Mormon Pamphleteering" (Ph.D. diss., Brigham Young University, 1982), esp. chap. 6. Whittaker cites the present essay in its typescript form; here I would be remiss if I failed to call attention to his important dissertation.

7. Condemnation of the prejudices and false traditions of the world are found especially in sermons by Brigham Young and Heber C. Kimball, as, for example, in *Journal of Discourses* 3:105; 8:243–52; 14:98. There was a potential cultural relativism in the denial of an intrinsic relationship be-

tween cultural traditions and eternal or natural morality, but seldom, if ever, was the idea carried to its logical conclusion.

8. *Journal of Discourses* 5:2. Amasa Lyman saw the physical benefits in terms of longevity. Average life expectancy, he said, was once that of a tree; now, thanks to the corruption of the seed, it was only about twenty-five years. Plural marriage was instituted "to check physical corruption and decline of our race" (*JD* 13:204).

9. Unsigned manuscript on more than a dozen pages of foolscap in the George Q. Cannon MSS., LDS Church Archives, Salt Lake City, Utah. Other discussions of man's natural drives for self-perpetuation are John Taylor, *On Marriage* (Salt Lake City, 1882), 1–8; Parley P. Pratt, *Marriage and Morals in Utah* (Liverpool, 1856), 2. Physical differences between men and women, with the woman's need for "certain periods of continence" contrasted with the man's lack of such a need, were set forth by Romania B. Penrose in 1881. B. H. Roberts, *Comprehensive History of the Church of Jesus Christ of Latter-day Saints*, 6 vols. (Salt Lake City, 1930), 5:299 (this work to be cited hereafter as Roberts, *CHC*). A remarkably frank statement of male-female differences is Belinda Marden Pratt, *Defence of Polygamy, By a Lady of Utah, In a Letter to Her Sister in New Hampshire* (Salt Lake City, 1854?).

10. Various assumptions and claims about the preponderance of females over males are found in Orson Spencer, *Patriarchal Order* (Liverpool, 1853); Parley P. Pratt, *Marriage and Morals*, 7–8; Amasa Lyman, in *JD* 11:208; George Q. Cannon, *A Review of the Decision of the Supreme Court of the United States in the Case of Geo. Reynolds vs. the United States* (Salt Lake City, 1879), 43; and Charles Carrington's foreword to *A Plea for Polygamy* (Paris, 1898). In 1882 George Q. Cannon said that in Utah Territory "the males outnumber the females; it [polygamy] cannot therefore be a practice without limit among us" (*JD* 24:46). One example emphasizing the superior character of women and the likelihood of having more women in the Church is the following: "Woman is naturally more virtuous, innocent, pure, and religiously disposed than man, for this reason, more women than men, will receive and obey the gospel in the last days, and be gathered out. . . . Therefore the Lord has revealed a law, whereby they can lawfully, honorably, and virtuously obey the great command, 'Be fruitful, and multiply, and replenish the earth.'" Jesse Haven, *Celestial Marriage, and the Plurality of Wives* (Cape Town, n.d.), 3.

11. Spencer, *Patriarchal Order*, 2.

12. Jill C. Mulvay, "Eliza R. Snow and the Woman Question," *BYU Studies* 16 (Winter 1976): 250–64.

13. Horace Greeley, *An Overland Journey from New York to San Francisco in the Summer of 1859* (New York, 1964; first published in 1860),

204. During the debate on the Edmunds Bill the claim was made that children of polygamous marriages were "neurotic and morons" (Poll, "Twin Relic," 218). See also "The Effects of Polygamy," *Anti-Polygamy Standard* 1 (Sept. 1880).

14. B. H. Roberts saw this as *the* purpose of plural marriage, namely, "to give to succeeding generations of a superior fatherhood and motherhood, by enlarging the opportunities of men of high character, moral integrity, and spiritual development to become in larger measure the progenitors of the race" (Roberts, *CHC* 5:295).

15. *JD* 3:291. See also *JD* 11:204, 207. One example of many Mormon claims of the phenomenal geometrical growth of their population due to large families is N. L. Nelson, "The Mormon Family," *The Mormon Point of View* 1 (Oct. 1904): 380–81. Heber C. Kimball speculated about his own posterity as follows: "A hundred years will not pass away before I will become millions of myself. You may go to work and reckon it up, and twenty-five years will not pass away before brother Brigham and I will number more than this whole territory . . . , which numbers more than seventy-five thousand. If twenty-five years will produce this amount of people, how much will be the increase in one hundred years? We could not number them" (*JD* 4:224). John Taylor saw the Gentile hatred of plural marriage as deriving partially from fear of Mormon expansion, a situation he compared to the Egyptian hatred of the children of Israel. *The Mormon Question Being a Speech of Vice-President Schuyler Colfax at Salt Lake City, A Reply thereto by Elder John Taylor; and a Letter of Vice-President Colfax Published in the "New York Independent," with Elder Taylor's Reply* (Salt Lake City, 1870), 9.

16. William Appleman Williams, *The Roots of the Modern American Empire* (New York: Random House, 1969).

17. Cannon, *Review of the Decision*, 31–33. The comparison of Mormon polygamy with suttee and thuggism was enunciated and repudiated in 1870 by Schuyler Colfax and John Taylor, respectively (*Mormon Question*, 4–7.) A good answer to the Mormon claim that their practice concerned only themselves and that there was no right of legislation against such "private" matters was offered by Colfax (*Mormon Question*, 4). The Mormons continued to emphasize that the plural marriage relationship was "voluntary," as stated, for example, by George Ticknor Curtis, *Pleas for Religious Liberty* (1886), 31. At least one modern student has agreed that the court was assuming instead of proving that anyone was harmed by the Mormon practice (Orma Linford, "The Mormons and the Law: The Polygamy Cases" [Ph.D. diss., University of Wisconsin, 1964], 519).

18. Among those who denied that Mormon polygamy was a threat to the rest of the United States was George Q. Cannon, *JD* 24:46.

19. *JD* 13:102.

20. Virtually every Mormon defense of polygamy said something about the moral iniquities of Babylon. In the sermon first publicly acknowledging plural marriage, Orson Pratt said, referring to the Gentiles: "It matters not to them how corrupt they are in females prostitution, if they are lawfully married to only one; but it would be considered an awful thing by them to raise up a posterity from more than one wife" (*JD* 1:61). See also *JD* 5:91; 9:331; 20:4–7, 199–201, 374–75; 24:4–7, 74–75, 115–16; 26:181–82. The theme was almost immediately picked up in Congress. When David L. Carter, Ohio Democrat, said that polygamy was bad enough to "make a Sodom of Salt Lake City," he was answered by Joshua R. Giddings, Ohio Free Soiler, who said, "While we authorize the sale of women here in this city, I am not to be told that we shall punish the Mormons for deeds of less enormity" (*Congressional Globe*, 32d Cong., 1st sess., 1413, 1414). See also *JD* 11:201–2; 13:102; 25:88; 20:374–75; 24:4–7; 26:181–82; 5:91; Cannon, *Review of the Decision*, 42–43.

21. Spencer was one of those who saw plural marriage as the cure for the social evils of monogamy (*Patriarchal Order*, 2). The point of view was expressed by an 1870 mass meeting of Mormon women, who said, "Resolved: That we acknowledge the institutions of the Church of Jesus Christ of Latter-day Saints as the only reliable safeguard of female virtue and innocence" (quoted in Roberts, *CHC* 5:232). In 1879 Franklin D. Richards said that polygamy was "the only potent remedy by which to eradicate the so-called social evil, with all its con-comitants, from the land" (*JD* 20:313).

22. Mormon defenses of polygamy on the basis of the Bible were numerous, including: William H. Hooper's speech before Congress, *Congressional Globe*, 41st Cong., 2d sess., Appendix, 173–77; Spencer, *Patriarchal Order*; Parley P. Pratt, *Marriage and Morals*, 3–7; *Scriptural Evidences in Support of Polygamy* (San Francisco, 1856); and Orson Pratt, *The Bible and Polygamy* (1870); and, in sermons, *JD* 6:351–64; 13:38–42; 23:225–30; 26:117–27, 171–85; 27:214–23. Apparently a non-Mormon defense was the anonymous *The History and Philosophy of Marriage* (Boston, 1869; Salt Lake City, 1885), which was republished in Paris in 1898 under the title *A Plea for Polygamy*. It would be interesting to discover some connection between Christopher Jencks, supposedly the author, and the Mormons. A more basic question, to my mind, is the derivation of the Mormon biblical arguments. Many, if not all, of the possible biblical arguments favoring polygamy were set forth in great detail in the Reverend Martin Madan, *Thelyphthora*, 2d ed. (London, 1781). The copy in the LDS Church Archives is inscribed "Presented to Brigham Young by S. W. Richards, G.S.L., Jan. 27th 1859." In 1853 it was charged that Orson Spencer plagiarized his ideas and arguments from a book entitled *Polygamia Triumphatrix. The Mormon Doctrine of Polygamy* (1853), 5. Of course the refutation of the biblical argument was equally unoriginal,

being found in *Reflection upon Polygamy and the Encouragement given to that Practice in the Scriptures of the Old Testament* (London 1737) as well as earlier works. See also G. P. Dykes, *To the Saints on the Pacific Slope* (Sacramento, 1863); *Opinion Concerning the Bible Laws of Marriage* (Philadelphia, 1871), Samuel Ellis Wishard, *The Divine Law of Marriage, or, The Bible against Polygamy* (New York: American Tract Society, n.d.). B. H. Roberts made clear that the Bible was not of itself sufficient basis for practicing polygamy (*Improvement Era* 1 [1898]: 473–74).

23. The passage is in Jacob 2:27–30. Schuyler Colfax was one who attempted to use this passage in refutation of the Mormon position; doubtless he was prompted by members of the Reorganized Church of Jesus Christ of Latter Day Saints standing in the wings. The Mormon loophole explanation was quite roughly dealt with by G. P. Dykes, *To the Saints* (1863), who gives signs of being involved with the Reorganization movement.

24. On the emergence of the Reorganized Church of Jesus Christ of Latter Day Saints, see Richard P. Howard, "The Reorganized Church in Illinois, 1852–82: Search for Identity," *Dialogue* 5 (1970): 63–75. Following are a few of the many books and pamphlets in which the Reorganized Church challenged the Mormon version of the plural marriage doctrine: Willard J. Smith, *Joseph Smith: Who Was He? Did He Teach or Practice Polygamy?* (Lamoni, Iowa, n.d.); Zenas H. Gurley, *The Polygamic Revelation: Fraud! Fraud! Fraud!* (Lamoni, Iowa, 1882); and Granville Hedrick, *The Spiritual Wife System Proven False* (Bloomington, Ill., 1856). Some Gentile crusaders against polygamy recognized the Reorganized Church as a potential ally and urged Congress to support its proselyting in Utah. See William Jarman's postscript to T. De Witt Talmage, *The Utah Abomination* (n.p., n.d.). Reorganized Church member T. W. Smith wrote for the *Anti-Polygamy Standard* 2 (Mar. 1882). The interconnections between Gentile merchants, the Godbeites, the Reorganized Church, and the antipolygamy campaign have not, to my knowledge, been adequately delineated. It is well established now, and accepted by all informed historians, that Joseph Smith did indeed originate the practice of polygamy prior to his death. See Foster, *Religion and Sexuality*.

25. The best exposition of some of these concepts, recognizing the various implications of Mormon metaphysical materialism, is Sterling M. McMurrin, *The Theological Foundations of the Mormon Religion* (Salt Lake City: University of Utah Press, 1965). Quite different in tone is the useful Kimball Young, *Isn't One Wife Enough?* chap. 5—on the "quantum theory of salvation." Another contribution is Gordon Irving, "The Law of Adoption: One Phase of the Development of the Mormon Concept of Salvation," *BYU Studies* 14 (Spring 1974): 291–314. Setting forth the theological justification in great detail was Mormon apostle Orson Pratt in *The Seer* (1853),

whose twelve articles on the subject are conveniently summarized in Whittaker, "Early Mormon Pamphleteering," 338–39.

26. *Speech of Hon. George Q. Cannon* (n.p., n.d.), 9–10. The Mormons frequently denied that lust was a motivating force in establishing or entering the system. See Jesse Haven, *Celestial Marriage*, 2; *Mormon Women's Protest* (Salt Lake City, 1886); G. T. Curtis and F. S. Richards, *Plea for Religious Liberty* (1886), 31, 76–68; and *JD* 20:38.

27. *Mormon Question* (1870), 7. Another statement of the problems and dangers of defining religion is George A. Cannon, *Review of the Decision*, chaps. 1, 8, 9.

28. The decision is the Reynolds case in *United States Reports*, 98:145. See the critical review by George Q. Cannon, *Review of the Decision*. By 1886 there was some modification of the Mormon position on these issues. Before the Supreme Court, George Ticknor Curtis said, "Of course I do not stand here to contend that a man's religious belief operates to prevent the legislative power from prohibiting conduct which that power deems injurious to the welfare of the society. The Mormons once made that contention, at least up to a certain point; but I am not asked to make that contention now, and I could not make it if I were" (George Ticknor Curtis and Franklin S. Richards, *Pleas for Religious Liberty* [1886], 25). Other Mormons continued to insist on the religious exemption and failure or malice of the Congress and the Court for not recognizing their constitutional rights. See also Ray Jay Davis, "Plural Marriage and Religious Freedom: The Impact of Reynolds vs. United States," *Arizona Law Review* 15 (1973): 287–306.

29. See Edwin Brown Firmage and Richard Collin Mangrum, *Zion in the Courts: A Legal History of the Church of Jesus Christ of Latter-day Saints, 1830–1900* (Urbana: University of Illinois Press, 1988).

30. F. S. Buchanan, "Yoder Case: Precedent for Polygamy?" *Christian Century* 40 (21 Feb. 1973): 223–24.

31. On the slavery controversy, standard works are William Sumner Jenkins, *Pro-Slavery Thought in the Old South* (Chapel Hill, N.C., 1935); Arthur Young Lloyd, *The Slavery Controversy, 1831–1860* (Chapel Hill, N.C., 1939); David Brion Davis, *The Problems of Slavery in Western Culture* (Ithaca: Cornell University Press, 1966); and the controversial Larry E. Tise, *Proslavery: A History of the Defense of Slavery in America, 1701–1840* (Athens: University of Georgia Press, 1987). Especially valuable in pointing out the parallels between the legislative-constitutional problems posed by polygamy and slavery—which is not necessarily the same as parallels in the rhetoric—is Richard D. Poll, "The Mormon Question, 1850–1865: A Study in Politics and Public Opinion" (Ph.D. diss., University of California at Berkeley, 1948).

32. The extremist and the apocalyptic nature of radical abolitionist

thought is well known. See Lloyd, *Slavery Controversy*, 49–101. Several significant examples of apocalyptic premonitions are found in Edmund Wilson, *Patriotic Gore* (New York, 1962).

33. Richard Hofstadter, *The Paranoid Style in American Politics* (New York: Knopf, 1965).

34. H. A. Overstreet and Bonaro Overstreet, *Strange Tactics of Extremism* (New York: Norton, 1965).

35. Reverend T. De Witt Talmage, *Mormonism, An Exposure* (London, n.d.). Besides appearing in Talmage's widely syndicated column, the sermon was reprinted in various forms. One of these was entitled *The Utah Abomination: All Sorts of Cruelty, Treachery, and Murder, Practiced under a Cloak of Religion. Its Blasphemy, Polygamy, and Incest*. The publisher, William Jarman, an apostate Mormon, appended this note: "The sooner an army is sent to Utah to compel obedience to the law the better. . . . I do not consider Mormonism a Religion. I have seen enough of it to convince me that it is an Infernal Despotism, which seeks only political power and aggrandizement under the cloak of religion. I see the whole of the so-called 'Church of Jesus Christ of Latter-day Saints' to produce one Christian Man or woman among the lot. Among the dupes there are sincere Mormons, but no Christians" (7–8).

36. *Congressional Globe*, 37th Cong., 3d sess., Appendix, 120.

37. *Mormon Question* (1870), 15, 23–25. See also Spencer, *Patriarchal Order*, 9, 12.

38. *Deseret News Weekly*, 28 July 1886.

39. Pratt, *Marriage and Morals in Utah* (1856), 8.

40. *JD* 20:37; 24:47.

41. Orson Hyde remembered Joseph Smith as having said that "the time would come when the Constitution and the country would be in danger of an overthrow; and he said, If the Constitution be saved at all, it will be by the Elders of this Church" (*JD* 6:152). As early as 1861, if not before, some Mormon leaders saw themselves as the true defenders of the Constitution. In this Civil War situation John Taylor said: "We have ever stood by it [the Constitution], and we expect when the fanaticism of false blatant friends shall have torn it shred from shred, to stand by the shattered ruins and uphold the broken, desecrated remnants of our country's institutions in all their purity and pristine glory" (*Deseret News*, 10 July 1861, 152). The same theme was eminently suited to the period of the antipolygamy legislation and prosecutions; far from being traitors, the Mormons were the true defenders of the constitution. See also *JD* 9:263; 20:6; 24:49; 26:39.

42. Some insights into this world of thought are provided by Klaus J. Hansen, *Quest for Empire* (East Lansing: Michigan State University Press, 1967); Boyd Eddins, "The Mormons and the Civil War" (M.A. thesis, Utah

State University, 1966); and Louis G. Reinwand, "An Interpretive Study of Mormon Millennialism during the 19th Century" (M.A. thesis, Brigham Young University, 1971); and especially, Grant Underwood, *The Millenarian World of Early Mormonism* (Urbana: University of Illinois Press, 1993). The attitude is represented by Franklin D. Richards, who in 1879 said: "Our appeal must be to the government of heaven, to which we have vowed allegiance. Jehovah will hold a contention with this nation, and will show them which is the higher and eternal law, and which is the lesser and more recent law" (*JD* 20:315). One Mormon saw the "social evil" as necessitating divine punishment: "When the inhabitants of Sodom and Gomorrah committed the same seething infamies that are now running right through the world, corrupting the life's blood of the nations, and cursing posterity, God destroyed them by fire" (B. H. Roberts, "Social Evils," *The Contributor* 3 [1882]: 311).

3

Zion's Rowdies: Growing Up
on the Mormon Frontier

BENJAMIN FERRIS, secretary of state in the Utah Territory in 1852–53, was not favorably impressed with the Mormon children there. These children were deplorably unhealthy, he said—"the combined result of the gross sensuality of the parents, and want of care toward their offspring." Nor was the problem purely physical; it was also behavioral. Nowhere outside of New York City's "Five Points," he continued, could "a more filthy, miserable, neglected-looking, and disorderly rabble of children be found than in the streets of Great Salt Lake City."[1]

Of course the Mormons did not look on their own children with such a jaundiced eye. Sharing general nineteenth-century attitudes, the Mormons regarded childless marriages as a disappointment if not a curse. Agricultural and domestic needs meant that children could be a distinct advantage in terms of labor. To this expected frame of reference the Mormons added religious teachings that for them enhanced the importance of children. They saw the whole question of children in terms of eternal existence. Families, if properly and authoritatively made up on earth, would continue in the post-mortal existence, and those who came closest to the divine plan, approaching divinity themselves, would have numberless progeny. God himself had created "worlds without number," and the process of creating worlds and peopling them was ongoing. Abraham had been promised that his own progeny would be as the sands of the seashore. And faithful Mormons, thinking in this same frame of reference, looked upon children not merely in the limited perspective but as evidences of their own divine creativity that would continue on in eternity. It was a poor, pinch-backed man, said George A. Smith who would chain himself down to the law of monogamy. Similarly, it was a poor, pinch-backed man and a shriveled, selfish woman who would choose to have no children or few. Increase, expand, multiply—these were the watchwords. One who was faithful over a small kingdom or family in this life was preparing to be faithful over worlds in the hereafter. In the whole scheme of things children were not only welcome, they were indispensable.[2]

In addition to their importance for eternal salvation, children could be seen as playing an enormously important role in the advance of Mormonism on earth. Here the millennialism of the movement meant a heightened sense of the significance of the generation in which they lived. These children that Mormon adults saw coming into their homes, in the 1830s, 1840s, and 1850s were to be a choice generation. Unlike their parents, the young would learn the true gospel of Mormonism from their mothers' knees. Brigham Young was sharply aware of the influence of values inculcated in youth, and usually when he described this phenomenon—"traditioning" as he sometimes called it—he was referring to the negative side of the experience. He and those to whom he addressed his words had grown up in families that had not known the true gospel of Jesus Christ. The result is that they had imbibed false ideas about God and man, about what was proper and improper; even after their conversion to Mormonism, some of the old ideas still clung on.[3] Fortunately their children would grow up in a society where they would learn truths and true values from the first. Great things were naturally expected of such young people, those born into Latter-day Saint homes. They were described in a later hymn as the "hope of Israel, Zion's army, children of the promised day."

The Mormons did in fact produce children in quantity. Reliable statistics are not available for the twenty years of Mormonism's history prior to 1850—the tumultuous series of settlements and flights in New York, Ohio, Missouri, and Illinois—but in the frontier environment of the Great Basin the children were unusually numerous. This may have been partially due to the death of the old and infirm that resulted from the rigors of the overland journey and the hardships of settlement. For whatever reason, the census of 1880 shows a population in which something like 44 percent was fourteen or under, with another 10 percent in the upper teens. This was a youthful population; the weight was on the lower end of the age scale. The contrast is not only with such frontier territories as Colorado and Idaho, where there were proportionately very few children, but also with the country as a whole. The state in 1880 that seems fairly close to Utah in its fecundity and child population is Iowa.[4]

As is always the case with a human population of any size, more males are born than females. In Utah this was the case, too, although by the age of fifteen females were dominant numerically. The fairly equal distribution of sexes after the years of highest infant mortality and the large number of children may simply reflect that Utah was further into its settlement cycle in 1880, having been settled for more than thirty years. In any case, children were numerous. If you walked down Salt Lake City's Main Street during a busy shopping day at conference time, almost every other person you passed would be fourteen or under. At least this would be the case if the shopping crowd represented the overall population. And there would be many tots; close to 18 percent of the population was four years old or less.

But if the quantity of children was impressive, what about their quality? Were they physically strong and, consistent with their parents' hopes, were they a noble generation, intellectually and morally superior? One way of getting at this question is through the eyes of travelers in Mormon country. Early in the Utah period J. W. Gunnison noted that Mormon youth "seem to care but little for the details of doctrine." The younger generation, he said, were not a "holy generation" but were "the most lawless and profane" he had ever observed.[5] Agreeing with this negative evaluation was Jules Remy, who said the Mormon children were "far from being models of candor and innocence." He admits that they are "handsome, well-made, and robust" but sees them as "godless, licentious, and immodest."[6] Physically, one gathers, they could be admired, but their behavior was deplorable. The fault, of course, was polygamy, which revealed to children the "mysteries of the harem." At least this was the standard explanation.

Other critics, while agreeing that Mormon children were guilty of outrageous behavior, were not willing to concede that they were physically robust. Benjamin Ferris, whose statement was cited at the beginning of this essay, was only one of those who insisted that there were deplorable physical consequences to polygamy. Writing soon after the census of 1850 had seemed to provide evidence of a death rate in Utah of 21 per thousand, with over a third of these among children under the age of five, the ex-Mormon John Hyde proclaimed "a fearful mortality among the Mormon children." Like Ferris, Hyde added a condemnation of juvenile misbehavior among Mormon boys: "Cheating the confiding, is called smart trading; mischievous cruelty, evidences of spirit; pompous bravado, manly talk; reckless riding, fearless courage; and if they out-talk their father, outwit their companions, whip their school-teacher or out-curse a Gentile, they are thought to be promising greatness, and are praised accordingly. Every visitor of Salt Lake will recognize the portrait, for every visitor proclaims them to be the most whisky-loving, tobacco-chewing, saucy and precocious children he ever saw."[7] In short, the Mormon children were being held up as Exhibit No. 1 whose physical debility and moral depravity proved polygamy a vicious system.

The travelers were not uniformly critical. Elizabeth Woods Kane noticed several beautiful family relationships as she traveled with the party of Brigham Young in a tour to southern Utah. There was playfulness among some of these children; others, especially the girls, helped prepare and serve meals to the visiting party; and the children were noticeably numerous in attendance at church.[8] Perhaps Mrs. Kane was slanting her perceptions, but I suspect that as a mother of two young boys she was more ready to recognize attractive traits in other children who befriended her sons. William Chandless was another visitor who enjoyed teasing and playing with Mormon children. He wrote, "Probably no people (speaking collectively) set a higher value upon their children than Mormons do; and . . . upon boys particularly: not certainly without a sort of Spartan feeling that their sons belong to their country and faith, to co-operate in the building up of the church and Kingdom." Chandless rejected claims that Mormon children were ill-behaved as "so much sheer nonsense."[9]

Sir Richard Burton, whose *The City of the Saints* appeared in 1861, did not challenge the assertion that Mormon children may have experienced a high mortality rate but did not think that polygamy was the explanation. As for the charge that Mormon children were a "filthy, miserable, and disorderly rabble," his experience did not provide confirmation: "I was surprised by their numbers, cleanliness, and health, their hardihood and general good looks." Burton responded directly to John Hyde's caricaturization of Mormon children, chalking it up to "the glance of the anti-Mormon eye pure and simple."[10]

Mormon children were being used as weapons in an ideological war. Objectivity was hard to come by. There are many problems with mortality figures. It has been estimated that throughout the United States unreported deaths approximated 15 percent of the total. Moreover, what is the basis of comparison? In 1880, according to census figures, one out of every ten Utah babies (10.2 percent) died before reaching their first birthday. The figure for the United States as a whole was 11.10 percent, for Sweden 13 percent, for England 15 percent, and for Italy 22 percent. In the absence of detailed analysis that differentiated monogamous Mormons, polygamous Mormons, and non-Mormons, it would be unwise to put much weight on these figures, but they at least suggest that sweeping condemnation of the Mormons based on the sickness of their children was premature and ideologically motivated.

But what about the other charge, that Mormon children were disorderly and ill-mannered? It is the kind of question that on the face of it cannot be answered in simple terms, and it does not lend itself to quantification. What is clear, however, is that Mormons themselves, full of hope for the rising generation, were more than a little distressed at much juvenile behavior. As early as 1819 Bishop John Murdock remarked, "I was never in a community in my life where there was so much disagreement in the famelys [sic] as I witness here. The children from a very small size are learning bad habits such as cursing, swearing, taking the name of God in vain."[11] In 1851 Bishop Edward Hunter remarked on the prevalence of "unruly youngsters." It is the duty of [ward] teachers, he said, "to make special enquiry of parents in regard to the conduct of their children." Several others seconded his observations about "the low state of moral and religious [standards?] existing among the youths of the church."[12] In 1854 at a meeting of the bishops in Salt Lake City the question was raised, "Should we ordain young men and boys who are wild, etc.?" (This referred to priesthood ordination which, in theory, was received by every Mormon boy at the age of twelve.) After some discussion the answer given was that the young hellions should be ordained in hope that "the ordination may make them the best of men."[13] In 1859 there were several incidents of street brawling.[14] In 1861, speaking at a meeting of the city's bishops, Brigham Young favored the construction of recreation halls that would attract youth "who would otherwise meet in small groups, and indulge in low, grovelling rowdyism."[15] In 1868 the custodian of the Tabernacle complained of "indecent words being written on the wall and the backs of the seats being very much cut up."[16]

In 1870 Martin Lenzi saw a group of teenagers tearing up foot bridges and jerking off the mail boxes from the fronts of houses and throwing them over the fence into the yards. He shouted to them, and they ran off. "He says they live in the lower wards of the city."[17] The local establishment failed to see any joke in willful destruction of property. About the same time Thomas Jones said that while people were at church on Sundays "mischievous boys" would break windows and damage property.[18] "We have a large juvenile population," wrote the *Deseret News* that same year as it called for provisions for some kinds of public recreation grounds.[19] The community lamplighter complained that boys were throwing rocks and breaking the lamps. "It's first rate to see boys full of fun and frolic," said the *News*, "but it's quite another affair to see them wickedly mischievous."[20]

In 1873, again, the public press deplored "the writings of the most disgusting and obscene words and sentences on the walls of public buildings and other places." In the same breath, now that the subject of youthful misbehavior was brought up, the newspaper added: "Many of the boys have also been in the habit lately of slinging pebbles through the windows of school houses and other buildings. This is not legitimate fun, but wanton mischief."[21]

This same year a Salt Lake City resident complained of boys that visited his stables at night, frightened his mules, and otherwise disturbed "him and his neighbors by hallooing and romping about the streets till a late hour in the night." The response of the public press, again, was a reprimand: boys should behave and parents should be responsible for their children. In the course of this news item an interesting phrase appears: "The hoodlum element in that part of the city ought to be checked."[22]

Also in 1873 a visitor from England noted that "he never was in a place in his life where there appeared to be so many people hanging around the streets, doing nothing."[23] Interestingly, this was in 1873, a depression year; jobs may have been scarce. But from the moralist's vantage point this was no excuse.

Some of the vandalism was a result of the prevalence of knives—jackknives, bowie knives, and so on—among boys. In 1873 the newspaper commented:

The other day we stated that a little spell of sunshine brought out the "bummers' brigade" in force. This delectable body has its subdivisions, one of which is the "whittlers' squad." The members of this department appear to have a large development of what phrenologists call the bump of destructiveness. They are not contented with the old Yankee custom of assisting a free flow of thought by whittling a piece of stick, but they employ their jack knives in other ways. For instance that street lamp post, at the bummers' headquarters, Exchange Buildings corner, is all but cut in two by their operations, and some of the posts which sustain the awning there have shared a similar fate.

Now those fellows should consider that those posts are useful, and that in that particular they are much ahead of those who whittle them. When they go to whittling, let them operate on that which is useless, which, however, would involve the question as to whether they could possibly find anything of less utility than themselves, which would bring in a second idea, as to whether they might not just as well commence whittling on each other.[24]

In a later article the "bummers' squad" was further described as including the "squirters' squad," a group which squirted tobacco juice on goods put out for sale.[25] Lovely young people, these.

I do not want to leave the impression that all of the young people of Utah were juvenile delinquents. Some of the "misbehavior" complained of was more in the area of annoyance and noise than in actual serious threat. Thus the sleighriding down the hill. Some old people were quite upset at the rapid speed of those sleighs coming down the hill, especially after dark when they could not be seen. They were concerned not so much for their own safety as for that of the children. One boy was killed when a wagon ran over him in this way. Another incident was described: "A day or two ago a boy came down a hill and a cow crossed the track just as he was coming down. Here a collision was imminent. The boy could not stop, nor had he a chance to steer around, consequently he went straight ahead. As good luck would have it, he shot right through between the legs of the cow, without collision and unhurt. Scared cow! Lucky boy!"[26]

In 1874 "a number of boys" were arrested. They had broken down fences, lifted gates from hinges, and written "various obscene and profane sentences" around the premises. They escaped with a reprimand from the police. A little later a group went "howling and hooting" along South Temple Street, lifting gates. The *News*, ever the guardian of public morality, opined, "A dose of coarse salt sent with sufficient propelling force against their posterior region would be as good as they deserve."[27]

On February 11, 1874, the parents were due for another appeal from the public authorities:

Parents, why do you allow your children to be out so much at night after dark? They there and then learn many things which they would not at home, and which are nothing to their benefit.

When boys and girls are verging on manhood and womanhood, and scarcely understand their new feelings, some of them are apt to be headstrong and wilful, and will not be controlled nor advised by their parents or other elder friends. But the younger children should have a little healthy parental restraint thrown around them, particularly as regards this out-at-night business. Young boys and young girls, who ought to be at home and in bed, are strolling around at night in each other's company, and there is smoking by the boys and in all probability language indulged in that would not be permitted at home, and should not be heard anywhere. Just look after these little ones, and have self-interest enough not to forget the proverb about "as the twig is bent," etc.[28]

This is typical of many such statements.

Without multiplying examples further, it can be observed that there are different possible approaches to this general question of rowdiness among Mormon children and teenagers. First, theoretically the phenomenon could be studied quantitatively. What were the kinds of misbehavior? How did it fluctuate from year to year and from season to season? But we do not yet have reliable studies of crime on the Mormon frontier, much less of an ill-defined activity like rowdyism. Since the evidence presented here is far less reliable than the usual crime statistics, any quantitative information could be used for comparative purposes only with the greatest caution.[29]

In the meantime, a second approach is to recognize that awareness of juvenile misbehavior was in part a function of the anti-Mormon crusade. Like other advocates of reform, the anti-Mormons were not in their minds making up evidence, but there is no doubt of their predisposition, of their determination to paint a negative picture. They saw what they were prepared to see.[30] It is a case study of selective perception and of caricature. The extent to which some degree of distortion occurred depends, of course, on the objective criterion against which the descriptions are measured, and we have already noted that such a criterion is lacking.

While recognizing some truth in the second approach, it is a half-truth at best. Whenever people are in a conflict, there is likely to be both a negative outside image and a positive self-image. The surprising discovery of the present analysis is that the negative description of Mormon children by outsiders had its counterpart in negative descriptions from the inside. Not that the two sets of observations were being seen through the same lens. Critics saw confirmation of the deplorable consequences of a despised social system. The Mormons might have answered that the practical demands of frontier living simply made it impossible to give adequate care and attention to their children, that it took time in a newly settled area for the institutions to become established and behavior patterns to become regularized, and that the Mormon young people were certainly no worse than those in other parts of the West. But among themselves the Mormons were experiencing a disconfirmation of their extravagant hopes. The children of the promised day were all too often behaving like ordinary nuisance-loving children and at times like thugs and ruffians.

If the Mormon perception of rowdyism is of more importance than the passing criticism of travelers from the outside, it is because the Mormons tried to do something about it. However one might dislike the Mormons of the past century, it was generally conceded that they were people who did things. Their theology was not simply a pie-in-the-sky affair; it required specific actions on earth, and these, or at least many of them, were organized by the church. Missionary proselyting, gathering immigrants, collecting tithes and offerings, laying out settlements, organizing the economy—such activities were organizational responses to various kinds of challenges. True to character, the Mormons in Territorial Utah, once they had clearly defined the problem, proceeded to come up with organizational responses. It was these, along with the general frontier conditions and the set of community expectations already described, that marked the parameters of what it meant to grow up on the Mormon frontier during the last three decades of the century.

Let us bring the camera in on 1871, when George Q. Cannon, editor of the *Juvenile Instructor*, made a few interesting editorial comments. Something has happened. Looking back, he noted:

> There are towns where the young men were indifferent about meetings or schools. They preferred to go riding, fishing, hunting or playing on Sunday to going to meeting. Faithful men and women were grieved in thinking of the future of these boys and young men. Did they leave Babylon and gather to Zion to raise their boys in this fashion—to see them grow up ignorant of the gospel, careless respecting its requirements, with no regard for

God, or even for their parents, rude in speech and manners? In coming here they hoped to be able to rear their children better than they could elsewhere. They hoped their boys and girls would have more of the faith and of the power and of the gifts of God than they had. But alas! they saw them growing up wild, uncouth, and ignorant, fonder of play and rioting than of prayer and meetings.[31]

This is a good statement of the contrast between the optimistic hopes and the behavior we have noticed above. But something had happened to change the picture. Sunday Schools had been organized; young people, especially boys and young men, had made a right about face, becoming interested in religion and centering their "hearts' affections" upon the church. "Violence and rowdyism have been checked," Cannon continued. "The reading of books has taken the place of the playing of cards. Amusements of a rational and innocent character have been adopted in the stead of drinking and carousing." If Cannon was overstating the degree of change, there is no mistaking his general sense of encouragement. The Sunday School was still new; those who lived in communities without this program—and where rowdyism presumably continued unabated—were encouraged to take steps to get things going in the right direction.

This was the decade, too, that saw the emergence of other programs. Along with the Sunday School there were for teenagers the Young Women's Mutual Improvement Association and the Young Men's Mutual Improvement Association and for children twelve and under the Primary Association.[32] Letters and speeches of contemporaries make it clear that each of these organizational developments was responding to the same perception: the young people were going to the dogs; they were growing up without testimonies or convictions of the truth of Mormonism; they were not living constructive, purposeful lives but were wasting their substance in riotous living.

"Young ladies, we are glad you are organized," said Eliza R. Snow at Ephraim, Utah, in 1875. "Come to meeting, learn the laws of life and salvation, never sacrifice the Spirit of God to marry a Gentile. Those young men who are hanging around the saloons, in Salt Lake City and elsewhere, defile their bodies with whiskey, tobacco and foul language; they are no more fit to be husbands and fathers than the heathen, and many girls are just the same."[33] It is already clear, of course, that these saloon-frequenting young people included more than a few Mormons. The important thing, in 1875, was that the response to the problem was organization: "Young ladies, we are glad you are organized."

What did the Mormons attempt to teach their children in the schools and in these organizations intended as responses to the problem of a disorderly younger generation? What, in other words, were the ideals the parents of the Mormon Israel were to encourage?

1. Religious training was of the highest importance. As George Q. Cannon said in 1881, it was "of the first importance, more important than anything else; more important even than teaching them to read and write."[34] Of course sometimes the religious teaching would not "take," but apostle Joseph F. Smith had some commonsense advice: "Teach your children so that they may grow up knowing what 'Mormonism' is, and then if they do not like it, let them take what they can find. Let us, at least, discharge our duty to them by teaching them what it is."[35]

2. Strong among the qualities that children were expected to develop was obedience. They should obey their parents, show respect for the standards of the church and community. Obey, obey, obey—the word was heard over and over again. It was qualified, however, by the advice to parents that they should be kindly and not use the rod when kindly words could accomplish the purpose.[36]

3. Mormon children were to learn to work. This was a practical fact of life for most people, one gathers, but it was also stressed in the sermons and manuals. Parents, said apostle Erastus Snow, should "begin the work of education with their offspring, and teach them to bear their own burdens at the earliest practicable day, and let them begin to learn and receive this practical education. . . . Let no mother, in her misplaced sympathy and love, and her anxiety to serve her offspring, wear herself needlessly out in waiting upon them when they are able to wait upon themselves."[37]

4. Cultivation was advocated as a goal of education, although it was not always defined with any precision. Somehow the younger generation was to become accustomed to the finer things, learning how to discuss ideas, becoming socially adept. "Every boy should be trained in such a manner as to fit him to move in the first circles of society," said George Q. Cannon in 1881, adding, "We should not be content to make our children like ourselves; that because we have lived in a certain way that they may do so also."[38]

5. Although both parents had responsibility to raise up their children in the proper manner, it was the mother who had the primary responsibility. "Mothers will let their children go to the Devil in their childhood," said Brigham Young, "and when they are old enough to come under the immediate guidance of their fathers, to be sent out to preach the Gospel in the world, or to learn some kind of mechanism, they are as uncontrollable as the winds that now revel in the mountains."[39]

It is of interest to notice how this compares with the larger American society. According to Robert Sunley's study of "Early Nineteenth-Century American Literature on Child Rearing," the literature on the subject before 1860 stressed the importance of the mother, recommended freedom of movement rather than restrictive swaddling, insisted upon neatness and orderliness, and warned against sexual practices. All of this could be found in the Mormon prescriptive literature as well, combined of course with the specific slant provided by the Mormon religion.[40]

The new organizations—Sunday School, Primary Association, the Mutual Improvement Associations for teenagers—did not suddenly introduce a Garden of Eden into the valleys of the Rockies. For one thing, attendance at these organizations, whether from lack of interest or involvement in work or fatigue, was something less than 50 percent.[41] For another thing, the quality of the programs varied widely, as did the ability of the teachers whose services were donated. Even when the children attended and when the programs themselves were of high quality, there was the problem of followthrough. Without reinforcement at home teenage toughs would remain incorrigible. On one occasion in 1898, apostle Brigham Young, Jr., said:

> I go again to the Sabbath school, and on one occasion I said to the presiding officer: "Who are those little boys on those back benches?" "Why," he said to me in a whisper, "those are our hoodlums. We work with them as best we can. You see that brother is a mild tempered man. He sits right there by those little fellows trying to keep them in order; and we use every effort and all the persuasion that we are capable of to get them to observe order, but I tell you, Brother Young, with all they get from here, their parents are indifferent as to what their children do. Parents neglect their children and they run hither and thither all the week long and when they come into the Sabbath school it is almost useless

to try to keep them quiet and orderly for the little fellows have been neglected and disorderly the whole week."[42]

Young went on to comment that there was "neglect in this department throughout the length and breadth of the land."

Mormon children were American children with a difference. The criticism of Mormon young people may be seen as a variation of the criticism of American young people by European travelers who thought they saw the baleful consequences of democracy.[43] The community's own recognition of antisocial behavior—the idleness and disrespect and wanton destruction of property—must have had its parallel in other communities across the country.[44] The difference for the Mormons was their tendency to see youthful behavior against a backdrop of millennial hopes. And the effort to organize programs as one means, along with improved schools, of combatting juvenile misbehavior was not unique to the Latter-day Saints. Indeed, much of whatever improvement took place may have occurred naturally as Utah society matured. But one can discern in the programs that sprang into existence on the Mormon frontier a strong element of religious awareness along with conventional instruction in manners and morals. As the programs continued to expand and mature, taking Mormon children at a tender age and shepherding them through the early teens, the life of young Mormons was more fully programmed than that of most young Americans. In this sense much of what remains true of Mormon group character even today was taking shape.

Notes

An earlier version of this chapter appeared in *Utah Historical Quarterly* 50 (1982): 182–95.

    1. Benjamin Ferris, *Utah and the Mormons* (New York, 1854), 47.

    2. See Kimball Young, *Isn't One Wife Enough?: The Story of Mormon Polygamy* (New York: Henry Holt, 1954), chap. 2.

    3. These ideas are stated and restated in the sermons printed in the *Journal of Discourses*, 26 vols. (London: Latter-day Saints Book Depot, 1854–86).

    4. Bureau of the Census, *Tenth Census of the United States Taken in the Year 1880* (Washington, D.C.), vol. 1, *Population*. "Of the population of Utah one quarter are under eight years old, one-third under eleven and one-half under seventeen. Utah has more children under five years old, in proportion to its population, than any other division of the country." *Bi-*

ennial Report of the Territorial Superintendent of District Schools for the Years Ending June 30, 1882–1883 (n.p., 1884), 73.

5. J. W. Gunnison, *The Mormons, or Latter-day Saints in the Valley of the Great Salt Lake* (Philadelphia, 1852), 159–60.

6. Jules Remy and Julius Brenchley, *A Journey to Great Salt Lake City,* 2 vols. (London, 1861), 150, 174–75.

7. John Hyde, *Mormonism: Its Leaders and Designs* (New York, 1857), 77.

8. Elizabeth Wood Kane, *Twelve Mormon Homes* (Salt Lake City: Tanner Trust Fund, University of Utah Library, 1974), 26, 43.

9. William Chandless, *A Visit to Salt Lake* (London, 1857), 192.

10. Richard F. Burton, *The City of the Saints* (1861), ed. Fawn M. Brodie (New York, 1963), 472–73.

11. Presiding Bishop Minutes, 18 November 1849, Church Archives.

12. Ibid., 13 July 1851, Church Archives.

13. Ibid., 31 January 1854, Church Archives.

14. *On the Mormon Frontier: The Diary of Hosea Stout, 1844–61,* ed. Juanita Brooks (Salt Lake City, 1964).

15. Presiding Bishop Minutes, 14 February 1861, Church Archives.

16. Ibid., 14 May 1861, Church Archives.

17. *Deseret News Weekly,* 2 March 1870.

18. Ibid., 9 March 1870.

19. Ibid., 16 March 1870.

20. Ibid., 7 December 1870.

21. Ibid., 2 April 1873.

22. Ibid., 6 August 1873.

23. Ibid., 17 September 1873.

24. Ibid., 10 December 1873.

25. Ibid., 17 December 1873.

26. Ibid., 14 January 1874.

27. Ibid., 4 February 1874.

28. Ibid., 11 February 1874.

29. As a study of crime a model is David J. Bodenhamer, "Law and Disorder on the Early Frontier: Marion County, Indiana, 1823–1850," *Western Historical Quarterly* 10 (July 1979): 323–36.

30. On the larger stage a similar example of slanted perception is studied in Richard L. Rapson, *Britons View America: Travel Commentary, 1860–1935* (Seattle: University of Washington Press, 1971), 93–105.

31. *Juvenile Instructor* 9 (1874): 234.

32. Among the histories of the church auxiliary programs are the following: *Jubilee History of Latter-day Saint Sunday Schools, 1849–1899* (Salt Lake City, 1900); Susa Young Gates, *History of the Young Ladies Mutual Improvement Association* (Salt Lake City, 1911); Leon M. Strong, "A History

of the Young Men's Mutual Improvement Association, 1877–1938" (M.S. thesis, Brigham Young University, 1939); Marion Belnap Kerr, "The Primary Association Yesterday and Today," *Improvement Era* 38 (Apr. 1935): 244–72; and Carol Cornwall Madsen and Susan Staker Oman, *Sisters and Little Saints: One Hundred Years of Primary* (Salt Lake City: Deseret Book, 1979).

33. *Woman's Exponent* 4 (15 Aug. 1875): 42.

34. *JD* 22:287.

35. *JD* 14:287.

36. "Bring up your children in love and fear of the Lord; study their dispositions and their temperaments, and deal with them accordingly, never allowing yourself to correct them in the heat of passion; teach them to love you rather than to fear you, and let it be your constant care that the children that God has so kindly given you are taught in their early youth the importance of the oracles of God, and the beauty of the principles of our holy religion, that when they grow to the years of man and womanhood they may always cherish a tender regard for them and never forsake the truth" (*JD* 12:221).

37. *JD* 17:365.

38. *JD* 22:282–83.

39. *JD* 1:68.

40. Robert Sunley, "Early Nineteenth-Century American Literature on Child Rearing," in Margaret Mead and M. Wolfenstein, eds., *Childhood in Contemporary Culture* (Chicago: University of Chicago Press, 1955), 150–67. One theme emphasized in New England but largely rejected or ignored by the Mormons was the depravity of man. See also M. Guy Bishop, "Preparing to 'Take the Kingdom': Childrearing Directives in Early Mormonism," *Journal of the Early Republic* 7 (Fall 1987): 275–90.

41. Information supplied by Jill Mulvay Derr and Carol Cornwall Madsen, based on their research.

42. *Conference Reports, October 1898* [Salt Lake City, 1898], 49.

43. Parson, *Britons View America*, 93–105.

44. Some illuminating examples are found in Joseph F. Kett, *Rites of Passage: Adolescence in America, 1790 to the Present* (New York: Basic Books, Inc., 1977). For a larger perspective, see John R. Gillis, *Youth and History: Tradition and Change in European Age Relations, 1770–Present* (New York: Academic Press, 1974).

4

Bard of Utah's Dixie:
Charles Lowell Walker and His Verse

"**B**ETTER THAN any other source, popular poems and songs capture the force of the early republic's religious populism." Thus Nathan O. Hatch sees the significance of a body of material not often used by historians. Such verse, he goes on to say, articulates "the interests of ordinary people"; such "poems, ballads, and songs are ingenious tools of communication, translating theological concepts into the language of the marketplace."[1]

In the 1850s Charles Walker, with other members of the Walker family, emigrated to Utah. He was called to settle the Dixie mission in 1862 and, except for trips to general conference in Salt Lake City, spent the rest of his life in St. George. Husband of two wives, father of ten or more children, he never became wealthy. A faithful ward teacher, he accepted whatever assignments were given him but never achieved any real prominence as a Church official. He was typical of thousands of humble, hardworking Latter-day Saints who were not the generals or colonels but the noncommisioned officers and enlisted men of the restoration.

Walker was a man of words. He enjoyed both speaking and writing. His diary, extending from 1854 to 1899, is one of the great diaries of pioneer and territorial Utah. He wrotes essays, toasts, hymns, and poems. The total literary production of Charley Walker, especially the poetry, entitle him to be known as the poet laureate of Dixie or, less pretentiously, as Dixie's bard.

Even while still living in Salt Lake City, Walker showed some of his literary flair, attending meetings and being called on to sing or recite something. On October 19, 1862, he attended a meeting in the Bowery and heard his name read as one of those called to settle "the Cotton Country." Ever the moralist, ever the dutiful Saint, he wrote in his diary:

"Here I learn'd a principle that I shant forget in awhile. It showed to me that obedeance was a great principle in Heaven and on earth. Well here I have worked for the last 7 years thro heat and cold, hunger and adverse circumstances, and at last have got me a home, a Lot with fruit trees just beginning to bear and look pretty. Well I must leave it and go and do the will of My Father in Heaven who over rules all for the good of them that love and fear him, and I pray God to give me Strength to accomplish that which is required of me in an acceptable manner before him."[2]

The incredible difficulty of pioneering southern Utah can only be suggested. Walker's first reaction to the new setting included the following description: "to look on the country it [is a] dry, parched, barren waste with here and there a green spot on the margin of the streams. Very windy, dusty, blowing nearly all the time. The water is not good and far from being palatable. And this is the country we have to live in and make it blossom as the Rose. Well its all right; we shall know how to appreciate a good country when we get to it, when the Lord has prepared the way for his People to return and build up the waste places of Zion" (241).

On June 21, 1863, it was "hot, windy and dusty." "Our crops this Season have been light; very light, in fact I might say a failure owing to the want of water." They got more water than they wished in September. A new little daughter had been born. Two days later "it rained and leaked thro the house to such a degree that the floor was a Pool. The Bedding, child, and her [Charley's wife] were wet thro and thro, yet By the help of God and the administering of the Elders she never took cold or the child either" (242).

In this harsh environment the Mormon settlers tried to keep their minds and spirits active. They followed the news of the Civil War as best they could. They had lectures in a new public hall, and Charley attended both as listener and speaker. A Lyceum and Dramatic Association were organized, and Charley joined up. A little handwritten newspaper circulated for about a year, and he wrote a column for it under the pseudonym "Mark Whiz." He taught a Sunday School class on the New Testament and gave talks on a variety of subjects. He delivered toasts ("The Mayor of St. George; may he never be hobbled"). And he wrote poetry. Sometimes this verse was simply recited; sometimes it was intended to be sung to a standard tune. Some of these productions were published in newspapers or magazines, while others appeared in his diary or were later preserved in his unpublished book of poems.

In such a setting at such a time what was the value of a bard, a man of words, a poet? What subjects would he treat? Unable to do more than sample, I wish to give examples of the main subjects treated.

The hard times of 1864 triggered "The Loafer's Lament," the opening stanza of which reads: " 'Tis the last greenback dollar left crumpled alone, / All the fives, tens, and twenties are gambled and gone, / No note of its kindred, no specie is nigh, / And I'm broke for sartin and heave sigh for sigh" (276).

The progress of settlement and the improvements had to be celebrated. He can be forgiven, I think, for believing that "progress" and improvement could best be appreciated by contrast with conditions in the country at the time of the settler's arrival. In 1864 he wrote the following in "Veprecula," intended to be sung to the tune of "Come, Let Us Anew":

> We are but a few
> I'll own it is true,
> Rolled down in the South
> And we've never stood still,
> Or been down in the mouth.
> The old chieftain's will
> We've endeavored to fill,
> And the desert improve
> By the patience of Job
> And no rain from above.
>
> Our life on the stream,
> the old virgin I mean,
> Glides swiftly away,
> And the old patched-up ditch,
> It refuses to stay.[3]

Walker's most famous song describing the bleak environment in 1862 was enjoyed by the people and even by visiting dignitaries from Salt Lake City:

> Oh what a desert place was this
> When first the Mormons found it.
> They said no white man here could live
> And Indians prowl'd around it.
> Twas said the land it was no good,
> And water water was no gudder,

> And the bare Idea of living here
> Was enough to make one shudder.
>
> CHORUS: Muskeet, soap root,
>   Prickly pears, and briars.
>   St. George ere long will be a place
>   That every one admires. (369)

By 1867 he could note a contrast; if it had not arrived, St. George was indeed becoming "a place that every one admires": "Some six or seven years ago this country looked forlorn, / A God-forsaken country, as sure as you are born. / The lizards crept around it, and thorns immense had grown, / As we came marching to Dixie." Sung to the tune of "Marching through Georgia," this song by Walker had the inevitable buoyant chorus: "Hurrah! Hurrah! The thorns we have cut down. / Hurrah! Hurrah! We're building quite a town. / St. George is growing greater, and gaining great renown, / Since we came marching to Dixie" (283).

How proudly the St. George settlers noted the erection of public buildings, and Walker was always on hand to supply memorable words. Even the construction was not too mundane to receive its literary tribute, as "Pounding Rock into the Temple Foundation" (362). As the construction proceeded, on July 24, 1873, a choir sang Walker's anticipatory anthem:

> Lo a Temple long expected
>   In St. George shall stand
> By God's faithfull saints erected
>   Here in Dixie Land.
>
> CHORUS: Halleluyah, halleluyah
>   Let Hossannahs ring.
>   Heaven shall echo back our praises,
>   Christ shall reign as king. (372)

On this same occasion in 1873 Walker recited lines in honor of the St. George Relief Society. Then when it was time for toasts he was there with tributes to the temple quarrymen ("God bless the quarrymen and tools, / And faithful 'Ed' with his four mules"), the pioneers ("The Pioneers of forty seven. / May every last one go to heaven"), and the Mormon Battalion ("God bless the old 'battallion Boys' / May God increase their peace and joys") (375).

Two years later, construction on the temple was moving right along, thanks to volunteers who had donated their time and effort. When they were ready to lay the roof timbers, a celebration was held. Not surprisingly, Charley had a song for the temple volunteers:

> Ye Saints throughout the mountains,
>   Pray listen to my rhyme,
> Of a noble Band of Bretheren
>   Who came to Dixie's clime
> To build a Holy Temple,
>   Just in a Stated time,
>   As they were counselled by Brigham.
>
> CHORUS: Hurrah! hurrah hurrah for Brigham Young.
>   Hurrah for all the Noble Boys who've pushed the
>   work along;
>   God bless them in their labors, and all their
>   lives prolong
>   To Build up Temples in Zion! (403)

Although jaunty optimism and good humor were characteristic of Brother Charley, he could be realistic, even sardonic. In July 1875 it was hot and dry, the crops were not doing well, and on the morning of Monday the fifth he had to unload machinery for the temple construction. In the afternoon his original song went like this:

> The Procession to the Bowery went.
> No Declaration read.
> There would have been some toast that day
> But the folks were short of Bread.
> 'Tis the driest fourth we ever saw.
> No Meat or cheese to buy.
> And all the fun the citizens had,
> You could stick it in your eye. (411–12)

Walker was, however, a loyal Latter-day Saint. He had no doubt of the truth of the latter-day work. With no reservations he accepted the prophetic leadership of President Brigham Young. In June 1876 he took a choir to Young's St. George home, where they sang an original song: "God bless thy chosen Seer, To the Saints of God most dear" (424). Then a group of little girls, including little Mabel Young, sang "God bless to

day, we children pray, / Thy Chosen Many years to come. / May Angels
day and night watch o'er him, / Until the Lord shall call him home."
Among other individuals receiving poetic tribute from Walker at different times were: Milo Andrus (529), stake president McAllister (534–35),
Zina D. Young (541–42), Erastus Snow and, not least of all, Joseph Smith.

In 1880 he composed a long poem in honor of "The Pioneer Sisters":

> When drove from Caldwell and Farwest,
> Like Birdlings sweet from cozy nest,
> Who! robbed of all, firm stood the test?
>   The pioneer sisters.
> Who was it when we left Nauvoo,
> That many trials waded thro
> And showed that they were firm and true?
>   Why, the sisters.
> . . . .
> Who carded wool, who spun and wove,
> Who taught their children God to love?
> God blessed them, and smiled from above
>   On these truehearted sisters.
> When crickets grain and crops devoured
> Whose smiling faces sunbeams showered?
> And strugled on, by God empowered?
>   Those ever gritty sisters.
> . . . .
> I heard a dream the other day,
> Of a man who went to hell:
> He thot the place looked dreadfull strange;
> But why, he could not tell.
> But as the fire and brimstone blazed,
> His eyes began to stare:
> He soon saw why the place looked strange,
> There was no sisters there. (496–99)

I am told that this tribute may be perceived as condescending today,
but it was an honest appreciation, and I have no doubt that the women
of 1880 loved it.

Charles Walker was a Sunday School teacher. He must have been
a good one. On one occasion his class memorized the entire eleventh

chapter of Hebrews. He often showed an interest in children and youth, in teaching them the restored gospel and inspiring them to be faithful. In January 1877 at a jubilee celebration, the children sang a song of his, each verse "substantiated by passages of scriptures and quotations from church works":

> The Lord decreed in Ancient days
> His glorious gospel should come forth
> An Ensign bright should shed its rays,
> To cheer the drooping sons of earth.
>
> For ages long it lay concealed,
> A Holy Book of sacred worth,
> And by the power of God twas sealed,
> In latter days to come from earth.
> . . . .
> And Joseph Smith in prophecey,
> Declared his truth with inspired tongue,
> The Leader of this church should be,
> Our Much loved Prophet Brigham Young. (446)

It was for the children, too, that he composed the hymn that was published in 1877 in the *Juvenile Instructor* and that remains in the hymnal today:

> Dearest children, God is near you,
> Watching o'er you day and night,
> And delights to own and bless you,
> If you strive to do what's right.
>   He will bless you,
> If you put your trust in Him. (466)

Not surpisingly a loyal Latter-day Saint like Walker would have his reaction to the various efforts of the federal government to bring an end to Mormon plural marriage. In 1876, when a convention in Cincinnati had included an antipolygamy plank in the party platform, Walker responded with:

> Should the 'Plank' be of oak,
> May it all end in smoke,
> And the ashes decay and get rotten.

> May its Author do well
> On his journey to Hell,
> And sink, sink and sink till forgotten. (429)

An especially eloquent poetic reaction came in 1879, the year of the Reynolds decision by the Supreme Court, which was really the beginning of the end for plural marriage. For Walker and others like him there was no doubt that the Supreme Court and the United States were on the high road to destruction. He wrote "An Address to the American Eagle":

> Illustrious Bird! Magestic Fowl,
>> Are you deaf?
> Cant you hear the Nation's howl
>> Their sighs of grief,
> I thought your pinions broad and strong,
>> Cant you hear?
> Would shield the right, redress the wrong:
>> Ah a tear.
> And why that tear most noble bird?
>> Aint you well?
> Or is it what we've lately heard
>> Sounds like hell?
> Illustrious Bird in doleful plight
>> Cant you cluck?
> Or are you meditating flight?
>> Say are you stuck?
> Your crest seems fallen, your plumage soiled;
>> What—no reply.
> What is the matter, are you riled?
>> What? going to cry?
> (REPLY)
> The sickly bird said, pray dont joke,
>> I dont feel well.
> My Constitution's nearly broke,
>> Cant break the spell.
> . . . .
>
> The Supreme Court of all the Land—
>> They'd better pause—
> Have deemd it right to Countermand
>> God's Holy Laws.

. . . .

The Noble Bird raised high his beak
And left them in the lurch
And made his home on Utah's peak
And Since has joined the Church. (488–89)

Having taken a second wife, Walker could not help but be sensitive to this issue. Other poems or songs on the subject were written, such as "The Spirit of the Times" (October 2, 1882), "What Shall We Do with the Mormons?" (December 23, 1882), "In Utah" (May 17, 1885), and "The Goddess of Liberty's Soliloquy" (July 4, 1888).

How did Walker see the passing years? He was your typical middle-aged person or senior citizen who shakes his head at the developments of the day, especially the interests and fads of young people. When a style of dress called the Grecian bend became fashionable, he could not help but write a work called "Burlesque on the Fashions of the Day, 1870":

Come all ye gents and ladies and listen to my rhyme,
While I relate a song to you to pass away the time;
It's of the modern fashions that seem to have no end,
And the latest on[e] that's all the rage, is this stylish
    'Grecian Bend.'
. . . .

In the good old times a lady counted ringlets no disgrace,
As they hung in rich profusion 'Round about her pretty face;
Now they shingle, crop, and frizzle it in styles that have no end,
And stick it out away behind, just like the 'Grecian Bend.' (300)

Later, dress was just one of the reforms advocated by feminists of the 1890s, including Walker's daughter Zaidee. Walker wrote, with humor but not cruelty and not rejection, of "The New Woman, Dress Reform, and Suffrage":

She's going to join the army,
Yes, join the light brigade,
And when the war is over,
She'll shoulder pick and spade.
The man, poor thing, must stay at home,
Bake, cook, and wash the tins,
Yes, rock the cradle, hush-a-bye,
And take care of the twins.

> She'll likely run for Congress,
> Or President-elect,
> And when she guides that ship of state,
> Guess what you may expect?
> The woman's rights and marriage bills
> Will pass without dissent;
> Old maids then all will married be,
> And hail the grand event.
> . . . .
>
> If I were called to rule the world,
> As to how they should be dressed—
> I'd let them have their own sweet way,
> And dress as suits them best,—
> For if I were to pass a law,
> Regarding form and style,
> They'd have their own way anyhow,
> 'Tis true, now watch them smile. (797)

He was not a sour misanthrope (or misogynist) and could enjoy the passing scene.

As for the deeper meaning of the events surrounding him, he experienced some dismay yet modulated it first into resignation and ultimately into faith and hope. He did not attend the conference in Salt Lake City in October 1890, but on October 12, when the stake president reported on the issuance of the Manifesto, Walker wrote in his diary: "Some cant understand why this should be, it looking like as tho we feared what man could do instead of trusting in the Power of God to enable them to carry out all his commandments, He being able to bring us off more than conqueror."

As 1891 began, he wrote (January 3): "Some say and have written that great things are to happen this year and the fulfillment of Daniels prophecies as to the prophetic numbers will be plainly Manifested this year 1891. Yea, dire and dreadfull things are to transpire. Some even declare that Christ will come and the Millennial Reign [be] inaugurated. I think some of these things will not happen as stated, but God holds all these things in his hands and at the close of 91, we shall tell more than now."

The same sense of impending cataclysm was expressed poetically. In

1894 (July 24), he composed two lengthy pieces. One looked forward to statehood. Grover Cleveland is the hero:

> Just please give your attention
> To what I now relate,
> We've been knocking at our uncle's door
> And asking for a State;
> Old Grover gently raisd the latch,
> Young Ute took off his hat,
> "Come in! you Rocky Mountain Chief,
> You saucy democrat."

At the end of the ninth stanza we have the Dixie poet's version of the elders saving the Constitution hanging by a thread:

> Young Ute said, "Should there come a time
> You get into a row;
> The Constitution we'll defend
> The best that we Know how,
> And should vile traitors swarm around,
> Which looks like soon they must;
> Young Ute will save our glorious Flag
> From trailing in the dust." (778–79)

That same day Miss Josephine Jarvis recited Walker's long poetic reflection entitled "As It Is." Eighteen stanzas long, the work can properly be described as apocalyptic. Here are some sample stanzas:

> What Mean these strange sounds of riots we hear,
> Of bloodshed, and murder, men's hearts fill'd with fear,
> Of floods, fires, and cyclones that sweep oer the Land?
> 'Tis but a beginning of those close at hand.
> . . . .
> There must be a reason these things have gone forth,
> From the Fair Sunny south to the Land of the North;
> They've regected [sic] the Gospel, the Message of Love,
> And God's angels of vengeance have flown from above.
>
> These Angels have now left the Portals on high
> To show forth the Signs that Christ's coming is nigh;

Their judgements are Sealed, and will surely go forth
And vex all the Peoples, who dwell on the Earth. (776–77)

After describing the darkening of the sun, the moon turning to blood,
pestilence, famine, earthquake, death, plague, dearth, and desolation,
Walker assures the Latter-day Saints that all will be well with them if
they are faithful and true: "Rejoice all ye Saints for the favors of God, /
The blessings of Peace, and your own quiet abode, / While Death and
destruction are sweeping the Land, / Ye are Kept and preserved, by the
Might of his hand" (777). Throughout his diary, but especially during
the last decade of the century, Walker faithfully recorded floods, fires,
and other catastrophes—his record of the "signs of the times."

What, then, is the significance of all this? There would seem to be
the following possibilities. First, we might come across a neglected poet
of genius, someone who deserves to be included in the anthologies. In
other words, there may well be poems whose range of subject, sensi-
tivity, verbal felicity, and inventiveness justify our admiration. By such
qualitative measures, it should be obvious, Walker's works do not deserve consideration. If at best they are sometimes clever, they are predictable in sentiment, either monotonous or, alternatively, clumsy in
prosody, and always devoid of that individuality and happy combination
of subject, diction, and meter that historically characterize the best of
a society's poetic output.

Second, works of this kind may have biographical value. The relationship of the life of the writer to the literature produced is not always
obvious, and indeed one school of thought insists that the attention
should be on the work, the poetry itself, and not on the poet's life.
But literary biography has seldom been able to resist the temptation
of noticing connections. Within Mormon history, Maureen Ursenbach
Beecher's *Eliza and Her Sisters* (1991)[4] provides an example of showing
how poetry, when read closely, may relate to the life experience of its
author. A biographer of Charley Walker could exploit his verse in this
same way, although I am not sure how much would be revealed that
would be otherwise unknown.

Third, this body of frontier rhyme can be seen as part of the rhe-
torical strategy by which Mormons were controlled. Or if "controlled"
seems too strong a word (I mean it in the neutral sense of "social control"), let us say encouraged, inspired, kept in the line of duty and instructed as to the meaning of their own experience and the events of the

larger world. Mormons on the frontier found themselves subjected to verbal bombardment, from outside as well as from within. From within there were converging and mutually reinforcing messages conveyed by books, newspapers, magazines, pamphlets, sermons, anecdotes and testimonies, orations, toasts, songs, and poetry. Although not all orchestrated from the top, these different forms and avenues of expression tended to work together for a common purpose.

Charley Walker was an "outsider," belonging to a group out of step with the rest of the country. He and his people were ridiculed and denounced, reviled and verbally spat upon. But whether he realized it or not, Walker was part of the Mormon establishment, doing his bit to promote the Kingdom of God on earth, as he might have put it. By the modest talent that "is death to hide" he would help to provide the Saints with encouragement and understanding.

Finally, we may see the corpus of frontier poetry as reflecting the attitudes, values, and standards of the community. Such a claim might seem to run counter to the preceding point, which emphasized shaping and influencing the audience, but a little reflection reminds us that one does not succeed in such efforts if the words are so distant from the group that they fail to be read or listened to or enjoyed. The historian is often at a total loss to know how "people" responded to literary works, but in Charley Walker's case we do have some clues. First is the simple fact that he continued to be invited to compose and recite, year after year in many public situations. It is implausible to imagine that he was forced on listeners who grumbled and complained. In his diary he noted that a poem or song "was well received" (493), "applauded by the vast assembly" (496), "warmly received" (807). On one occasion, he commented, "from the boisterous demonstrations of applause I judged it pleased the audience" (744–45). In 1894 he "received rounds of applause" (775). When the time came for toasts, the following notes were handed in to be read: "Our Inspired Dixie Poet, Long may he live, and may his mind grow brighter to bless us with his sentiments"; and "Bill Nye is not in it with our Charlie" (779–80). Insofar as it is possible to judge such things, I think we can say that Walker both inspired and reflected his people. He put into words feelings that they, or at least many of them, shared.

The social role of a popular poet turns out to be not so minor.[5] Tributes to individuals, the commemoration of anniversaries and various celebrations, recognizing special groups within the community, understanding current events of special impact on this people, casting the changes of fashion into a meaningful interpretation, using humor as a release from distress, encouraging the young to be true to the faith, refusing to see the old fade into forgetfulness but instead repeatedly reminding the coming generation of their parents' heroic accomplishments—all of this, done with a dash of individuality and occasional flashes of self-effacing humor, is not, after all, an insignificant accomplishment.

Many human societies have had their bards, their wordsmiths, who would channel into rhyme or other patterns the significant events and experiences of the group. Other poets of teritorial Utah, from Eliza R. Snow and John Lyon, to a host of those whose rhymes appeared only in letters or diaries or perhaps newspapers, performed this same function to a greater or lesser degree. But for dogged consistency of output, variety of subject matter, and popularity probably none of these pioneer poets surpassed the bard of Utah's Dixie, Charles Lowell Walker.

Notes

1. Nathan O. Hatch, *The Democratization of American Christianity* (New Haven: Yale University Press, 1989), 227.

2. A. Karl Larson and Katharine Miles Larson, eds., *Diary of Charles Lowell Walker,* 2 vols. (Logan: Utah State University Press, 1980). All poems in the present essay are from this work, as of course are all the diary quotations. Page numbers or dates in the text are considered sufficient reference. Another work of relevance, not used here, is Charles Lowell Walker, "Poems," original owned by Dr. Walter Woodbury, Salt Lake City, Utah, according to *Diary,* 43n.

3. From Davis Bitton, *Wit and Whimsy in Mormon History* (Salt Lake City: Deseret Book, 1974), 27–28.

4. Salt Lake City, Utah: Aspen Books, 1991.

5. For examples of verse coming from the broad spectrum of Protestant dissent, including Mormons, see Hatch, *Democratization of American Christianity.*

5

Mormonism's Encounter
with Spiritualism

FOR THE FIRST twenty or thirty years of Mormonism's existence one of its main appeals was the claim to modern-day revelation from God. Whereas other Christians were limited to hearing the word of God only through the pages of the Bible, obscured by problems of translation and theological controversy, the Mormons could hear the voice of God speaking directly to their needs in their day. Such was the message that was proclaimed confidently in the early Mormon proselyting literature and by the hundreds of missionaries that carried the good news to the world.

Around the middle of the century another movement set forth claims to direct communication with the unseen world. This was spiritualism, one of the significant enthusiasms of the nineteenth century. It was in 1848 in upstate New York that modern spiritualism had its origins. At Hydesville, in Wayne County, a Mr. and Mrs. J. D. Fox and their two daughters heard mysterious knockings or rappings, which they discovered to be in some way intelligent, that is able to respond to questions. A little later, when Kate and Margaret Fox went to live with a married sister at Rochester, they established communication, as they said, with dead relatives and even famous figures of the past. The messages were conveyed by rappings—one for no, three for yes—and were transmitted through "mediums," persons having some special quality enabling them to receive messages from the "other side." The three Fox sisters were the first mediums of the new movement.[1]

The spiritualist movement spread, as one authority has said, "like an epidemic." Spirit circles were formed. Soon there were mediums holding seances all over the country. Publications were established. Professional mediums from America carried the message to England and other countries, where the movement caught on. Variations in the form of supernatural communication included, in addition to the rapping already mentioned, such forms as spirit writing (in which the medium wrote but supposedly only as the passive instrument of a spirit), trance-speaking (in which the medium's voice was supposedly used by the spirit), and various kinds of table-turning, table-raising, or the well-known planchette (later the Ouija board), which through the slightest of physical contact with a living person could become a means of an-swering questions posed to the spirits on the other side.

A large part of the appeal of spiritualism was its supposed ability to provide assurance of life after death, the well being of departed loved ones, and the existence of a divine power and a real meaning for human life. The messages received through a medium were intimate, personal, directed to the individual. At the same time, according to the claim, the spiritualist activities were thoroughly scientific. Almost from the be-ginning there were investigations of the various psychic phenomena at-tempting to find natural explanations for them. Some examples of fraud were found, of course, and many of the spiritualist experiences could be explained quite adequately by some kind of subconscious influence. But almost from the beginning, also, there have been people, including scientists of repute, who have concluded that some of the spiritualist communications were indeed of supernatural origin. Spiritualism, in a word, offered the unusual combination of religious fervor, emotional satisfaction, and intellectual respectability.

It is not surprising that the territory of Utah began to hear rumblings. Several prominent Mormon leaders were natives of the area in upper New York where the Fox sisters lived. Letters from relatives told of the spiritualist excitement. During trips to the native state, or missions to different parts of the United States or to Europe, Mormons began to hear about the spiritualists and their ability to receive messages from the other side of the veil. Through newspapers and periodicals received through the mail—some of which were used by the Utah newspapers as a source of national news—Mormons were made aware of the existence of the new rival. Unlike the Protestant and Catholic churches, which did not choose to claim modern revelations of their own, the spiritualists did claim present-day communications addressed to individual needs.

As early as 1852 Mormon leaders were remarking on the popularity of spiritualism. Heber C. Kimball told of hearing from a brother-in-law in Rochester, New York, that there were 135 "spiritual writers" in that one city. He saw this as a sign that "the invisible world are in trouble; they are knocking, and rapping, and muttering."[2] The following year, in April 1853, Parley P. Pratt delivered a major address on the subject of spiritualism, by which, as he said, the world was "agitated."[3] In February 1854 Jedediah M. Grant, just back from a mission in New York and Pennsylvania, told of there becoming acquainted with the "spirit rappers."[4]

It is more difficult to know what ordinary members of the Church knew about the subject. Did the printer's devils at the *Deseret News* talk about it? Was it of any interest to new immigrants, some of them working on the temple block? Did it arouse the curiosity of families in American Fork, in Parowan, in Hebron, in Cache Valley? We do not have the complete transcripts of sacrament meetings or high council meetings or home teaching conversations that would give a solid answer. Nevertheless, there are a few glimpses indicating that Mormons, like other people, were interested in these claims to communication from "the other side." Apostate or lapsed Mormons at Kirtland were attracted to the "spirit rappers."[5] The same was true in San Bernardino after the withdrawal of the loyalist Saints in 1857.[6] In missionary diaries we get some hints. David Holladay found that a member had been "carried away" by the spiritualist movement in 1855.[7] Two years later Henry G. Boyle encountered some spiritualists during his preaching mission in California.[8] In 1859 Oscar O. Stoddard told of meeting a family who believed in spiritualism because their daughter had been cured of consumption by it.[9] In 1858 Charles L. Walker was attending a grammar school class in Salt Lake City, where, one evening, the subject of spiritualism was discussed. Later the same year he spoke in church on the subject of "spirit rappings." He was quite disturbed the following year to find that his own father was favorably impressed by a spiritualist book written by a Mr. Arnold. Gradually, much to the dismay of Charles, his father became more and more interested, reading other spiritualist books and a spiritualist periodical. Even after he moved to St. George, in 1862, Charles Walker still found the subject to be a lively issue; his diary continues to include disapproving references to spiritualism for several years.[10]

A new phase in the incursion of spiritualism into Mormon Utah followed the coming of the railroad in 1869. This was the year of the Godbeite schism. The general lineaments of the Godbeite movement— its renunciation of economic dictation by the Church, its advocacy of mining and other industry for Utah, and its alleged championing of free speech and enlightenment—have been known. But the movement had strong religious motivation as well. In essence the religion of the New Movement was, in Ronald W. Walker's phrase, a "grafting of their [the Godbeite leaders'] concept of spiritualism upon the roots of Mormon organization."[11] Use of the planchette by curiosity seekers about this time is clearly established; one William Cogswell received special instructions from it to join the Mormon Church.[12] The device found such a ready acceptance among the Godbeites that Brigham Young denounced them contemptuously as the "Harrison-Godbe-Planchette church."[13]

As for mediumistic communications with the beyond, William S. Godbe and E. L. T. Harrison told of a series of seances in New York City in the fall of 1868.[14] By 1870, according to some rumors, Charlotte Ives Godbe, William's wife, was acting as a medium.[15] A more important medium entered the movement with the conversion of Amasa Lyman, excommunicated Mormon apostle.[16] His diary gives clear indication that during 1869 he was quite friendly with Harrison, Godbe, H. W. Lawrence, and T. B. H. Stenhouse.[17] In 1870, when he announced that he was going to "resume the preaching of the gospel," the Authorities of the Mormon Church, including his son Francis Marion, were upset. Within a matter of weeks we find Lyman circulating among followers of the New Movement and proselyting, meeting a medium by the name of John Murray Spear, and attending a seance. His reading during 1871–72 includes such works as Henry J. Horn's *Strange Visitors;* A. J. Davis's *Stellar Key to the Summer Land; Spiritual Pilgrim; Biography of Mr. J. M. Peebles;* and the *Religious Philosophical Journal*— all of them written with a spiritualist orientation.

Lyman's involvement in seances became more frequent. At first he seems to have been there as an observer, with someone else acting as the medium, probably Spear and on one occasion a Brother Carlile. During 1871 he even sent questions to a medium named Charles H. Foster in New York, who contacted Lyman's dead relatives and sent back the results. Quickly, however, the gift of mediumship was more widely shared. His daughters Josephine and Hila were "entranced." Sometimes his comments on these seances are quite general: "encouraging manifestation," "had private seance with happy results," "had pleasant time with our friends from beyond." Others are more specific, as this communication from Chief Walker through Lyman's daughter Hila: "Me big Chief. American. Me Walker, me much shine in spirit life, on big hunting ground. Me write big lots in Spirit life. Me Walker sure. Me no fool·you. No, me good." Others from the spirit world who communicated to Amasa Lyman and his coterie were Kit Carson, Henry Lyman, Mother Phelps, Perez Mason, Cornelia Lyman, Joseph Smith, Heber C. Kimball, and Hyrum Smith.

Lyman himself began to function as a medium. Between 1870 and 1873 he traveled from town to town, meeting with interested persons holding seances. Lyman and his associates seem to have been quite hopeful of attracting numerous followers. In 1874 Richard R. Hopkins wrote to Lyman that their movement, known as "harmonial philosophy," was "making such inroads among the faithful that it is a subject of condemnation in the various ward meetings."[18] Orson Hyde and Franklin D. Richards called on Lyman to inform him of his excommunication. "Why my dear brethren," he replied, "you here now are simply, as it were, at the foot of the mountain, whereas I have been where you are now, but unlike you, I have gone to the summit of the mountain, and traversed its plateau, and gone far beyond, making the heights of another mountain far beyond and removed from this one."[19]

Part of the appeal of New Movement spiritualism to dissident Mormons was that it allowed them to retain some elements of their Mormon beliefs, or to see Mormonism as a preliminary phase of spiritualism that had now moved, in Lyman's phrase, to the summit of the mountain. T. B. H. Stenhouse was especially articulate in giving a spiritualist interpretation of early Mormonism. Joseph Smith was "no more and no less than a 'spirit-medium.'" He did receive genuine communications but mistakenly interpreted as divine revelations messages that came from departed spirits. His seclusion behind the curtain when translating the Book of Mormon corresponded, said Stenhouse, to "the dark seances so common in the experience of modern Spiritualism." Even the extraordinary manifestations at the dedication of the Kirtland Temple were rejected out of hand by most people living at the time, but modern spiritualists "will credit the thousand spectators and witnesses at the dedication with having had a 'wonderful experience.'"[20]

If Ronald Walker's interpretation is ultimately persuasive, as it is to me, then the Godbeite leaders may not have at first recognized the implications of pursuing the spiritualistic experience. It seems clear enough that at first their intentions were veiled under the guise of modern reform of Mormonism, that they recognized the need for adding the genius of Mormon organization to the emotional appeals of spiritualism, and that "the logic of spiritualism ultimately was antithetical to the Mormon faith they believed themselves preserving."[21] For present purposes, such crosscurrents and motivations are less important than the fact that this was a major channel for the inroads of spiritualism into the Mormon membership. Formally at their own meetings, through informal conversations and study groups, by development of mediumistic talent among their number, and by the sponsorship of prominent spiritualist mediums and lecturers from the outside such as Spear and Foster, the Godbeite spiritualists could appear as a formidable challenge to the Mormon position.

As they contemplated the popularity of spiritualism and saw its introduction into Utah, Mormon leaders could respond in different ways. One refrain that was heard over and over again as the Mormon leaders mentioned the subject, was that people who earlier had rejected the Mormon message by insisting on the impossibility of modern revelation were now accepting the spiritualist claims without compunction. After recalling how people had rejected the Mormon gospel, George Q. Cannon added: "But as soon as something came along that gratified them in the way they wanted—something that could tip a table or give some other singular manifestation of power, such as feeling invisible hands laid upon them, or hearing music played by invisible performers, or something of this character, they were convinced immediately that it was possible for spiritual beings to communicate with mortals, and now the Spiritualists number their converts by millions; they probably number more than any other denomination, if they can be called a denomination. They boast of their success."[22] The inconsistency and irony were enhanced by stressing the popularity of spiritualism.[23]

In such statements there was an element of the I-told-you-so attitude, some sarcasm, and some understandable delight at pointing to what seemed to be a huge inconsistency on the part of their opponents. But the Mormon answer could scarcely stop with such superficial nudging. Were the spiritualists' experiences, which had an abundance of personal testimony in their favor, fraudulent or were they genuine? This was what the Mormon leaders were called upon to explain so that their people would not be lead astray.

There were some suggestions from the Mormon pulpit that the spiritualists were frauds. In 1853 the *Latter-day Saint Millennial Star* labeled the movement as "transparent, blasphemous imposture."[24] In the *Deseret News* in 1859 the following brief notice appeared: "Dr. B. F. Hatch gives it as his opinion, after nine years' acquaintance with spiritualism and its leading advocates, that many of their theories are founded in wild delusion, and productive of the most direful results; that he is determined to 'flee from his errors,' and though he once threw Christianity overboard, he thanks God that he has again been made its recipient. For his wife Cora he professed the profoundest respect and tenderest regard, but asserts that spiritualism (of which she was a medium) is fifty per cent self-delusion, twenty-five per cent psychology, fifteen per cent intentional imposition and the remaining ten per cent yet a matter of uncertainty."[25] For N. L. Nelson, writing in the 1890s, spiritualism was a "superstition," explainable in large part as the result of "unconscious cerebration." He told of an experience he had had with a lodger, a "woman of strange mien," who turned out to be a spirit medium. He heard strange noises in the night from her quarters. When he objected to the "quality and number" of her visitors, she sought other quarters.[26] The tone here is one of mild ridicule.

Occasionally humor was used in the Mormons' denunciation of spiritualism. In 1889 an amusing story in the *Young Women's Journal* was entitled "Spiritualism, or What Became of Murphy." The best of the humorous stories I have found was published on February 22, 1859, in *Valley Tan*, where it was undoubtedly seen by a good number of Mormon readers:

> An enthusiastic believer was relating to a skeptic, the spiritual performances to which he could testify, and among other things said that on a certain occasion the spirit of his wife, who had been dead several years, returned to him, and seated herself upon his knee, put her arm around him, and kissed him as much to his gratification as she used to when living.
>
> "You do not mean to say," remarked the skeptic, "that the spirit of your wife really embraced and kissed you?"
>
> "No, not *exactly* that," replied the believer, "but her spirit took possession of the body of a female medium, and through her embraced and kissed me."

Nudges and knowing winks would follow such a story, which was not calculated to treat the spiritualist claims with much seriousness.

But simply writing off the new movement as a fraud was too easy. Such terms as "delusion" came with ill grace from the Mormons, whose claims had repeatedly been disposed of with the same cavalier expression. As Parley P. Pratt recognized in 1853, the Mormons found themselves on the horns of a dilemma: "If on the one hand we admit the principle of communication between the spirit world and our own, and yield ourselves to the unreserved or indiscriminate guidance of every spiritual manifestation, we are liable to be led about by every wind of doctrine, and by every kind of spirit which constitute the varieties of being and of thought in the spirit world. . . . If, on the other hand, we deny the philosophy or the fact of spiritual communication between the living and those who have died, we deny the very fountain from which emanated the great truths or principles which were the foundation of both the ancient and modern Church."[27]

The general Mormon position on spiritualism was worked out to meet this dilemma. Besides many brief references to the subject, there are three fairly substantial statements. An editorial entitled "Try the Spirits," which appeared in the *Times and Seasons* in 1842, preceded the rise of spiritualism in its specific form with the Fox sisters, but several of the principles there discussed were found to have relevance to the question later on. A full sermon on the subject of spiritualism was delivered by Parley P. Pratt in 1853, when some of the first stirrings were taking place. Finally, near the end of the century, N. L. Nelson published a series on "Theosophy and Mormonism" that contained a fairly thorough discussion of spiritualism. It is mainly in these articles that the Mormon leaders gave their reasoned response to the spiritualist challenge. Other statements in the sermons or in Church periodicals repeated the basic Mormon position with only occasional variations.[28]

Rather than rejecting all of the spiritualist claims out of hand, the Mormons therefore allowed that at least some of the communications from the spirit world were genuine. But evaluating their worth did not stop there. One clear possibility was that the spirits responsible for the messages were inferior spirits. N. L. Nelson was not so extreme as to maintain that only "evil" spirits were involved (although he saw only these as capable of "possessing" a human body when that phenomenon occurred). He was prepared to admit, in other words, that the spirits of people who had lived on earth were communicating. But he reasoned that it was unlikely that "men and women of intelligence would hang about clairvoyants and mediums for the miserable chance of gratifying the curiosity of earthly friends and relatives." The spirits moving the planchette or working upon earthly spirit mediums were "low-caste spirits."[29] Other Mormon statements did not differentiate quite this carefully but simply labeled the spiritualist phenomena as coming from the devil and his minions.

Once genuine communication was admitted, the basic question became the means of discriminating between the good and bad, the lawful and the unlawful, channels. Pratt listed five characteristics of true and lawful communications. The privilege is granted (1) to those who believe in direct revelation in modern times; (2) to those who have repented of their sins; (3) to those who act in the name of Jesus Christ; (4) to those who hold the Priesthood; and (5) in the temples dedicated to God.[30]

The Mormon leaders were confident of the superiority of the priesthood. Heber C. Kimball indicated his opinion in unmistakable terms: "I never heard a knocking, or saw a table dance, only as I kicked it myself. I do not want them knocking or dancing around me." After mentioning the claim of some to automatic or spirit writing, he said, "I do not thank any person to take my hand and write without my consent; we do not like such proceedings."[31] Brigham Young was especially confident that the powers responsible for the spiritualistic phenomena simply could not operate in the presence of a Mormon Elder, for this would mean that a lesser power was dominating a greater. "You may assemble together every spiritualist on the face of the earth," he thundered, "and I will defy them to make a table move or get a communication from hell or any other place while I am present."[32]

What about such words or ideas as the spiritualists did receive? The Mormons were not impressed. Some truths were conveyed, of course, but these were only such truths as the devil used to disguise and make palatable the basic error he wished to peddle. In most instances the Mormon leaders were obviously contemptuous of the feeble "truths" conveyed through the mediums. N. L. Nelson gave the one systematic analysis when he listed twenty "ethical principles" of the spiritualists. These included, among others, the following: that man as a spirit is immortal; that there is a spirit world; that the "process of physical death in no way essentially transforms the mental constitution or the moral character of those who experience it"; that happiness or suffering in the spirit world depends on "character, aspirations, and degree of harmonization, or of personal conformity to universal and divine law"; that progression continues beyond the grave; that there are different grades in the spirit world; and that as offspring of the Infinite Parent man has in his nature "a germ of divinity." Nelson asked what all of this had to do with Mormonism and answered his own question: "Three-fourths of it *is* Mormonism and not Spiritualism." The remaining one-fourth could be accounted for, he thought, by "unconscious cerebration."[33]

The most obvious characteristic of the messages, as the Mormons saw them, was their confusion. This was closely related to the lack of any real organization among the spiritualists, who were seen as flying off in all directions, believing anything they wanted to, receiving messages that said almost anything, contradicting each other, a helter-skelter stumbling after some kind of guidance but with a bumbling confusion as the result. "God has spoken now, and so has the devil," said Brigham Young. "Jesus has revealed his Priesthood, so has the devil revealed his, and there is quite a difference between the two. One forms a perfect chain, the links of which cannot be separated; one has perfect order, laws, rules, regulations, organization; it forms, fashions, makes, creates, produces, protects, and holds in existence the inhabitants of the earth in a pure and holy form of government. . . . The other is a rope of sand; it is disjointed, jargon, confusion, discord, everybody receiving revelation to suit himself."[34]

In a sense what the Mormon leaders were saying was, "By their fruits ye shall know them." "The difference between the two systems is apparent," said George Q. Cannon. "The Latter-day Saints are united, just as Jesus Christ prayed that His followers might be. It is true that we are not yet one as the Father and the Son are one; but we are approximating thereto. The principle of oneness is in our midst and is continually growing. But how is it with those who are the base imitators of the servants of God? Why a thousand vagaries are indulged in by them. There is no form of belief in which they unite. . . . Are the inhabitants of the earth benefitted by them? Is the earth better, more beautiful or lovely by their labors or by the revelations they receive? No, there are no fruits of this kind to be witnessed among them; but all is division, confusion, and chaos. There is nothing to cement them together or make them one."[35]

In 1871 Gustave Henriod wrote of a man, once a Mormon, who was attracted to spiritualism and then later died under the influence of alcohol or opium. Such an example was thought to be ample warning to any Mormons who might be tempted by "the delusive influence of this new sect."[36]

In 1874, at a meeting of the Retrenchment Association, Sarah Decker "exhorted the sisters not to attend these Spiritualist meetings that were held in the Liberal Institute." She was "sorry to see so many of the saints drawn there."[37] This, of course, was the immediate aftermath of the Godbeite enthusiasm, and we may suspect that what she considered "many" may have been a hundred or less curiosity seekers. That Utahns could still follow spiritualism if they were inclined is suggested by a letter of 1888 in which Mrs. B. Raymond, a clairvoyant from Denver, asked about obtaining a license to practice in Salt Lake City.[38] As late as 1900 an interesting comment appeared in the record of the Salt Lake Stake. An Elder J. Selley, a city employee, told that he had recently visited a "spiritual medium," who told him that she had been in town only about two weeks but had already received visits from "hundreds" of Mormons who came to ask her whether or not they should be baptized for their kindred dead.[39]

Such indications notwithstanding, it would be hard to prove that spiritualism proved to be a serious threat to Mormonism if we judge it in terms of conversions. Spiritualism hovered on the periphery, a reality of which the Mormon leaders were aware and which for brief periods did bid fair to become a craze in the Mormon community. When the meetings, private conversations between individuals, and the Mormon sermons on the subject simmered down, however, it is apparent that spiritualism had never been more than a flash in the pan in Mormon country. Brigham Young was quite right in recognizing the confusion and disunity among the spiritualists. While their numbers may have been considerable throughout the world, they were never effectively organized. As a later authority said, spiritualism "failed to maintain its early promise . . . because of its failure to develop either organization, ritual or doctrine,"[40] a general observation that was doubly true when it faced a powerful, functioning organization like Mormonism.

Another reason for Mormonism's relative immunity has not yet been suggested. I refer to the fact that the church had already provided for many, if not all, of the experiences that spiritualism offered to those longing for them. Reading statements in the spiritualist periodicals gives ample evidence of what these experiences were and of the widespread complaint that Christianity in general had become too rational, too proper, too arid to answer emotional-spiritual yearnings. But Mormonism was different in some respects. Was modern revelation speaking to modern needs desired? Mormonism had it. What about personal contact with God and departed spirits? Mormonism allowed for such encounters and, under the necessary controls, even encouraged them in the form of dreams and individual revelations for the guidance of the individual. Patriarchal blessings and other similar blessings were an effective way of communicating a precious experience that was seen as highly individual. The longing for contact with departed loved ones, aside from the possibilities already mentioned, was given rich fulfillment in genealogy and temple work, which was seen and experienced as an activity that actually did something to knit the relationship with one's family and in some cases to perform services for those souls who were dead and gone. Anyone familiar with the folklore of Mormon temple work—I am referring to the rich variety of intimate personal experiences almost always transmitted by word of mouth—knows that actual appearances of spirits, along with voices and other kinds of manifestations, occurred frequently enough and in a beautiful setting, sanctified and permeated with awe, to make a trip to a medium seem anticlimactic if not superfluous and lacking in propriety.

I am referring of course to the resources of the two systems as they were seen by those who participated in them, the kinds of experience they offered, the needs they seemed to fulfill. When the problem is considered in these terms, the failure of spiritualism to gain much of a following in Mormon country is scarcely surprising.

Whatever the reason, spiritualism did not succeed in winning substantial numbers of Mormons to its ranks. And on the world scene it has not since measured up to the anticipations of some of its early proponents. The failure of spiritualism in nineteenth-century Utah is therefore an instructive case study dramatizing the inherent disadvantage of a faddish, quasi-intellectual, loose movement in competition with a movement that had its own theology, its own internal consistency, its own satisfactions and appeals, and above all its own firm organizational base.

Notes

An earlier version of this chapter appeared in *Journal of Mormon History* 1 (1974): 39–50.

1. A standard treatment of spiritualism is Sir Arthur Conan Doyle, *The History of Spiritualism*, 2 vols. (New York, 1926). A popular account is in Carl Carmer, *Listen for a Lonesome Drum* (New York: Farrar & Rinehart, Inc., 1936). A lively, well-researched biography is Early W. Fornell, *The Unhappy Medium: Spiritualism and the Life of Margaret Fox* (Austin: University of Texas Press, 1964). An interesting debunking of spiritualist claims is Ruth Brandon, *The Spiritualists: The Passion for the Occult in the Nineteenth and Twentieth Centuries* (New York: Knopf, 1983).

2. *Journal of Discourses*, 26 vols. (London: Latter-day Saints Book Depot, 1854–86), 1:36. Hereinafter abbreviated as *JD*.

3. *JD* 1:6–15.

4. *JD* 2:10.

5. For later spiritualism in Kirtland see the report of Thomas Colburn, who in 1855 found there a "few that call themselves Saints, but very weak, many apostates, who have mostly joined the rappers" (*St. Louis Luminary,* 17 Feb. 1855 and 2 May 1855). In 1869 Apostle Orson Pratt reminisced of a time several years earlier when he was in New York City. Spiritualism, he said, "was all the order of the day. Almost all those old members of the Church that had been in Nauvoo and Kirtland and had apostatized, had fled into New York, Philadelphia, St. Louis, and throughout the Eastern cities; and in going through any of these cities, if you heard anything about these apostates, you would hear about them being great mediums; there was scarcely a case but what they were spiritual mediums" (*JD* 13:70).

6. "We have had some curious manifestations under the head of Spiritual communications by working table tipping and writing but the people are generally satisfied that God is not in the whirlwind nor the storm but in the spirit that whispers peace to the contrite heart." Amasa Lyman and Charles C. Rich to Brigham Young, 1 September 1853, Historical Department, Church of Jesus Christ of Latter-day Saints, Salt Lake City, Utah, hereinafter cited as Church Archives. See also Rich speech as summarized in San Bernardino Branch Record, 26 August 1855, Church Archives. Benjamin Grouard's defection to spiritualism is noted in Louisa Barnes Pratt's journal, *Heart Throbs of the West* 8 (1947): 309–81. Later spiritualism in San Bernardino is reported in *The National Spiritualist,* 1 January 1931. On San Bernardino generally, see Edward Leo Lyman, "The Rise and Decline of Mormon San Bernardino," *BYU Studies* 29 (Fall 1989): 43–63.

7. David H. Holladay Diary, typescript, Church Archives.

8. Henry G. Boyle Diary, Harold B. Lee Library, Brigham Young University, Provo, typescript, Church Archives.

9. Oscar O. Stoddard Diary, microfilm, Church Archives.

10. *Diary of Charles Lowell Walker,* 2 vols., ed. A. Karl Larson and Katharine Miles Larson (Logan: Utah State University Press, 1980), pass.

11. Ronald W. Walker, "The Commencement of the Godbeite Protest: Another View," *Utah State Historical Quarterly* 42 (Summer 1974): 216–44; and "When Spirits Did Abound: Nineteenth-Century Utah's Encounter with Free-thought Radicalism," *Utah Historical Quarterly* 50 (Fall 1982): 304–24.

12. William J. Cogswell, "Was Brigham Young a Spiritualist?" 24 September 1900, Bancroft Library Manuscript; microfilm copy in Church Archives.

13. Journal History, 2 February 1870. This is a huge, multivolume compilation of newspaper clippings and other primary sources located in the Church Archives.

14. *Utah Magazine,* 27 November 1869. For Orson Pratt's critical comments on these alleged manifestations, see *JD* 13:72–73.

15. Ellen Pratt McGary to Ellen Clawson, 23 April 1870, in papers of Hiram B. Clawson, Western Americana, Marriott Library, University of Utah, Salt Lake City, Utah.

16. See Loretta L. Hefner, "From Apostle to Apostate: The Personal Struggle of Amasa Mason Lyman," *Dialogue: A Journal of Mormon Thought* 15 (Spring 1983): 90–104.

17. Amasa Lyman Diary, Church Archives.

18. Richard R. Hopkins to Amasa Lyman, 14 November 1874, Church Archives.

19. Clinton D. Ray Reminiscences, typescript, Western Americana Collection.

20. T. B. H. Stenhouse, *The Rocky Mountain Saints* (Salt Lake City, 1904).

21. Walker, "Commencement of the Godbeite Protest."

22. *JD* 12:370.

23. It was estimated that there were about ten million "followers" of spiritualism by the mid-1850s (Fornell, *Unhappy Medium*, 107). Mormon references to this popularity are found in several sermons printed in the *Journal of Discourses* and also, for example, in the *Latter-day Saints Millennial Star* (Liverpool), 7 March 1868, 30 December 1873, 27 December 1886, and 11 July 1887.

24. *Millennial Star*, 7 May 1853.

25. *Deseret News*, 9 March 1859.

26. N. L. Nelson, "Theosophy and Mormonism," *The Contributor* 16 (1894–95): 487, 483n.

27. *JD* 2:43.

28. "Try the Spirits," *Times and Seasons*, 1 April 1842; also in Joseph Smith, *History of the Church of Jesus Christ of Latter-day Saints*, ed. B. H. Roberts, 7 vols. (Salt Lake City: Church of Jesus Christ of Latter-day Saints, 1932–51), 4:571–81. Pratt's sermon is in *JD* 1:6–15 and was reprinted in the *Millennial Star*, 11 February 1865; see also Pratt's sermon in *JD* 2:43–47. N. L. Nelson is cited in note 26.

29. Nelson, "Theosophy and Mormonism," 488.

30. *JD* 2:45–46.

31. *JD* 2:223.

32. *JD* 14:72; see also 3:370.

33. Nelson, "Theosophy and Mormonism," 485–88. These were resolutions passed by the American Association of Spiritualists at their 1868 convention in Rochester, New York.

34. *JD* 13:281.

35. *JD* 12:371.

36. *Deseret News*, 10 May 1871.

37. Minutes, Senior and Junior Cooperative Retrenchment Association, 31 October 1874, Church Archives.

38. Letter dated 27 November 1888, City Council files; xerox copy in possession of author.

39. Salt Lake State Historical Record, 25 April 1900, Church Archives.

40. Geoffrey K. Nelson, *Spiritualism and Society* (New York: Schocken Books, 1969), 83.

6

"These Licentious Days":
Dancing among the Mormons

In an official statement of the First Presidency of the Church of Jesus Christ of Latter-day Saints, church members were instructed to avoid "dances that require or permit the close embrace and suggestive movements." Also condemned was immodesty in dress, "the shameless exhibitions of the human form purposely presented in modern styles of dress, or rather undress." Here was the ringing conclusion: "Let not the brilliant prospects of a glorious millennium be clouded with such shadows as are threatened by customs and costumes and diversions of these licentious days."[1]

When was this statement written? Nineteen ninety? Nineteen fifty? In the roaring twenties? Actually it was part of the Christmas message of 1912. But it could have been written at various other times, for the behavior of young people, especially as shown in dress and dance, had long been and continues to be a matter of concern in a church that sees itself as in the world but not of the world. The question of dancing among the Latter-day Saints is of no import theologically, but it is a beautiful example of the interface between religion and popular culture with its inevitable stresses and strains.

On one level, the story of dancing among the Mormons is simply told. The Saints love to dance. From the Nauvoo period, if not before, they found that getting together and kicking up their heels in time to music was welcome relief from their cares. Crossing the plains and in many settlements of the Great Basin, it was a form of amusement that had the tremendous advantage that little was required for it to succeed—a floor would help (although dancing was on the ground during the trip westward) and some kind of music was necessary (as little as a violin or, in one extreme situation, a good whistler).[2] Some kind of combination of males and females was standard, but the ages of those participating could extend from the very young children to old folks in their sixties and seventies. Often there were separate dances arranged for the "primary age" children and the adults.

We have little glimpses that tell us of much hilarity and good fun in these dances. In Cedar City an eccentric bachelor was asked to do a step dance, and he agreed if Josephine Wood would dance with him. She consented and in her preparations managed to pin her switch on his coattail. The results are described by an eyewitness: "When they began to dance, the loud applause convinced him that he was putting on a wonderful performance, and turning himself loose he cut 'high pigeon wings' and executed fantastic capers while the switch waved behind him like the tail of a wild mustang and the party laughed till they had to wipe the tears from their eyes."[3] This was not the only incident that showed that the Mormons knew how to have a good time.

Yet there were signs very early in the history of the Church that everyone was not enthusiastic about dancing. Helen Mar Whitney recalled that in Kirtland—this would be in the 1830s—those "guilty of indulging in so gross a sin as dancing were considered worthy of being disfellowshipped."[4] By the 1840s in Nauvoo the attitude was generally favorable to dancing, but with some reservations. An editorial in the *Times and Seasons*, probably written by John Taylor, approved of dancing both as a religious activity and a physical exercise but expressed concern over unduly late hours and the mingling in bad company.[5] Another reason for not dancing was its inappropriateness for a time of mourning, but the following statement of Brigham Young a few weeks after Joseph Smith's death suggests that everyone may not have been enthusiastic about allowing dancing in the first place: "And so far at least as the members of the Church are concerned, we would advise that balls, dances and other vain and useless amusements would be neither countenanced or patronized; they have been borne with, in some instances heretofore for the sake of peace and good will. But it is not now a time for dancing or frolics but a time of mourning and humiliation and prayer."[6] So dancing had been "borne with . . . for the sake of peace and good will." It is impossible to tell whether this refers to the dancing that had taken place in Nauvoo during the previous four years or the few dances that might have taken place between the martyrdom and the editorial.

Brigham Young's attitude toward dancing was probably affected by his New England background. If he had long since broken away from assuming that such things were sins, he occasionally was uneasy about them. There was a moment after the completion of the Nauvoo Temple when musicians played a Fisher's Hornpipe at the request of Joseph Young, who "broke the gravity" by dancing and asking others to join in. At this same meeting on January 2, 1846, Brigham Young seemed quite lenient: "We will praise the Lord as we please. Now as to dancing in this house—there are thousands of brethren and sisters who have labored to build these walls and put on this roof, and they are shut out from any opportunity of enjoying any amusement among the wicked—or in the world, and shall they have any recreation? Yes! and this is the very place where they can have liberty!"[7] A week later, however, Brigham was demanding that dancing and merriment should cease in the temple "lest the brethren and sisters be carried away by levity."[8] A month later a dance was held in the Nauvoo Temple with music provided by the brass band; several of the Twelve participated.[9] After leaving Nauvoo and starting on the journey west, Young spoke as follows: "There is no harm in dancing. The Lord said he wanted His saints to praise him in all things. It was enjoyed on Miriam and the daughters of Israel to dance and celebrate the name of the Almighty, and to praise him on the destruction of Pharaoh and his host. For some weeks past I could not wake up at any time of the night but I heard the axes at work. Some were building for the destitute and the widow; and now my feelings are, dance all night, if you desire to do so, for there is no harm in it."[10] But a month later he was instructing the brethren to "cease dancing and commence prayer meetings."[11]

One can look upon President Young's statements as representing inconsistency, or on the other hand, as reasonable reactions to different situations. It is clear enough that he was seeking some kind of moderate position, avoiding unseemly levity and some of the dangers of wild abandon while at the same time leaving open the possibility of recreational rejuvenation within the proper limits. In addition to the question of timing, as the impropriety of dancing during mourning or during some of the attempted spiritual reformations while crossing the plains, the main reservations or concerns that were expressed during the first generation of the Church's history were: (1) the danger of mingling with bad company, associating with nonmembers, those whose social and moral standards were not those of the Saints; and (2) the late hours of some dances. Both of these matters continued to be a cause of concern through the remainder of the century; those who frowned on dancing would cite these reasons, and efforts to bring dancing under control would usually include rules on closing times and on standards of admission.

Another problem arose in connection with the introduction of new dances, especially the round dance, and was the center of concern roughly during the last quarter of the century. It will be helpful to remind ourselves that the introduction of new dance steps had sometimes presented problems in the past. In early eighteenth-century England, for example, Beau Nash led the way in introducing French dances that caught on and virtually replaced the traditional and simpler English dances. An English father who observed his daughter in one of the new French dances could not believe his eyes and wrote to a friend:

> As the best institutions are liable to corruption, so, sir, I must acquaint you that very great abuses are crept into this entertainment. I was amazed to see my girl handled by and handling young men with so much familiarity, and I could not have thought it had been my child. They very often made use of a most impudent and lascivious step called setting to partners, which I know not how describe to you but by telling you that it is the very reverse of back to back. At last an impudent young dog bid the fiddlers play a dance called *Moll Patley*, and, after having made two or three capers, ran to his partner, locked his arm in hers, and whisked her round cleverly above ground in such a manner that I, who sat upon one of the lowest benches, saw further above her shoe than I can think fit to acquaint you with. I could no longer endure these enormities, wherefore, just as my girl was going to be made a whirligig, I ran in, seized my child, and carried her home.[12]

This was a century and a half before the Mormons encountered round dancing in pioneer Utah.

In early nineteenth-century America most dances were either square dances or line dances. For the square dance, usually called a quadrille or a cotillion, the basic pattern was four couples to a set. For the line dance, or reel, the men and women lined up in opposing lines. Naturally there were variations, such as the Lancers Quadrille, the Virginia Reel, the Scotch Reel, and others. These dances were lively and fun, as present devotees of square dancing will still attest.

Even such dances had their opponents. Many ministers regarded any form of dancing as a sin. Peter Cartwright, the itinerant minister, liked to tell of how many dances he had successfully interrupted.[13] Ministers of other denominations too denounced dancing as a pastime that was extravagant, harmful to health, a waste of time, and dangerous flirting with immorality. They went on to warn that cheap dance halls were dens of liquor, gambling, and prostitution. All ministers were not equally outspoken, but such opposition was common, especially among evangelical Protestants.

During the second quarter of the century a new dance was catching on in America. This was round dancing—dancing all around the hall, the gentleman and his lady in close proximity—and especially its most popular variant, the waltz. From Napoleonic France the waltz first leaped the Channel and then the Atlantic. In 1827 Senator John Tyler (later president) first saw a waltz and wrote to his daughter that it was "a dance which you have never seen, and which I do not desire to see you dance. It is rather vulgar, I think."[14] Round dancing continued to grow in popularity, not displacing square dancing but providing a popular alternative. Those who disapproved of all dancing naturally did not like the round dancing, but in addition there were those who had found the older styles acceptable but who disliked the newer ones. "The waltz is a dance of quite too loose a character, and unmarried ladies should refrain from it in public and private," said one book of manners in the 1830s.[15] Later, George Templeton Strong, the opinionated New York architect and critic, described the polka as "a kind of insane Tarter jig performed by a disagreeable music of an uncivilized character."[16] Among the Latter-day Saints the waltz had occasionally been allowed in crossing the plains and in Utah during the 1850s and 1860s. We read of Danish waltzes and other round dances on the plains.[17] In American Fork in the 1860s a man was not allowed to waltz with a woman other than his wife—which must mean that waltzing with one's wife was permissible.[18] Such dances must have been infrequent before the 1870s, a decade in which the popularity of the new styles aroused opposition from several groups. The Episcopal Church failed to pass a proposed canon that would forbid holy communion and confirmation to those who "habitually indulge in round dancing," but a resolution was adopted recommending that round dancing be discontinued by all good members of the Episcopalian Church.[19] About the same time a New York newspaper warned against male tempters who would take advantage of round dances: "They find all their opportunities ready made to their hands in the liberty allowed, and the intoxication of giddy female heads, already weakened and turned by the fumes of flattery, the over-powering effect of the close embrace of the waltz and the gratification of the sense in the associations and incidents of the night."[20]

In this context it is understandable that Brigham Young felt it neces-sary to make his position known. In an article published in the *Woman's Exponent* on January 1, 1876, George Reynold quoted President Young as follows: "With regard to round dances, he was opposed to them, from beginning to end, from top to bottom. Round dances were first com-menced in and still continue brothel-house dances."[21] The next month George Q. Cannon published an editorial in the *Juvenile Instructor* criticizing round dancing as "not conducive to health" and "considered improper by the servants of God who are placed to teach us."[22] Both statements also urged closing dances at an earlier hour—nine or ten in-stead of after midnight—and Cannon warned against strangers "with vile purposes in mind." Obviously round dancing was part of the specter —unwholesome outsiders, immoderate hours, extravagance, tempting and improper physical familiarity—these leaders wished to exorcise.

Some of the issues were discussed by a *Deseret News* editorial. Advo-cates of the waltz had claimed that it was a graceful and pleasant activity, impure only to the evil-minded. Admitting that most young people did not have impure intentions, the Church newspaper said: "But at the same time it must be admitted that the close embrace of the modern style of this whirling, giddy, seductive dance is not proper for the mod-est maiden, and is not exactly the position in which a prudent wife should place herself." But could it not be indulged in among friends? This might be permissible, leading only to a "dizzy brain," the news-paper continued, but if allowed in private circles it would quickly spread to public balls where evil people were present. Those who would waltz with a pure mind should abstain for the sake of others, the editorial con-tinued, for waltzing "adds nothing to health, longevity, respectability or anything that is permanently beneficial."[23]

At first glance the response of the Saints to these prohibitions seems loyal and enthusiastic. At least as early as 1874 a number of Young Ladies' Retrenchment Associations included in their resolutions some strictures against round dancing, and these continued to the end of 1876. Some Young Men's Mutual Improvement Associations were also being formed, and often they announced their willingness to cooperate in abandoning round dancing. The reasons given were predictable. Injurious to health, originating from an evil source, demoralizing in their influence, round dances received the final and decisive condemnation in that they were "not approved of by the Presidency of the Church."[24]

Closer examination reveals a mixed reaction—efforts at obedience and a general feeling of loyalty combined with the recalcitrance of human nature. At meetings of young people it was common for leaders to present a resolution condemning round dancing and asking for a vote of those who would refrain. Usually the vote was unanimous, but sometimes it was noted that a "majority" agreed. What does such a simple term tell us about the probable grumbling and behind-the-scenes criticism of the old-fogey ideas of their leaders? One unanimous vote was on the proposition that they be "willing to try and refrain from it"—which gives more than a little leeway. One group hedged by voting not to indulge in round dancing "to excess." On the other hand, there were groups so zealous that they voted not only to refrain from such dancing but also to "abandon their desire" for it.

Suggestive of some of the generational tension and the difficulty of imposing a flat prohibition is a report from Nephi: "We are striving to put down round dancing, but we meet with a great deal of opposition, but hope with the help of God to carry out the resolutions we have formed."[25] And from Draper came the following revealing statement: "We had been counseled to cease the round dances, but as they had become the favorite and almost universal dance, it appeared at first, as though it would be a hard matter to get the young to comply with the request. But after being organized the sisters immediately resolved to cease dancing them. The young men complied without the least resistance, so there is no more round dancing among us."[26] One is tempted to speculate that the young women of Draper had learned something from Lysistrata. That round dancing had become "the favorite and almost universal dance" is openly admitted, and all settlements would not so easily suppress its popularity.

The difficulty of enforcing an absolute ban on round dancing quickly became evident. Brigham Young's statement in 1876 sounded iron-clad enough, but Heber J. Grant later remembered an incident during the last year of Brigham Young's life when the Thirteenth Ward was trying to raise money for the benefit of the St. George Temple.[27] Heber J. Grant headed the young people's committee and had to talk things over with Bishop Edwin Woolley, who was anxious to have his ward beat all the others in raising money by this event. Young Heber responded:

"I will do my best, but you must agree to pay the loss if there is one."

"Loss?" he said.

"Yes, you cannot have the party in the Thirteenth Ward and make any money; the young people won't come any more. In other places they allow them to have three round dances, and you won't have any. I would rather dance three round dances and throw all the rest away. You have got to have three waltzes."

"All right," said Bishop Woolley, "take the three waltzes."

Then Heber said: "You won't allow Olsen's Quadrille band; they are the only people who can play the Blue Danube Waltz well; that is one of the things that draws the crowd. When you say Olsen's full band, that means the finest cornetist in Salt Lake will be there to give some cornet solos during the evening."

The bishop said: "Take Olsen's Quadrille Band; take your three round dances; wax your floor."

As the story continues President Grant recalled how he had sold tickets for $1.50 each instead of the usual dollar and made special invitations to bring the Young family and the employees of Z.C.M.I., the Church-owned department store. President Brigham Young came and paid ten dollars.

President Grant obviously enjoyed recalling the results. "We scooped the town, and we had four round dances. The fourth round dance was a waltz quadrille [a quadrille which concluded with the couples waltzing around and around the square]. I said, 'I am going to sit by the President [Brigham Young] and see what he says.'

"I said to the leader of the band: 'Now when you get through with the waltz quadrille, stop playing.'

"President Young said: 'They are waltzing.'

"I said, 'No, they are not waltzing; when they waltz they waltz all around the room; this is a quadrille.'

"He turned to me and laughed and said: 'Oh, you boys, you boys.' "

This little glimpse shows that even before Brigham Young's death in 1877 there were exceptions to the "no round dancing" idea. And we get a charming glimpse of Young, who had always sought some kind of moderation in dancing.

A slight but significant relaxation of the rule on round dancing was expressed soon after Brigham Young's death in an article on "Dancing Parties" published in the *Deseret News*.[28] Complimenting President Young for his desire "to guide and regulate, not to suppress, the rational enjoyment of the Latter-day Saints," the article went on to outline certain rules:

1. A limited number of parties could be held in the ward houses until more social halls could be built.
2. These parties would be under the supervision of bishops.
3. Order and decorum were to be maintained.
4. No "disreputable or immoral persons" were to "mingle in the society of the Saints."
5. Parties should not continue past midnight but should usually close at ten or eleven.
6. Dancing parties for raising money were prohibited, since they would have to let undesirable people in to make them a financial success. (Was this an indirect slap at the very party that Heber J. Grant later remembered so fondly?)
7. Invitation lists should be submitted to the presiding authorities in the ward.
8. Those who attended dancing elsewhere, in "public balls," should not be invited to ward dances.

Clearly more than just the question of the kind of dances was at stake here; it was a concerted effort to shield the Mormon youth from outside influences, to allow dancing parties to continue while imposing certain restraints of attendance and time and establishing responsibility for proper behavior. On the matter of round dancing, this same article commented: "There has been among all correct feeling people a strong prejudice against them, as they tend, though not always intentionally so, to demoralize our youth, and operate prejudicially to those innocent enjoyments which ought to characterize the recreation of the Latter-day Saints. We do not wish to be too restrictive in relation to these matters, but would recommend there be not more than one or two permitted in an evening."

Attitudes among the Latter-day Saints actually continued to be rather varied. That some were not enthusiastic about dancing at all is suggested by a recommendation that young people seek amusements "of a more intellectual tendency" than dancing, which offered only physical exercise and social intercourse.[29] And it would be rash to scoff at the fears of allowing the young people to mix socially with those whose standards of behavior were quite different. "Recent developments in the Police Court of this city," announced one news article, "reveal the fact that balls and dancing parties of a more or less public and mixed character have been the means through which the ruin of a number of young girls has been accomplished."[30]

Even President John Taylor may not have been entirely consistent. At a meeting on November 24, 1879: "Round dances was deprecated and Prest Taylor said he was not willing to submit to the influences of the adversary but to hold ourselves aloof from Wickedness and he wanted the Bishops to be firm in the discharge of their duties—yet if the Bps are desirous of taking the responsibilities of ruining our youth by over indulgence, let them do it at their own peril."[31]

One does not know exactly how to interpret this statement. Either Taylor was saying that he preferred no round dances at all and the idea of even having one or two was a concession to the bishops, or (more likely) he was saying that he had gone as far as he could in allowing one or two and that further requests coming from the bishops would not be approved. In any case there is evidence of friction.

Denunciations of waltzes and round dancing continued through the 1880s and 1890s. In the Riverdale branch of the Young Ladies Mutual Improvement Association, one young lady spoke in tongues, the message being that round dancing was displeasing in the sight of God.[32] Some of the statements are obviously responses to arguments that were being used in favor of allowing round dancing. To those who had said that round dances were necessary if the evening party was to be enjoyed, George Q. Cannon wrote that just as Adam and Eve could be happy while having all the fruits but one, so "round dancing is not absolutely necessary to enjoyment." To those who saw no immediate harm, he explained that, like tea, it is pleasant but will eventually bring "dreadful evils." To those who argued that round dancing was a national dance in some countries, he explained that national dances included the "hula hula" and the can-can, both immodest and debasing. If it were permissible to indulge in any national dance, where would it stop?[33]

No new reasons were given during the last-ditch stand, roughly from 1890 to 1910. The *Young Woman's Journal* repeated some of the older arguments but almost always ended with a flatly authoritarian position: round dancing should be avoided because the authorities say so. In 1896 an article noted that some young people thought that the Church's position on this dancing was a means to crush or afflict them, but it was really for their own good. Doesn't the Lord have a right to dictate in all things? How could anyone take pleasure in something displeasing to his heavenly parent? Round dancing allowed for too close an intimacy, was detrimental to health, and produced desires for other light-minded pastimes. Besides—here was always the clincher—even if none of these undesirable effects should result it would still be wrong "for the simple reason that it is not allowed."[34]

At the end of the century a writer described the desire to waltz as a love of selfish gratification, like indulging in tea, coffee, beer, or card-playing. Young people feared being called religious fanatics or being thought too pious. Besides, they enjoyed it and could see no harm in it. "Everyone else waltzes," they said. "Why shouldn't we?" Well, the writer responded, those who might well indulge with no harm to themselves should avoid it so that the weak would not stumble. The physician and the psychologist could point out other dangers, the article continued, but the one "simple yet most potent reason why our young people should not indulge in round-dancing, and which is here given: it is against counsel! And the moral effects of disobedience are often worse for a human character than the performance of the act which is forbidden. . . . our leaders have condemned it, and that should be enough for our Mutual Improvement girls and boys."[35]

Reading between the lines of these statements one can readily perceive an uneasy tension between many of the young people and those who frowned on round dancing. Once in Porterville, after the dance had been going for an hour or two, the boys got together in a huddle. When the next set was called for square dancing, the boys chose their partners, quickly explained things to them, and then all stood at the edge of the dance floor. The floor manager told them to take their places on the floor, but no one moved. He warned them that they would lose their turn to dance. Still no one moved. He motioned to the musicians to start the music. After they had played it through, the next set was called with the same results. Finally, in exasperation, the floor manager said, "All right you can have your remaining number of round dances and then you can go home." And that is what they did.[36]

Actually young Latter-day Saints were receiving mixed signals on the question of round dancing. On the one hand, there was the concession that one or two an evening would be allowable, which understandably led to the conclusion that they were not absolutely evil. On the other hand, there had been earlier statements indicating that the dances were in fact objectionable because of their origin, their associations, their unwholesome results, and the temptations they presented. It was easy to conclude, as some did, that those who were really "following the brethren" would desist from all such dances.

The actual practice varied, it seems. Most widespread was the assumption that two dances in an evening would be round dances. Variation in the direction of greater tolerance or laxity usually took the form of finding loopholes such as those already noted: making the two waltzes unusually long, so as to be equivalent, say, to four or five normal dances; getting the musicians to play an "encore" that would not be counted as a new and separate dance but as a continuation of the dance; or defining certain dances as square if they started that way (the "waltz quadrille" of Heber J. Grant's recollection).[37] Those who were so resistant to the Church standards that they wanted all or most of their dances to be the new round style could go to public dancing halls, but that would be equivalent to abandoning Church standards and association with active Latter-day Saint youths. It is hard to estimate how many of the young people disliked the moderate policy (allowing two round dances). Many may have considered it something they could live with, although it must have been extremely common to grumble and think of church dances as old-fashioned.

The other extreme—not those who tried to find loopholes or those who went along with the recommended policy—was to exclude all round dances. The experience in the Bear Lake Stake is a most interesting example of what could happen.[38] It all started on January 29, 1876, when Apostle Charles C. Rich asked the bishops to follow Brigham Young's counsel by doing away with round dancing entirely. The young people of the stake were not nearly so enthusiastic about this policy as the older generation, but on January 3, 1880, at stake priesthood meeting the following rules were accepted by unanimous vote:

We will not practice waltzes or any other round dances in our assemblies.

Persons dancing out of turn shall be considered violators of good order and may be requested to retire and if persistent may be ejected.

We will not use liquor in our assemblies nor suffer any person inebriated to participate in the dances.

Swinging with one arm around the lady's waist shall not be permitted in our assemblies.

To swing a lady more than once against her will shall be con-

sidered ungentlemanly. To swing more than twice under any circumstances [not against her will] shall be considered disorderly
and if persisted in the offender may be requested and retire and if
necessary may be ejected by force.

Were the stake leaders confused? Or were they remaining true to what
they regarded as President Young's attitude, disregarding President John
Taylor's relaxation of the rule? Or did the general suspicion of round
dancing that was found in many of the statements mean, for these stake
leaders, "We would rather that you did not participate in round dancing at all"? In any case, here was an effort to be more royalist than the
king—more stringent than the president of the Church had required.

By 1882, under pressure from the young people, President William
Budge announced that although President Taylor preferred no round
dances, he considered one or two permissible. If Church dances did not
provide some of these well-liked round dances, people would simply
have private dances. It seemed that Bear Lake Stake was just about
ready to make the concession that was common elsewhere when President J. H. Hart spoke out. He was in favor of the rules already adopted,
he said, adding that "the feeling which should govern the bishops and
heads of families should be 'let others do as they will but for me and my
house we will serve the Lord.'" Not surprisingly, perhaps, when a vote
was taken the result was that there would still be no round dancing.

In 1887 Bishop W. L. Rich tried to get the stake to allow one or two
round dances per evening. Even though he read John Taylor's statement
that made such a concession acceptable, he was voted down in priesthood meeting; the absolute prohibition was continued. In the meantime
it was not only the Gentiles that were offering round dances. Some LDS
people built a private dance hall and allowed round dances while prohibiting liquor. Nor was it only teenagers who chafed under the strict
rule. After the play *William Tell*, a group of Swiss people had arranged
to use the hall for dancing. The dancing they knew was round dancing.
When the sheriff tried to stop them, he was told that many of them did
not know how to square dance. By special permission they were allowed
to round dance until midnight.

During these same years—roughly the 1880s and 1890s—some wards
in the stake allowed one or two round dances, while others allowed
none. At one dance two of President William Budge's children observed
that the rule against round dancing was broken. What should they do?

They decided not to walk out but to refrain from dancing: "The next morning President Budge asked his daughter, 'Were you at the dance last night?' 'Yes Sir!' 'Did you waltz?' 'No, sir.' 'Why didn't you get up and walk out?' 'We talked it over and decided it would be better not to.' President Budge next called on Jesse and received the same answers. Just as he was leaving he met his son Frank. 'Were you at the dance last night?' 'No, sir!' 'Well, if you had been, you would have been just as bad as the others.'" This anecdote carries overtones of family loyalty, generational tension, and the whole range of feeling in the community.

It is hard to pin down the exact transition to Mormon acceptance of round dancing. In 1902 a statement in the *Juvenile Instructor* indicates that the main concern was not the waltz per se but the closed position: "Certain dances such as the waltz are used by young people as an excuse for assuming an attitude that is sometimes shocking, and those who are so frivolous as to be devoid of a high sense of propriety should be warned by the Bishop in a kindly spirit and in a proper manner in a private way to refrain from any and all unseemly and indelicate attitudes in the ballroom."[39] There were undoubtedly differences from one area to another on this question, with some of the outlying settlements perhaps lagging and still trying to enforce the old rules. By 1910 the waltz and two-step were favorably accepted by the Mutual Improvement Association, and by 1910 the polka and schottische were added as acceptable forms of dancing.[40] There continued to be uneasiness about the closed position, however, and often floorwalkers would be assigned to walk up and down and make sure that daylight could be seen between the partners.[41] By at least 1916, new, popular dances were included in the program. Ironically, the Virginia Reel was now considered a little too boisterous.[42]

Some would see the Church leaders as reactionary in trying to prevent new styles of dancing that were not those they had learned in growing up. Since we have come to accept not only the waltz but other kinds of round dancing as perfectly wholesome, it is easy to ridicule the fears of moral license. Personally I do not see the issues in these terms. Often in human history there is a series of developments that brings about a confrontation between a system of order and control and what is perceived as a tendency on the part of the young to abandon time-honored values and behavior patterns. The young appear "wild," unrestrained, irreverent and disrespectful. Many people of the older generation (some might say those beyond their teens and with responsibilities of marriage and family) see the world in a "topsy-turvy" state. Almost always the defensive reaction consists of attempts to tighten up, to establish rules, to reassert the old ideas and values with renewed emphasis. This situation—old versus new, order versus disorder, control versus license, stability versus change—has recurred over and over again on many different levels.[43]

The round dance policy at the end of the past century provides a case study of just such a perceived conflict. Many were then looking with more than a little dismay at the younger generation. Ideas and values were at stake as well as fashions and morals. Dancing, while only one aspect, was highly symbolic of the whole situation. The old dances (the square and reel dances) were carefully ordered, planned, and controlled. If the squares and reels did not have the same dignity as the minuets of the preceding century, they were alike in that every step was clearly defined. In a brief moment of time was staged a pageant of grace and order and harmony. The round dances, on the other hand, were characterized by whirling turns free of formation. They could be seen as symbolic of the breakdown of order and structure in society. The closed position, the physical contact between the partners, was not only tempting to those participating but was symbolic of moral laxity in general.

When seen in this context, the Mormon Church's reaction to the new dance styles was understandable. The desire to provide structured aids for young people—the new Mutual Improvement Associations, the lesson manuals in Sunday Schools, and the carefully graded steps in priesthood activities—was part of the same impulse. Rather than saying "anything goes," leaders and the young people were agreed that rules were necessary. It might even be argued that the Church's position was one of commonsense and moderation. From Nauvoo days it had been a posture of allowing dancing and encouraging wholesome recreation of all kinds but of drawing lines so as to maintain propriety and good taste. The same general feeling obtained throughout the century: not to abolish dancing but to encourage it within proper limits. The balance was somewhere between a dour prohibition of all dancing and a free abandon that would allow any dance step whatever its associations and whatever the degree of intimacy. Seeking such a balance was not as old-fashioned as it seemed, but neither was it moving blithely with the fashions. Inevitably there were tensions and adjustments.

It is quite erroneous, of course, to see the issue in terms of theological truth. A white shirt is not "truer" than a colored shirt. A square dance is not "truer" than a waltz. Taste in music and art, fashions in dance and dress—these are matters not in the area of truth and error but of prudence. From the prudential point of view President Joseph F. Smith was quite right in 1912 to warn: "Let not the brilliant prospects of a glorious millennium be clouded with such shadows as are threatened by customs and costumes and diversions of these licentious days." There are always threatening shadows, and "customs and costumes and diversions" are usually among them. But the exact details, the precise rules to follow, will vary with shifting circumstances.

Notes

An earlier version of this chapter appeared in *Sunstone* 2 (Spring 1977).

1. James R. Clark, ed., *Messages of the First Presidency of the Church of Jesus Christ of Latter-day Saints*, 6 vols. (Salt Lake City: Bookcraft, 1965–75), 4:281.

2. Whistling for dances is described in Joel E. Ricks and Everett L. Cooley, eds., *The History of a Valley: Cache Valley* (Logan: Cache Valley Centennial Commission, 1956), 414–15.

3. *Our Pioneer Heritage* 8 (1965): 464.

4. *Woman's Exponent* 12 (15 Sept. 1883): 57–58.

5. *Times and Seasons* 5 (Mar. 1844): 460.

6. Ibid. 5 (1 Oct. 1844): 668.

7. Stanley B. Kimball, ed., *On the Potter's Wheel: The Diaries of Heber C. Kimball* (Salt Lake City: Signature Books, 1987).

8. Journal History, 9 January 1846. This is a huge, multivolume compilation of newspaper clippings and other primary sources located in the Church Archives.

9. Samuel W. Taylor, *Nightfall at Nauvoo* (New York: Macmillan, 1976), 352.

10. Journal History, 5 February 1847.

11. Ibid., 4 March 1847.

12. *Encyclopedia Britannica*, 11th ed.

13. Peter Cartright, *Autobiography of Peter Cartright* (New York: Carleton and Potter, 1857), 75, as cited by Joseph E. Marks, *America Learns to Dance* (New York: Exposition Press, 1957), 69.

14. Lyon G. Taylor, *The Letters and Times of the Tylers* (Richmond: Whittet & Shipperson, 1884), 1:390, as cited in Marks, *America Learns to Dance*, 74.

15. Marks, *America Learns to Dance*, 74.

16. Ibid., 75.

17. Kart Edward Wesson, "Dance in the Church of Jesus Christ of Latter-day Saints" (M.A. thesis, Brigham Young University, 1975), 46.

18. *Treasures of Pioneer History* 2 (1953): 390.

19. *Deseret News,* 29 May 1878.

20. *Deseret Evening News,* 16 January 1877.

21. *Woman's Exponent* 4 (1 Jan. 1876): 117.

22. *Juvenile Instructor* 11 (15 Feb. 1876): 42.

23. *Deseret News,* 20 September 1877.

24. *Woman's Exponent* 2–4 (1874–76), especially in section "R.S. Notes."

25. Ibid. 4 (15 Sept. 1875): 58.

26. Ibid. 4 (1 May 1876): 180.

27. This whole episode is taken from Heber J. Grant (as told to his daughter, Rachel Grant Taylor), "When Brigham Young Watched a Waltz," *Improvement Era,* November 1941.

28. *Deseret News Weekly,* 28 November 1877.

29. *Deseret News,* 13 November 1877.

30. *Deseret Evening News,* 16 January 1877.

31. L. John Nuttal Diaries, 24 November 1879, typescript, Church Archives.

32. *Woman's Exponent* 12 (15 Jan. 1884): 127–28.

33. *Juvenile Instructor* 19 (15 Feb. 1884): 56.

34. *Young Woman's Journal* 12 (Feb. 1896): 242.

35. Ibid. 11 (Feb. 1900): 89–90.

36. *Treasures of Pioneer History* 2 (1953): 379–80.

37. One other technique sometimes worked in small halls. Since it was impossible for all the dancers to dance every dance, numbers were drawn or a ticket entitled one to so many dances. In such situations in order to allow every dancer two round dances it might be necessary to play four to six during an evening. From this point it took little imagination for some dancers to buy two tickets or otherwise contrive to get onto the floor for several of the round dances.

38. The information on Bear Lake Stake comes from Bear Lake Stake Historical Record, Church Archives. It is conveniently summarized in Russell R. Rich, *Land of the Sky-Blue Water* (Provo: Brigham Young University Press, 1963), chap. 7.

39. *Juvenile Instructor,* 15 April 1902.

40. Ruth E. Yashko, "An Historical Study of Pioneer Dancing in Utah" (M.A. thesis, University of Utah, 1947), 21, 47, 49.

41. *Treasures of Pioneer History* 2 (1953): 377–80.

42. E. L. Roberts, "Social Dancing and Its Direction," *Improvement Era* 19 (Jan. 1916): 255–60.

43. My thinking along these lines has been especially stimulated by William J. Bouwsma, *Venice and the Defense of Republican Liberty: Renaissance Values in the Age of Counter Reformation* (Berkeley: University of California Press, 1968).

7

The Ordeal of
Brigham Young, Jr.

ONE OF THE trials of life is to be the child of a great man. The burden is greater if one carries his father's name. To the difficulty of parent-child relationships under the best of circumstances is added the additional tension created by the constant question, "Are you so and so's little boy?" Or, "You must be the son of so and so." Under such pressure, not surprisingly, many are the sons who turn out as rebels, choosing extreme means of establishing their own identity, while others, having no stomach for outright rebellion, grind out their lives as attenuated persons, never quite sure of themselves or their position. Others, of course, manage the difficult balancing act of maintaining a more or less positive relationship with parents while growing to be their own person. In this last category was Brigham Young, Jr., whose nickname of "Briggy" stuck throughout his life, perhaps preventing historians and biographers from giving him the attention he deserves.

》   《

Born in 1836 to Brigham Young and Mary Ann Angell Young, he was just eleven years old when the Mormons, under the leadership of his father, arrived in the Salt Lake Valley. His boyhood prior to arriving in Utah had been eventful. His memory would not have held much, if anything, of the Missouri persecutions, but he remembered growing up in the new settlement at Nauvoo, Illinois. As a small boy of five or six or seven, he remembered Joseph Smith, the prophet. He stood in the streets and watched the construction of houses in the new city. He helped around the home and ran to welcome his father back from his frequent absences as an Apostle. By 1842–44 he was old enough to be aware of the persecutions. He watched the Nauvoo Legion at drill. He was eight years old when Joseph Smith was killed. He saw the bodies of Joseph and Hyrum Smith brought to the grief-stricken city. The return of his father and other apostles from the East helped restore calm, but in the months following, refugees from surrounding settlements streamed into town.

The early months of 1846 saw the Mormons evacuate Nauvoo. During the rest of that year the migrants moved out in small companies and large, established camps and settlements across Iowa and Nebraska, planted crops, and finally wintered as best they could. In the spring of 1847, the pioneer company under President Young pushed on to the Salt Lake Valley, arriving in July, with a few other companies following that year. Young Briggy and his mother remained at Winter Quarters, where President Young returned in late 1847. In early 1848 they moved on to Utah.

Two anecdotes have come down in the family regarding Briggy's experiences during the evacuation from Nauvoo and the trek west. Although they seem at best half true, there may be psychological meaning that deserves notice. During the hours when his family was leaving Nauvoo, the first of these stories goes, young Brigham had been playing with some other children at Knight's mill. Returning home, he found the door swinging open and furniture still in the deserted house. In his absence his mother and the rest of the children had been transported across the river by ferry. Panic-stricken, the nine-year-old boy rushed down to the river and saw a last ferry boat just pulling away. It was loaded with men, women, and children. In the bow was a barrel. Quickly Briggy jumped on the barrel and was thus taken across the river. On the other side was unforgettable confusion: "Dogs, chickens, cows and pigs ran bellowing and grunting in every direction, men, women, and children by the thousands ran hither and thither in the utmost confusion, wagons were scattered about, here was one hitched up, the driver cracking his whip and pushing recklessly through the crowd; babies screaming for their mothers, and mothers calling piteously for lost babies and children. Weeping and groaning sick ones lay here and there, while anxiety was in every heart."[1] For three days the boy remained lost, living off the meat of an ox that had been drowned in the river. Finally, when he heard that his father and mother were at Sugar Creek, ten miles away, he walked that distance to join them. The family wagon was fully occupied, and there was no extra bedding. We get a picture of the lad huddling against an inadequate barrier of saddles and cooking utensils, trying to gain some protection from the cold wind. Then with some other boys he built a little brush hut that provided some shelter.

The other incident allegedly occurred in 1848, when Brigham Young returned for his family. The boy was twelve. Like other boys of that age he was given the responsibility of driving oxen across the plains. The anecdote tells of President Young's impatience with the grumbling in the company. Suddenly in the middle of the afternoon he announced that he and his coach were leaving; if anyone wished to follow, the road was open. Then the president "put the whip to his horses and gave not a glance behind." Young Brigham hastily yoked up his two teams of oxen, hitched them to the wagon and started after his father, determined not to lose sight of his wagon wheels, "while the day lasts." Against wind and storm, and later through the darkness and increasing cold, the boy pushed his wagon forward, much to the consternation of one of his father's wives, who was clinging to her seat on the wagon.[2]

Neither of these stories rings quite true. Were Briggy's parents so unfeeling as to move from Nauvoo without finding a son? Would the father drive off on his own, leaving his family to fare for themselves? Probably there is a kernel of truth here. The confusion of moving, the possibility of becoming separated, the irritation at delays—all of this is quite consistent with what we know of the events. But the remainder of the stories, perhaps the more important essence, describes a father who moves on ahead of his son. The son does not shrug his shoulders and go off on his own but instead doggedly follows in the father's footsteps. Although never great and strong enough to move dramatically into the lead position occupied by his father, young Brigham could follow along behind with patience and loyalty. Whether intended by the stories or not, such was the leitmotif of Brigham Jr.'s life.

What was it like to grow up in Utah as a teenage son of Brigham Young during the 1850s? It was hard work for one thing. Briggy seems to have early developed a stocky, strong figure, able to put out when it came to hard work. Among other things, he herded stock and went into the canyons after lumber. As a teenager he was one of the "minute men" designated to serve as guards and to be ready for expeditions against hostile Indians.

The journal of Hosea Stout gives us some interesting glimpses of young Brigham at about the age of nineteen. The U.S. troops on leave in the city were attending the theater on December 25, 1854, when a policeman attempted to discipline one of the soldiers. Other soldiers came to his defense, and Mormon young men rallied to help the policeman. This small riot was followed two days later by a larger one when drunken soldiers strolled the streets spoiling for a fight. Soon there were several dozen hot-bloods lined up on two sides. There was shouting, scuffling, throwing stones, swinging sticks, and even some firing of guns. Almost miraculously army officers and city police managed to quell the disturbance before it degenerated into a pitched battle. The final sentence in Stout's description of this incident is: "Hopkins Pender, E. Everett & Brigham Young Jr were some hurt but not seriously."[3]

A few weeks later, on March 22, 1855, Stout noted that some U.S. Army officers went before Mayor Jedediah Grant with a complaint "of Brigham Young Jr, Heber P. Kimball, Lott Huntington, and Stephen Moore . . . for riding violently by them & bowing, while they were riding the streets with some Ladies &c."[4] One gets the picture of young Mormon toughs—Lott Huntington later got into serious trouble with the law and lost his life to pursuing police—riding their horses like maniacs, galloping right up to the carriages, and taunting the officers and their ladies. It may be enough of an explanation to say that boys will be boys, remembering modern hot-rodders and their antics. Or the behavior of the drunken troops may be enough to excuse some of the Mormon boys' desire to demonstrate that they were not to be pushed around. In any case in the midst of this activity was young Brigham, a young man with little polish, little real education, but with physical strength and ability as a horseman.

This general impression of rowdiness is confirmed by a recollection of William Jennings, who had been mayor of Salt Lake City. Making the point that the coming of the railroad was "a great blessing as an educator," he recalled conditions prior to the railroad: "Boys eighteen or twenty years old, sons of Brigham Young and other dignitaries, satisfied their highest ambition when they would ride about the town on horseback, dressed fantastically, with leathern leggings, Spanish spurs, soft slouch hat with fur twisted around it and hanging down like a coon's tail. A Bowie knife would be stuck in his legging, and he would race about the place shouting and halloaing as he went. They were in no way above the cowboy of today and played the part of a Mexican or Spanish rough."[5]

That the young man may have been keeping bad company and well on the road to being a juvenile delinquent is at least a possibility. A few years later, when writing to his father, young Brigham expressed his gratitude "for the care that you have shown for me heretofore when I had forsaken the pathe marked out to me by example and would do wickedly."[6] On another occasion he referred to the "horrible gulf" he had

just missed falling into. "I realize to some extent how wild I've been—
and perhaps wicked in many instances," he wrote, "and how patiently
ye both [his father and mother] have waited for me to change. My constant prayer is that I may never cause you another pang of sorrow, or that
you may ever have cause to blush through any act of mine hereafter."[7]
These statements probably refer to bad company, late hours, a tendency
to rough language, and general rowdiness during his late teenage years.

On November 15, 1855, when he was only nineteen, Brigham married
Catherine, daughter of Orson Spencer. Nine months later Alice Roxy
was born. In the fall of 1856 Brigham served as one of the relief company
that went to the rescue of the handcart pioneers. He was a messenger
in the Territorial House of Representatives in the 1856–57 session. In
1857–58 he served in the militia during the Echo Canyon activities of
the Utah War, his physical strength, bravado, and horsemanship skill
being put to use as a scout assigned to "reconnoiter in the mountains."[8]

Meanwhile his family responsibilities were increasing. He took Jane,
daughter of Albert and Rhoda Carrington, as a plural wife in March 1857.
By 1859 he and his two wives had four children. He was only twenty-
three years old. But responsibilities in the Church were slow in coming.
The young man felt his educational deprivation and the roughness of
his background. Once when called upon to speak in Farmington, he ran
out the door.[9] In April 1861 Brigham Jr., then twenty-five, was called
to serve on the high council of Salt Lake Stake. The following year he
traveled to Washington, D.C., with the party of Latter-day Saints seeking admission of Utah as a state of the Union. In the nation's capital he
toured the prominent landmarks.[10] To his surprise there wasn't much
of a celebration on Independence Day. Lonesome and unfavorably impressed with the nation's capital, he wrote in his diary, "This city seems
to be one big whore house. I wish I was a thousand miles from here, or
in my mountain home."[11]

While in Washington he received a letter from his father suggesting
that it might be appropriate, before returning home, to fill a mission in
Great Britain.[12] Young Brigham agreed. In that foreign land he could try
out his own wings, could develop spiritual strength and independence,
and could start to show the sense of his own identity in the diary that
for forty years chronicles not only the life of a man but also the tor-
tured course of his Church and people. As he also found out, however,
in England he would not escape the fact of being the son of the famous
Brigham Young; there, too, he would be following in the footsteps of his

father, who had participated in the mission of the Twelve to England in 1840–41.

After the adjournment of Congress, George Q. Cannon accompanied the young man on his journey across the ocean. In England there was more sight-seeing. The Great London Exhibition, the Zoological Gardens, the Crystal Palace—all were visited and commented upon. After visiting the exhibition, he wrote to his father, "I am unable to give any account of it, my head is crammed so full and wedged in so tight that I can get nothing out."[13] Then came church conferences, of course, and some clerical work in the mission office. When he heard news of the Confederate advance on Washington, he wrote, "We can see the Lord is gradually withdrawing his Spirit from the nations of the earth." In 1863, when he heard of his father's arrest by U.S. marshals, he wrote, "Who can tell what my feelings were?"[14] We can guess that his feelings were a mixture of distress and anger; there was still some of the tough horseman in young Brigham, and some of the resentment against anti-Mormons that had been nurtured by the riots and the Utah War in the 1850s. As part of a self-improvement program he took swordsmanship lessons.

Although Brigham Jr. wrote dutiful letters repeatedly expressing how grateful he was to have such a father, he was always conscious of following along behind. "Father I can in part realize what a time you had, when you first came to this country," he wrote. "My mission will be a perfect pleasure trip, compared with yours." The closest he came to expressing any feelings of frustration was on October 13, 1863: "Here I am in England and I am doing my duty. I have been afraid that more is expected of me than I can do. They consider the idea that such a father, had ought to have a Smart Son, I cant help it if they are disapointed in their expectations but I will do my best to answer the prayers of my frinds." Once, after going through the Thames tunnel, he wrote, "I felt, (when looking upon and treading the Same pathe that you had so long ago) like foweling in, and Striving to accomplish the desire of your heart, the Same as you had done, and I could all most imagine that I could See you walking through the Tunel before me." *I could all most imagine that I could See you walking through the Tunel before me*—in a sense this was the inescapable challenge of Brigham Jr. throughout his life.

Young Brigham had had a conversion experience. The rowdy young man was no more. He wrote to his father of his deepened sense of gratitude: "I never could appreciate those blessings before and I am afraid

I do not sufficiently at the present time, but I know I thank God from my very *soul* that he has given me such a father and altho' I may err in many things, yet my desire will ever be that I may be a source of rejoicing to you and never for a moment give you pain or grieve the spirit of God within me." In his diary he summed up what his mission had meant to him: "I feel very like I had been in a deep sleep all my life and had just waken up. If I live a thousand years, I will never have anything happen to me so opportunely as this mission has."[15]

After visiting the Isle of Man[16] and traveling on the Continent— Louis Bertrand, a recent convert, serving as a guide in Paris—Brigham was ready to return to the States. A voyage across the ocean and then overland (the journey described in a small pocket diary) brought him home by August. A large family group was there to welcome him home. Catherine (now the mother of four children) was home ill and unable to join the throng. Jane, the mother of two, was doing better. In many ways the most important individual for twenty-seven-year-old Brigham to see was his father, on whom he made a special call. Already some of the close affection and respect between this prominent father and his namesake are observable. Brigham wrote in his diary of his gratitude for such a father. In just a few days President Young asked Brigham and his older brother Joseph to "assist him in the ministry . . . to live with him and not set up for ourselves." A great future seemed in store for the young man.

In the spring of 1864 he was again called to serve a mission in Europe. He traveled eastward to New York and Philadelphia with Catherine, who had left her children with her sister wife and who would give birth to a child in England. An ocean trip brought Brigham and his family to England by August 1864. Officially there as assistant to President Daniel H. Wells,[17] he found time for both reading and travel. "Spent the fore part of the day studying French, Grammar, D[eseret] Alphabet &c."—is a typical entry. His reading (or at least the books he bought) included historical works by Hume, Gibbon, Arnold, Milford, Chambers, and Mosheim. Literature was represented by Homer, Plutarch, Shakespeare, Milton, and Goldsmith. He also read newspapers and essays. He often related his reading to his Mormon beliefs, as when commenting on the books on Central America by J. S. Stephens and Frederick Catherwood: "I have no doubt but we will yet explore those ancient ruins, and find they are familiar through our reading the book of Mormon." Alexander Pope's *Essay on Man*, he said, "has many good things in it, and before the Gospel was revealed through Joseph Smith might have struck the reader as being the best thing extant, but now much of it is nonsense in consequence of the truths revealed in these the latter days; for Gospel light has made many things and arguments transparent which were before considerably opaque." The young man from the frontier, now approaching thirty, was becoming less of a country bumpkin.

His travels in 1864–65 included visits to the Isle of Man, travels to conferences in different parts of England, and, in the summer of 1865, a tour of the Continent, including Rotterdam, Cologne, Zurich, Constance, Geneva, and Paris. This was not purely a pleasure trip, for there was an examination of mission finances in Zurich, and the party included missionaries some of the time. But they also enjoyed visiting the "sites." Another trip was made to the Continent in 1866.

Returning to England, Brigham took over the editorship of the *Millennial Star* and, after the departure of President Daniel H. Wells in 1865, the presidency of the British Mission. Much of his time was now taken up not only with planning emigration, chartering ships, recording the arrival of new missionaries and the departure of old missionaries—all of which he had done before—but increasingly also with such concerns as mission finances and disciplinary problems. One missionary was imprisoned for assault, and Brigham considered him to have been justly condemned. An employee of the mission office had to be fired for "whoring it."[18] Obtaining paper for the printing needs of the mission—the Book of Mormon, Doctrine and Covenants, the *Spencer Letters*, and Parley P. Pratt's *Voice of Warning*—was a concern. There were also social obligations, as, for example, a call on U.S. Minister Charles Francis Adams.

The British Mission was no longer enjoying the flush of its original success back around 1840. Things were settling down. A diary entry that speaks volumes is the following statement overheard in the mission office: "Bro. [Orson] Pratt said 'bro Franklin [Richards] it is not now as it used to be in this mission. At one time the cry was send us more elders, but now the cry was from the Conferences for Godsake don't send any more elders here.'"[19]

In the fall of 1866, Brigham decided to return to the States.[20] Before leaving, he made another trip to the Continent and bought an Enfield rifle.

After the ocean crossing and a railroad and stage journey across the United States, Brigham arrived back in the Salt Lake Valley, where a joyful family—including his wife Jane and her three children—greeted him. For the fall and winter months he remained in Utah. As a Brigadier-General of the First Division of the Nauvoo Legion, he attended a three-day muster and sham battle. "Never before were the men & officers of the Nauvoo Legion so well uniformed, drilled, & armed as at present," he wrote. It was during these months that the telegraph, which had reached Utah in 1861, was being stretched north and south as a means of quick communication between the different Mormon settlements. Like other young people, Brigham took lessons in telegraphy. He also took fencing lessons, dined with the Albert Carringtons (his parents-in-law), attended the Salt Lake Theater, and enjoyed the festivities of a military ball. And he noted his attendance at religious meetings and appreciated the sermons. On the afternoon of November 4, 1866, for example, he remarked that "Prest Young delivered a very interesting discourse or revelation."

Brigham Jr. was steadily gaining experience in Church and state. He did some writing for his father, drafting a circular letter to bishops and the official governor's message of 1867.[21] He was elected to the Territorial Legislature as a member of the House, the first of seven consecutive terms he served in this body. He was also inducted into "this church municiple board, or in other words this council of fifty." Thus Brigham Jr. gained formal entrance into the body thought by many Latter-day Saints to be the future governing body of the Kingdom of God on earth.[22]

In February 1867 he started on a third trip to Europe, there to rejoin Catherine and her children. Stopping in Washington he was introduced by Utah delegate William Hooper to many members of Congress, who talked "freely about Utah affairs, but . . . abstained from mentioning polygamy."[23] Arriving at Liverpool, he went right to work on emigration matters, writing a circular of instructions for emigrants, visiting the bank to make financial arrangements, and giving Franklin D. Richards the authority to transact business. He visited Parliament and heard a speech by Benjamin Disraeli. He called on John Bright, the prominent liberal Parliamentarian. Having just finished reading Samuel Bowles's book, *Across the Continent,* with its supercilious treatment of the Mormons, Bright was not in a cordial mood but received Brigham rather "stiffly."[24]

This was the year of the Paris Exposition of 1867. The Utah Territorial Legislature had designated Brigham to see to it that an exhibit showing Utah at its best was set up at the exposition. He called on the American Minister to France, John A. Dix, and tried to obtain the necessary permissions. But red tape presented incredible problems. Just in going to the French Ministry of Interior to pick up the package of specimens that had been sent by freight for the purpose, Brigham was surrounded by confusion. "When they found that we were from Utah their astonishment was unbounded," he wrote. Finally, some Utah specimens (rocks, minerals, flora) were forwarded from Liverpool and taken by Brigham to the officials responsible for the various American exhibits. One gains the impression that a Utah exhibit was eventually on display but that, through no fault of Brigham Young, Jr., it was smaller than desired.[25] Even such a simple matter as donating books to the French Imperial Library (now the Bibliothèque Nationale) was not accomplished as easily as expected.

During these weeks in France, Brigham found time for some recreation. He attended the races, shopped, and undoubtedly enjoyed the romantic appearance of Paris during the Second Empire. He was not averse to broadening his experience. At the Théatre Gaité he saw *Pirates of Sarama*, in which "Miss Menken sustained an important part, and appeared as usual almost naked."[26] On another occasion, at the Jardin Bullier, Brigham and his friends were disgusted by "the dancing of the crazy French, women kicking higher than their heads, and men throwing themselves into all manner of shapes, wriggling and twisting their bodies in a distressing manner." The atmosphere of *gaité parisienne* evoked in the work of Toulouse-Lautrec, which many Americans of moralistic bent condemned, found even less sympathy in the eyes of one whose people were still eking out an existence in distant Utah.

A few weeks later, when back in France, Brigham saw the Emperor Napoleon III in a carriage with Czar Alexander II. The rough-hewn American was not impressed. On another occasion he saw from a hotel window William of Prussia and his son, the crown prince. In his diary he wrote, "The King appeared a hard featured old sinner, and neither did I like the looks of his son; his countenance did not foreshadow a noble mind, but was rather the harbinger of selfishness and contracted ideas." It would not be long before the French, prostrate after the Franco-Prussian War, would have reason to agree with this assessment of the German ruler.[27]

After other visits to the exposition, Brigham visited the newspaper *La Liberté* and had an article published. The lack of complete freedom of expression is indicated by his need to obtain permission from the Minister of Interior before giving a lecture. Brigham did not give up easily. He talked with many people and finally arranged with a printer named Fonville to publish a pamphlet, the manuscript to be submitted later. "People in Paris are very willing to hear of our worldly prosperity but care nothing for our religion," he noted.

It was June 1867. Returning to England, Brigham Young, Jr., gathered his family and prepared to leave the country. The return trip was uneventful except for an interview with railroad leaders anxious to court favor with Brigham Young. The party arrived in Salt Lake City on September 23.

>>   <<

The next ten years of the life of Brigham Young, Jr., were spent in Utah under the shadow of his father, President Brigham Young. It was on October 9, 1868, that he entered the Quorum of the Twelve Apostles, his earlier ordination as an Apostle, in 1864, now becoming more meaningful.[28] Brigham Jr. would not have to have been a Young to be a Mormon leader. His mind had been broadened by travel and reading. Administrative responsibility had been his in the British Mission. He was a zealous, sincerely committed Church member. But there was no denying the fact that his close relationship to the Mormon president gave him *entreé* where otherwise he might have been unwelcome and led to his being treated with special consideration. If this was fairly natural, similar to the treatment given the son of any national president or governor, there must have been those who explained his prominence as the result of favoritism. He continued to follow his eminent father down the road or through the tunnel, but he followed diligently and tried to acquit himself well of the responsibilities assigned to him.

During 1868 and 1869 he was mainly occupied with helping the Church president, participating in the annual musters of the militia, attending a theological class in Salt Lake City, and acting as contractor (or liaison) between the Church and the Union Pacific Railroad Company. In 1869 he made a trip to New York, Boston, and Philadelphia; in this last place he called on Thomas L. Kane, who still wished the Mormons well.[29] On whatever visits the Church Presidency made to outlying settlements during these years, Brigham Young's son and namesake usually accompanied him. In fact, Brigham Jr.'s diary, commenting on his father's health and on the content of the sermons, is very close to being an unofficial journal of the president's trips.

In 1872 a new phase in the life of Brigham Jr. began when he was set apart to preside over Cache Valley settlements, replacing Apostle Ezra T. Benson, who had died in 1869. Anyone interested in the history of Cache Valley during these years will find the Brigham Young, Jr., diary a valuable source of information.[30] Visits to the different northern Utah and southern Idaho communities are described. At one meeting of the Cache Valley bishops there was an agreement to cooperate with the railroad that would soon come through. Interesting and sometimes perplexing property matters frequently came up. In Hyrum, for example, Brigham Young (the Church president) owned a farm of 10,000 acres. That such ownership was not always what it appeared is suggested by Brigham Jr.'s conscientious efforts to examine "the claims of land which were preempted and paid for by Prest. B. Young but belong to the citizens in Millville and vice versa" (14 Jan. 1873).

While retaining an interest and responsibility in Cache Valley, Brigham Jr. found his sphere of activity enlarged once again at April conference in 1873, when he was named one of five counselors to the president of the Church. Following conference he made a trip to the East. Thomas L. Kane was host for a while in Philadelphia. Then Brigham traveled on to upper New York, seeing the historic sites around Palmyra and visiting relatives. He visited his brother Willard Young, now a West Point cadet. Continuing westward to Illinois, he visited the Carthage Jail and then Nauvoo. One entry reads: "Met young Joseph [Joseph Smith III] just at the foot of the hill. He was then on a visit to his mother" (13 June 1873). Arriving back in Utah, he probably reported on his trip to President Young and then rejoined his family in Logan.

Trips to Salt Lake were frequent. Not only was Brigham a counselor to his father, but he was an official in the Utah Northern Railroad Company. He served in the Utah legislature and participated in the militia muster. Now living in relatively tranquil Cache Valley, he was not favorably impressed with the trends in Salt Lake City. "Lawyers, Doctors, miners, loafers and drinking saloons are plentiful," he wrote, asking, "Why not prohibit the licensing of these sink holes of iniquity?" (16 Apr. 1874). After hearing a lecture by Victoria Woodhull, a noted feminist and advocate of free love, he commented that she was "mad, mad, decidedly a brawling woman influenced by a set of bad spirits which will probably drive her to the mad house" (12 May 1874).[31]

This was the year in which the United Order of Enoch was revived in the Church, and Brigham Jr. was one of those promoting it in Cache Valley. Signs of opposition were apparent from the beginning, and later that year, after a visit to St. George, he wrote, "Some brethren seem to think U.O. is a failure in St. George."[32] Disappointed with the failure of the United Order in Cache Valley, he expressed the hope that the Indians would now come into their period of flowering: "My hopes are in the Lamanites to build up Zion more than in this people. The aborigines of Mexico 'Aztecs' know more about the Gospel than all Christendom."

As director of the Utah Northern Railroad, he was involved in the important intra-territorial railroad expansion of the 1870s and made many trips to and from Salt Lake City for the purpose. When President Young went on trips northward or southward, Brigham Jr. continued to accompany him. Thus it was that at the end of 1874 he was participating in a Christmas celebration at St. George. While there he observed the new temple under construction.

Family affairs occupied much of the attention of Brigham Jr. He followed with great interest his father's state of health and his various confrontations with federal marshals. The Ann Eliza Young divorce case interested him. That Brigham Jr. functioned in some ways as family business manager is suggested by lists in his diary of livestock on different Brigham Young farms and a record of Z.C.M.I. stock.

It was as a representative of President Young and also in his own role as railroad investor that Brigham Jr. traveled east in late 1875. In New York he met with his brother John W.—who had become more and more of a business tycoon and was heavily entangled in financial dealings regarding the Utah Western Railroad. "It was a joyful and sorrowful meeting," Brigham recorded. "We thought and talked of our dear brother Joseph, our parents, home, the Kingdom" (29 Dec. 1875). On this trip he traveled to different towns and kept a careful record of his conversations and observations. In Washington Delegate George Q. Cannon took him onto the floor of the House of Representatives; Brigham was not favorably impressed with the quality of congressmen.

Back in Utah he encountered a heartrending problem in his family when his daughter Alice eloped and married Charles Hopkins. "I would not acknowledge her husband," Brigham wrote, "but told her when she wanted a friend I was to be found. . . . Sorrow has come upon us" (7 Feb. 1876). Later Alice returned home and asked forgiveness while Hopkins and some loud friends were outside the house shouting and cursing. Eventually a divorce was obtained.

The travels of 1876 took him back to Cache Valley and visits to such communities as Clifton, Weston, and Richmond. Then he accompanied

his father on a spring trip to St. George. The temple there was now nearing completion. While in the southern part of the state, he was called
to visit the new Mormon settlements on the Little Colorado in Arizona
then known as Ballenger's camp, Lot Smith's camp, and Lake's camp.[33]
Rejoining the party of President Young at Kanab, he accompanied it
northward through the settlements to Salt Lake City and on to Logan.
In the fall he returned to St. George for the dedication of the temple.

The role of Brigham Young, Jr., in the resumption of temple work is
not without significance. Although ceremonies had been performed in
the Endowment House, there was now an effort to standardize what was
done during the endowment. To this end Brigham Jr. met with Wilford
Woodruff, with L. John Nuttall as scribe, to work out their recommen-
dations. These were then read aloud to President Young, who made
some few corrections.

The most important event of 1877, however, was the fatal illness of
the great leader, President Brigham Young. Throughout this difficult
time Brigham Jr. was by his father's side. Finally, on August 26, the
long-awaited death occurred. One can imagine the swirl of emotion in
the soul of Brigham Jr. All through his growing-up years he had been
called "Briggy." The name had stuck, still used by people who didn't
necessarily mean to be disrespectful. Always in the shadow, always
introduced as the son of Brigham Young, sometimes having to explain
that he was not *the* Brigham Young—how must he have felt? The relationship was one of dependency. Brigham Jr. knew full well that his
apostleship, his counselorship, and his important assignments had been
his because of who his father was. For such recognition he felt gratitude,
but, if he was human, also some frustration.

»   «

During the ten years from his return from Europe in 1867 to his
father's death in 1877, Brigham Young, Jr., was in an excellent position
to observe important incidents of Mormon history: railroad construction, settlement in Cache Valley, the United Order, tours by the First
Presidency, contacts with the East, and others. His diary was not kept
between 1877 and 1882, but after its resumption it continues to be a
valuable lens through which several facets of Mormon experience are
refracted: Mormon activity in Arizona and Mexico, missionary work
among the Indians, the antipolygamy activities associated with the
Raid, negotiations with national leaders in an effort to obtain a settle-

ment. In addition, of course, Brigham Jr. had his more private, personal life to live, with its share of trials and adjustments. His strong and eminent father was no longer on the scene. Finally Brigham Jr. could stand on his own feet, and in fact he did face serious challenges during the twenty-five years he lived on after his father's death.

With other prominent Mormon leaders of the period he experienced a time, about three weeks in August 1879, of incarceration in the penitentiary, not for polygamy or unlawful cohabitation, but for refusing to deliver some Church property into the hands of a federal receiver. Regrettably, we do not have a prison diary from him; it would undoubtedly be a fine addition to the rich Mormon collection of prison diaries of those who served terms "for conscience' sake."[34]

During 1881 and 1882 he was gone from Utah much of the time. First he spent a year in Arizona, taking his wife Catherine along with him. Since this was still early in the history of the Mormon settlements along the Little Colorado (1876 was the time of their founding), his presence there was an important factor in the early history of those colonies.[35] Soon his responsibility in the Southwest was expanded to include New Mexico and Old Mexico. While visiting the Yaqui Indians in Mexico he contracted yellow fever and almost died. In Arizona, too, the Mormons were engaged in missionary work among the Indians. "I find that many of the brethren manifest a decided affection for the Lamanites," he wrote (18 Mar. 1883). "I like them but cannot go around those who are dirty like some of the brethren [do]."

As early as his mission to England during the Civil War he had developed a strong sense of the contrast between God's people, the Saints, and the surrounding evil of the world. This was a common view among Latter-day Saints, of course, but if anything Brigham Jr. was more rigid, more militant than the average, perhaps because of his own flirtation with infidelity and corruption prior to his resounding conversion. This two-valued orientation continued to characterize him throughout his life and in some ways became more pronounced when the trends of the time were least encouraging. On July 4, 1883, he wrote, "I am pained to have our city council mix up with outsiders to celebrate 4th of July. 12000 of us disfranchised and yet we are invited to sit up at Camp Douglas, hear the patriotic howls of those who have been instrumental in depriving us of our citizenship. All the whores, whoremongers and rif raf of this city are invited to camp to celebrate this national day and it is expected that I will take my wives and children to sit at a general table provided at camp and mix up with creatures as low as Eli H. Murray, Gov. of Utah." On June 27, 1884, noting that forty years had passed since the martyrdom of Joseph Smith, he pleaded, "How long oh Lord shall the blood of the righteous be unavenged."

This was the period of the Raid, when Mormon polygamists were either in hiding or risking indictment for breaking the federal laws. As a polygamist Brigham lived in constant apprehension of being seized by the federal marshals. A trusted senior apostle, he was called upon to make important trips in efforts to improve the situation. One of the most interesting sections of his 1884–85 diary describes a trip with Charles W. Penrose. At Detroit they stopped at the House of Correction to call on the Mormons who had been imprisoned there. At New York, they visited the church of Henry Ward Beecher and heard the famous minister deliver a sermon. More important, they met private lobbyists and important political leaders such as Daniel S. Lamont and Grover Cleveland. It was part of a complicated behind-the-scenes effort by Mormons to persuade national leaders to pull back from the anti-polygamy persecutions and to pave the way for Utah's admission as a state.[36] One person they talked to proposed "that we use the political influence of merchants, steamship and R.R. companies with whom we do such a vast business to help us out of our political difficulties" (26 Jan. 1885). Other meetings were held, including an audience with President Chester Arthur.

In 1885 he was called to go to Mexico to find a possible relocation site for Mormons in a land that would not persecute them for their social practices. After a train ride to Mexico City where he called on the U.S. consul and then visited the Minister of Colonization Don Carlos Pacheco, Young posed a series of questions to which answers were given. "If a man came into this country with more than one wife and used prudence would he be interfered with?" he asked. "Not unless the wife complained," Pacheco answered (14 May 1885). After a profitable interview with President Porfirio Diaz, Young recorded, "Prest Diaz has been chosen, in my opinion, to subserve the interests of the Kingdom just as Prest Cleveland has been chosen in the U.S." (22 May 1885). Obviously he still held fast to a providential interpretation of history and saw God "overruling" various events in the long-range interest of his people. Later in 1885 he returned to Mexico with Moses Thatcher to conduct more interviews and select sites for Mormon colonization.

The excommunication of Apostle Albert Carrington for "lewd and lascivious conduct and adultery" occurred on November 6, 1885. Carrington, it will be remembered, was Briggy's father-in-law. If the distress was great among Carrington's colleagues in the Council of Twelve, who voted to discipline him, it must have been doubly great in his family. Briggy, who filled both roles, carried a double burden. When serving as president of the European mission he had had to discipline a few young missionaries for misconduct. His father had written to him back in 1865: "It is grievous to hear of the misconduct and transgressions of the elders, and their deviations from the path of honor. . . . It is nevertheless strange that men who receive the holy priesthood, and are called to be teachers of men, should act so utterly at variance with all their knowledge and professions."[37] Brigham Jr. had been able to avoid or resist temptation, but now this on the part of his own father-in-law! Carrington's rebaptism in 1887 helped to soothe the suffering but did not remove all of the shame and dismay.

Much of the time during 1885 and 1886 Brigham was in hiding or at least "lying low" in Arizona or Mexico. The Mormon settlements on the Little Colorado were ten years old now. When a real fracas developed at Sunset because of charges and countercharges involving the United Order there, Brigham Young, Jr., conducted the investigations that eventually led to a settlement.[38]

As roving apostle in the Southwest he naturally had frequent encounters with Indians and played a leading role in choosing Mormon missionaries to work among them. The mood of eschatalogical crisis is suggested by a conversation of some Mormons with Chief Alchisa of the White Mountain Apaches: "He wanted Mormons to visit and talk with them as they did with the Navajos. He said the Lord would come in four years. Said Mormons, Navajos, and Apaches all one. They would kill all the gentiles that persecuted them." Even if inaccurately reported, this statement indicates the tenacity of ideas of Mormon-Indian alliance against Gentiles as part of the winding-up scene.[39]

During the presidential interregnum between the death of John Taylor and the official presidency of Wilford Woodruff, 1887 to 1889, Brigham Young, Jr., now in his early fifties, participated in many important meetings in which the Council of Twelve Apostles wrestled with the basic question facing the Church. An insight into the emotionalism of these sessions is provided in his account of one held October 5, 1888:

> The point in question, Shall we repudiate plural marriage to save the half million dollars the U.S. has seized or give them pretext to seize it as fund which sustains polygamy.

Every fiber in my body cried out, "We will sacrifice no principle to save property or life itself, God being our helper." I let others do the talking, so long as they go right I am satisfied. I would rather reach the point by much thinking than much talking. The younger members of our Quorum seem to think otherwise. Decided to let the lawyers do the best they could and we retain our honor before men and our integrity to God.

Interestingly this passage betrays a tension not only between the Mormons as defenders of principle and the Gentiles who were persecuting them, but also between older church leaders like Brigham Jr. and "younger members of our Quorum." As time went on this dichotomy, the sense of belonging to a vanishing species, would become stronger in his consciousness.

Besides the general problems facing the Church, Brigham Young, Jr., faced turmoil within his own family. Immediately after his father's death he had had to play a central role in the settlement of the Brigham Young estate. Some family members were anxious to keep everything for themselves, while others saw that in large part their father had functioned as trustee for the Church. After lengthy court battles a settlement was finally reached. One family member praised Brigham Jr. for maintaining a "just and amicable disposition," but others undoubtedly saw him in a less friendly light. Even if they had not had reason earlier to envy his name, his advancement in the hierarchy, his being favored, there were hard financial reasons for hating him now. He tried to exert a conciliatory influence, once attempting to arrange a lunch with Brigham Young's surviving wives. But some were not ready to accept the proffered olive branch. Harriet Cook, he noted in his diary, "sent an insulting no!!! to the invitation" (30 Apr. 1890).

Even in his own immediate family there were problems, possibly because he had added four more wives besides Catherine and Jane.[40] "My wives must soften their hearts towards each other," he wrote. One part of the problem was the belligerent mood and behavior of his first wife Catherine Spencer. She had sold property without his permission, he recorded. When he wanted to turn over the Forest Farm to his brother John W., following the wishes of his father, she would not sign the deed. "The U.S. Government has restored the first wife's right of dower and my wife Catherine Spencer is determined to take all the advantage of my wrong possible. I am sore distressed over her course, and greatly fear she will bring distress and sorrow on herself and children." Behind such statements must have been hard feeling, many arguments, and a general breakdown of good relations within the family. It is not surprising, perhaps, that in 1889 Brigham wrote, "I am very lonesome at times and have difficulty to keep up my flow of spirits."

Brigham still held fast to the eschatological hopes shared by many Mormons during 1890–91.[41] But bright promises that the Savior would soon come appeared against a background of despair. The general movement of the times was not encouraging. Salt Lake City was lovely, he noted in 1890, but "alas our streets are full of strangers. Gazing through the window blinds I seldom see a familiar face. The class that made the country are proscribed" (25 May 1890). Even in his Church quorum he sensed some uncomfortable discrepancies. In noting the feebleness of President Wilford Woodruff, he called him "the last representative of that sturdy, manly race whom the Father sent out to bring forth his Gospel to this generation." He continued, "I am essentially a Woodruff man for, when I compare my simple ideas with the effrontery of the rising generation, it seems to me that I had better join those noble plain God-fearing men who have passed behind the vail" (15 May 1890). It was an eloquent expression of the generation gap being felt by the older Mormon leaders.

In some ways it must have been a relief when he was called to return to Great Britain as mission president. He had not been there since 1867; now he would go back. Leaving Salt Lake City on August 18, 1890, Young and his family—two children, Hattie and Frank, and their mother, Young's third wife, Mary Elizabeth Fenton—traveled east. At New York they paid a visit to Coney Island. Then they boarded ship for England.

During the three years of his presidency there, supervising not only missionary activities in England but also in Europe, Brigham Young, Jr., traveled much, visited missionaries, addressed conferences—in general the kinds of activities of all mission presidents. But he found that the old fervor was dead. The quick conversions and enthusiastic responses to the early missionaries of the 1840s and 1850s had been on the wane when Brigham Jr. had been there back in the 1860s. But at that time there had been a sense of impending upheaval that would possibly mean a downfall of the United States and the counterpoint themes of building the Kingdom, returning to the Missouri Zion, and witnessing the dramatic Second Coming of Christ. The emigration of Saints from "Europe's shore," many of them helped by the Perpetual Emigration Fund, had been motivated at least in part by such considerations.

But now times had changed. Following events at home as he heard of them by mail, Brigham Young, Jr., was anything but encouraged. The Manifesto had not ended harassment of the Church, whose enemies continued relentlessly. When he read in the newspaper that the U.S. District Attorney contemplated seizing the temples in St. George, Manti, and Salt Lake City (the latter nearing completion), he exploded: "I was so disturbed when reading of their mean[n]ess that I could scarcely contain my feelings. I would rather fight if it is the Lord's will than submit longer to these curses who disgrace the Gov[ernment] they represent. If it were in my power I would stand by those Temples and kill the first hound from the President of the U.S.A. down to the dastardly U.S. Marshals . . . before they should desecrate those sacred buildings. These were my thoughts until I was worked up to a pitch seldom reached by one of my temper" (26 Feb. 1891). Finally, reminding himself that "the Lord was managing this business," Young uttered a silent prayer, "O Lord, give the Government and the people of the United States something to chew besides the L.D.S."

As a polygamist himself, he could not be indifferent to what was going on back home, as it had implications for his future domestic life. To gain amnesty the Mormon leaders made promises that disturbed Young, the rationale being (as it was for the Manifesto itself) that something must be done to save the temples. Some might ask, he wrote, whether God could not save them. "I answer Yes, and Zion might even now be redeemed had the people obeyed the counsel our leaders were inspired to give them in the past. I will do whatever my leaders counsel, but the bare thought of taking clemency from U.S.A. that has destroyed the prophets and thrust us out to perish pains me more than I can tell."

Closely related to clemency was the difficult question of what those who had taken plural wives earlier should now do about their family obligations. "What right has a first wife to enjoy all [the] blessings when her sisters who had suffered and ventured as much as she are wickedly thrust out from all rights of wives and mothers given them of their Father who is in heaven?" (14 Nov. 1891). That this was not an empty question is suggested by the abandoning of some plural wives by their husbands, by the pressure of U.S. officials in Utah to insist that the end of polygamy meant the end of existing plural relationships, and by the reluctant statements of high Church officials that could be interpreted as going along with the demands.[42] Like other polygamists among the high Church officials, Young would have none of this. "I will have all of my wives or none, God being my helper," he wrote (19 Dec. 1891).

His ample family was still growing. His first wife, Catherine, had had eleven children; Jane (married 1857), eight; Mary Elizabeth (married 1868), three. For nearly twenty years no more wives were added. Then Rhoda Perkins became wife number four in 1886 and had one child. In 1887, he married seventeen-year-old Abigail Stevens, whose seven children came along regularly between 1888 and 1902.[43] There was even a marriage in 1890 to Helen Armstrong, who had one child. All in all, when we consider new babies coming on the scene and, on the part of the older children, their own marriages and children, Brigham Young, Jr., had an ample progeny, to say the least. Family concerns would occupy much of his emotional energy right to the end of his life.

The question of polygamy was more than personal; it also had to be dealt with in terms of missionary proselyting. What should be said by the missionaries? Should they defend polygamy? Should they bring it up or mention it only when asked? Should they give different statements to Church members than to investigators? Brigham Young, Jr., wrote an answer to such questions in a letter, which he summarized in his diary: "Advised them to avoid the subject [as] much as possible but to stand by the revelation. The Lord has said cease and we stopped its practice, for we have always obeyed the laws of the land, but when the laws of the land are made to specially abrogate the commands of God, it takes the word of the Lord, as in this case, to render Congressional action effective. God will deprive those wicked men of every vestige of family, indeed of every private and national virtue, for their hypocrisy towards His saints" (26 Oct. 1891).

Then there was the question of immigration. This was the decade between intense promotion of immigration by the Mormons and the efforts to discourage European Church members from going to Utah that were announced in 1899.[44] The long-standing concern of anti-Mormons with the continual flow from Europe to Utah finally culminated in a more restrictive immigration policy. Young was irate when he heard about it: "The provisions of it are so dastardly discriminating against all immigrants and I think point expressly towards shutting out Mormons from U.S. that I feel like it would be right to close our immigration until we can make arrangements to ship them direct to Mexico" (1 Apr. 1891).

Actually, proselyting success was not great anyway. On March 8, 1892, he wrote to President Wilford Woodruff: "The missionaries are doing but little in proselyting. Leaving the people without excuse is most we hope to do. We do not average one convert to the missionary in a year. If more are baptized, it is Saints['] children or rebaptisms. The people have fortified themselves so strongly, entrenched behind their ramparts of '1 am saved,' 'Infidelity,' 'Pleasures of the table,' 'Women and women,' etc. that [they] do not want the gospel and are disgusted at the mention of the name of the prophet Joseph." Although the missionaries preached the words of Jesus and his apostles, Young wrote, those who stopped to listen to street meetings would immediately say, "Oh that's a Mormon speaking. Hear them quite enough."

Added to repeated problems of poor health, these things did not add up to a positive mission experience. Still, Brigham was conscientious in doing his duty as he saw it. In 1893 he was released and allowed to return home for the dedication of the Salt Lake Temple.

» «

Ten years remained in the life of Brigham Young, Jr. It was an exciting decade of adjustment for the Mormon Church and for the "Woodruff man" who saw himself as belonging to a dying breed.

In 1895 he attended a social gathering. President Wilford Woodruff appeared "very feeble." People came straggling in late so that it was not possible to start dining at the appointed time. Finally, George Q. Cannon was called on to deliver a blessing on the food. "He did so and prayed that Prest Woodruff might suffer no permanent inconvenience in consequence of going so long without food occasioned by waiting for those guests who came so late—so long after the appointed time for dinner." "Many smiled," Young added, "and I fear some few audibly" (11 Apr. 1895).

Bearer of a famous name, he received some favorable publicity and attention. On January 12, 1897, he received three applications for his photograph and biography from compilers of biographical dictionaries. "I don't like it much," he wrote. "It [is] too much work to be famous." The previous year he had attended a national irrigation congress at Phoenix, Arizona. He gave a speech before it and was complimented by many people afterwards. After his nomination as vice-president, the vote was unanimous in his favor. But such fame he knew to be not entirely his own attainment. "I know it was in the heart of every man present to honor my father's name and memory in my person," he wrote (17 Dec. 1896).[45]

The Church's apparent reversal of policy on the question of plural marriage still left him ill at ease. "Rulers in this nation will have a heavy bill to settle when they reach the spirit world," he wrote. On the other hand, he did not join with Mormon leaders—notably Matthias Cowley and John W. Taylor—who persisted in encouraging polygamy until they were finally excommunicated or disciplined.

On one question Young found himself standing on the progressive side—this was the question of female suffrage. On the losing side of this issue was fellow General Authority B. H. Roberts, of the First Council of Seventy, who in 1895 gave a long, fully reported talk against female suffrage in the Constitutional Convention while preparing for statehood in early 1896. One day Young ran into Roberts in front of the Constitution Building and let his feelings be known, saying,

> The Government of the U.S. has forced me, with many other polygamists, to put away our wives. We have given them their property. They now stand at the head of their families, pay their taxes, and are, to all intents and purposes, pillars of the body politic. Bro. Roberts, what argument can I bring which will satisfy these persecuted, much enduring women that we are right in withholding the franchise from them? I cannot do it, for their votes would be in the interest of morality and good order and would thereby thwart a class who enjoyed but ought never to have had the franchise. (1 Apr. 1895)

Young was of course expressing the dominant view of the Church and that which became accepted at the convention.

Later, when he had a chance to see some of the behavior of women, he was not so enthusiastic. Martha Hughes Cannon, elected state senator over her own husband, Stake President Angus Cannon, especially disgusted him in that she consistently voted for Judge Orlando Powers and Moses Thatcher, both Democrats but high on the list of those who wished the Church no good. "It was remarked by one of my friends that so far women's suffrage seemed to be a failure," he wrote, adding, "I fear many of our sisters will prove to be as big fools in the political arena as many of the brethren have proved themselves."

Other changes were harder for him to accept. The Mormons had been united in the Peoples party for many years. Now, as one of the prices paid for statehood, they had to divide into the two national parties. This had led to some partisanship and hard feeling, even among individuals in the high councils of the Church leadership. One day, Young was approached by Emmeline B. Wells, a Republican and women's rights advocate, who whispered in his ear, "We are talking of putting you in nomination for Governor of the new state" (9 July 1895). He had earlier been approached by Democrats, but he was not about to accept a nomination from either party, even to be President of the United States. In his diary he wrote: "So much good and so much bad figure together in politics nowadays that the dose seems too drastic for an honest man to swallow unbiased by the prevailing spirit in politics. Good, honest men shout themselves hoarse with urging party cries, but it is not the calm, sober spirit of God that makes howling maniacs of High Priests, Seventies, elders and teachers of the pure religion of the meek and lowly Jesus" (9 July 1895). He was absent on a trip to Mexico for several weeks. Upon his return he found that his name had again been proposed by both parties. He explained to his friends that there was only one way that such solicitations could have persuaded him—to be called by the President of the Church. And under these circumstances he "would not go in as Democrat or Republican but a free lance under no party control. I must belong to the people, not party nor sectional." On September 28, 1895, President Wilford Woodruff told him, "I would rather not that you be Governor or rather that you do not mingle in politics. You are not so suitable for that department." If politics is the art of compromise, Woodruff was clearly perceptive if not inspired.[46]

The immediate background of Young's aversion to political partisanship was the fracas over activities by Democrats B. H. Roberts and Moses Thatcher.[47] In one discussion Thatcher told Brigham Jr. that he was "too pliable," as were the other apostles, and that "they failed to maintain their individuality, their God-given rights—their manhood." Young showed no disposition to sympathize with Roberts and Thatcher. He had been conditioned to the virtue of following counsel. Not that he thought it was proper for the Church to "interfere" in politics, but for him it was simply a question of Church discipline: one should not accept an appointment as a General Authority without being willing to fulfill the duties—which meant that permission must be sought before accepting political candidacy or other responsibilities that might compete with Church obligations. At an emotional meeting on February 13, 1896, after Roberts had refused to recant, Young went outside and walked to the south side of the temple and "sobbed aloud." These were difficult days for Mormon leaders and especially for those who had the old ways, the old values, as part of their personal code. Later,

Roberts submitted to the Church position, for which Young was "glad and thankful," but Thatcher did not. Throughout Young's position was consistently that of the hard-line Kingdom builder.

But there was more to it than this. Young was not sympathetic to the new order of things, which would allow political differences between Church leaders who had earlier been united in the Peoples party. "Politics has made many foolish brethren," he wrote. "They have lost their heads and are more foolish than the wicked gentiles. I fear for many who have been faithful men but are now blatant politicians [who] don't know a Saint's face from a gentile's backside" (14 Oct. 1895).

Even when Utah became a state, in January 1896, Young's reaction was guarded: "I am not enthused—to use a familiar phrase, though I have waited and prayed for nearly half a century." At the inauguration address, he heard polygamy "cuffed about too much" and wondered in his heart how he could support a state constitution and men in office who would "stamp upon that sacred principle."

On other occasions we get glimpses of the "Woodruff man"—a Mormon of the old school—who was having some difficulty in adjusting to the accommodation era that characterized the turn of the century. In April 1896 he proposed that the First Presidency and Twelve operate a farm according to the principles of the United Order. That discredited system, which had failed when President Brigham Young had made a last-ditch effort to establish it in 1874, still had its appeal for Brigham Jr. For him the idea was intimately connected with the expected last days and the return to Jackson County. "My mind opens to visions of presidents of stakes, High Councils, Bishops, etc. gradually—unsolicited—following our example, coming to us for council, and thus a core of men and women who have received through their faithfulness, all the blessings in the House of the Lord being prepared to inhabit and build up the center stake of Zion in Jackson County, Miss[ouri]" (2 Apr. 1896). To say the least, his intense hopes were disappointed.

As he looked around him, Brigham Young, Jr., was disturbed by the increased gentile influence in the state. Benjamin Cluff, president of Brigham Young Academy, proposed employing a gentile professor of geology and civil engineering. Favoring the decision to hire the non-Mormon were President Wilford Woodruff and counselor Joseph F. Smith. When the vote took place, Young abstained. He wrote, "It is the first time I have failed to go with my leaders. I went my way sorrowfully. There is a growing disposition with the teachers to introduce into our

Brigham Young Academy the spirit of the world. The refined touches and whisperings of the Holy Spirit are becoming less frequent and in my spirit I fear we are drifting further from God in that institution" (31 July 1896). Interestingly, the next day the First Presidency rescinded the earlier decision, effectively agreeing with Young.

In the fall of 1896, the Quorum of Twelve met to decide whom they should support in the election. They decided that they could "morally" support a Gentile. Young was not sanguine about this decision and encouraged the group to "wait upon" the Lord until they were fully satisfied, "for apparently we are powerless in this wild political turmoil."

It was the old sense of being overrun by wickedness from the outside, a theme popular among Mormon leaders in the 1850s and at the time of the railroad's coming in 1869, that was still strong in Young's consciousness. Concerned about the danger to morals of young people, he and his apostolic brethren discussed the advisability of prohibiting the sale of liquor at Saltair, at least on Sunday, and of forbidding mixed swimming at the lake. At a Mutual Improvement Association conference in Preston, Idaho, after agreeing to speak for just a few minutes, he lost track of time and spoke for three quarters of an hour. That evening he wrote in his diary: "Good liberty but rather severe upon the wicked gentiles. The moral men and women I sustain. I was verging on dangerous ground if we consider the policy to placate the obnoxious element. I cannot look up[on] the adulterer, whiskey men, whores and profaners with any degree of patience only as the Lord gives it to me in answer to prayer. God help me to be longsuffering and set back in the breeching so far as taking vengeance into my own hands" (13 June 1897). Of course being disturbed about modern trends is not a new experience, but the strength of Brigham Young, Jr.'s, opinion, his inflexibility, seems to set him apart.

One specific modern development he opposed was public high schools supported by tax monies. "District free schools [elementary schools] are sufficient tax upon us," he wrote (13 Dec. 1897). Despite his outspokenness on the subject, the measure had passed, for the Gentiles banded together and voted almost unanimously in late 1897.[48] Young still saw things in black and white terms; his was a two-valued orientation. And often, as he experienced it, he was fighting a losing battle.

It must be admitted that as one of the senior members of the Church's apostolic quorums he had more than his share of frustrating, emotionally charged problems to face. The Thatcher case dragged on for several years and produced untold anguish. Similar were the questions of what to do about the Church's finances, inevitably entangled in attitudes toward the responsibility or lack of responsibility of Counselor George Q. Cannon. Relations among the Apostles were cordial, but at times animosities surfaced. At a meeting on January 6, 1898, Young spoke out strongly against Cannon. The latent hostility could not always be suppressed.

In early 1898, Young with other Americans, heard the news of the sinking of the U.S.S. *Maine* in Havana harbor. Unlike most Americans, however, he resisted the war fever that followed. He wrote, "The excitement over the destruction of the *Maine*. It seems to me that Americans are determined to provoke a war with Spain. I know it is to sell papers. Hence I think it wicked to lie the people into an excitement of perfect frenzy for war" (22 Feb. 1898). Most modern historians would agree with this assessment—the war was largely a public relations put-on[49]— but in 1898 Brigham Young, Jr., was out of step. When one prominent Church official told him that Mormon young men might "distinguish themselves" in the war, Young responded, "They would undoubtedly extinguish themselves. If I knew of any young men who wanted to go to this war I would call them on a mission to preach the gospel of peace. Our mission is to preach and to save souls" (21 Apr. 1898).

Soon he was called on the carpet by President Woodruff. He should have sought counsel before undertaking to "defy the government." Young replied that he had not really defied the government but was just trying to "make head against the spirit which is going through the people. . . . that spirit is not of God" (26 Apr. 1898). Without much discussion, it was ruled that Willard Young, a brother, and Richard W. Young, a nephew, both professional soldiers, should continue to recruit Mormon youths for the military service. "The feeling among the gentiles and some of the Mormons is strong against me," Brigham Jr. wrote. "God help me to be humble and take reproof in proper spirit. I will be one with the president, God being my helper" (ibid.). Was it a persecution complex that led him a few days later to note that he was ridiculed by "sometime friends and now maligners" and that the *Deseret News* was treating him with "silent contempt"? Judging from what usually happens in times of war, he probably had reason for his feeling.

Even his position of seniority in the Council of Twelve Apostles was insecure. Many years earlier, way back in 1864, he had been ordained an Apostle by his father but had not actually become a functioning member of the quorum until 1868. At the quorum's meeting in 1898, before it named Lorenzo Snow as the new president of the Church, the two counselors of the preceding president came back and took their places in order of seniority. This raised the question of where Brigham Young, Jr., should properly sit. After the meeting Heber J. Grant expressed his view that Brigham Young, Jr., should sit after Joseph F. Smith. Young answered, "I am willing to take any place in the quorum. [I] never felt I was fit to be an apostle." He went on to explain that he had raised this question with his father, President Brigham Young, many years earlier, who had replied, "It is just right the way it is, and you let it alone." Nevertheless, the decision was now made for Young to change places with Joseph F. Smith. "I am anxious for God through my brethren to decide this question and I yield my views to theirs with all my heart," Young wrote. He seems to have accepted the decision quite willingly. Significantly, however, he also wrote, "Still, I am of the opinion that when a man is ordained an apostle and seeks to magnify that office no new man can rank him in being set apart to fill a vacancy in the Quorum of the Twelve." It would be a human reaction for him to be at least slightly rankled at having been singled out for a "demotion."

But such pique, if it existed, was slight in comparison to his dismay at what was happening to the Church and kingdom to which he had dedicated his life. He had looked for a dramatic wind-up scene; it had not occurred. He had expected the revived United Order system to herald the great millennial reign; that experiment had failed. He had looked with hope to the Indians, the people of promise, to lead the way in re-establishing God's kingdom; the few of them who had converted had not fulfilled such great expectations. He had been proud of the Mormon commonwealth and now saw increasing numbers of Gentiles flowing in and corrupting the atmosphere, much as the troops of Colonel Steptoe had done with their drunken disturbance back in 1854. The Church was abandoning its earlier political unity, its staunch defense of celestial marriage. A younger generation was coming to the fore. Woodruff men like Brigham Young, Jr., saw themselves in a doom-shaped world.

His attitude toward the Gentiles was not friendly. How can the children of light fraternize with the powers of darkness? When he preached a sermon on "beware of the leaven of the gentiles" in which he compared them to ink poured into the pure water of Latter-day Saint faith, some of them complained. "My, what a row my sermon, has created," he wrote. "If the brethren will keep their hands off me, as true as the Lord liveth I will preach what He gives me" (14 Oct. 1898).[50]

When he preached a sermon looking forward to the fulfillment of prophecies, he was dealing with a favorite theme—the contrast between the degeneration of the world and the forthcoming glorious day of the Lord. This had long been a topic of interest to the Latter-day Saints, and during the brief administration of Lorenzo Snow the imminence of the return to Jackson County and the Second Coming of Christ were often discussed. It was starting to be apparent, however, that such hopes, while not officially abandoned, would receive less and less attention. In this sense Brigham Young, Jr., was one of the old guard in quoting scriptural passages that envisioned the return of the tribes of Israel from the north. "Then," he was quoted as saying, "a nation would be born in a day, and the influence of the faithful Saints would be extended politically and otherwise until all things promised to them would be literally fulfilled and they would become rulers over many things."[51] It was this sermon that the *Salt Lake Tribune* ridiculed in a cartoon showing Brigham Young, Jr., standing in sandals, robe, and an attached metal halo, his mouth sending up vapors labeled "That One Day Nation." Sending up smoke into the same cloud were an opium pipe and a hot air furnace. The caption announced, "All Three Produce the Same Thing."[52]

He was not in tune with the times, to say the least. After meeting with the University of Utah alumni he commented: "I found the company fine but there seems to be no God in it. Just as it seemed to me this morning at Theater where Diplomas were given. Not one word of God. All seemed to center in the nature around them and all the Pioneer work and hardships were endured, this country redeemed, for the sole and explicit purpose of giving these young gentlemen and ladies an education" (19 June 1901). These young people, he seemed to be saying, have not sacrificed and do not appreciate the cost of providing such things as universities. More important, they did not, for Brigham Jr., see their lives at all in relation to God and his purposes. Often he lamented the apparent increase of crime and immorality.

In another area Brigham Jr. found himself defending the good old ways against change. The issue was compulsory vaccination for smallpox, which he opposed, while other prominent Latter-day Saint leaders favored it. His reasons are interesting. "God alone can avert the contagious diseases and calamities coming upon the people," he wrote (6 Feb. 1901). On the same ground earlier Mormons had opposed going to medical doctors at all, and one has the impression that he would have agreed with them. More significant was his statement that gentile doctors were "trying to force Babylon into the people" and to "disease the blood of our children." The compulsory vaccination was symbolic, representing all that he disliked about the trends in the world around him, especially the powerful, irresistible intrusion into Zion of a foreign element with different values.[53] Within such a conceptual framework, it was shocking for Young to discover that fellow apostles were agreeing with the vaccination programs. But it confirmed his general pessimistic evaluation of his times.

Brigham Young, Jr., died on April 11, 1903. His life had been an ordeal. He had faced up to most of his challenges successfully. He had survived a hard childhood. He had crossed the plains. He had grown up tough and assertive on the frontier. He had been matured and tamed by marriage and family and by foreign missionary assignments. His religious faith had started from a small flame but had grown with the years. Additional assignments in Great Britain and in Utah had meant continued growth and maturing. As an apostle, a member of the Church's leading council, he had taken on important leadership assignments. Although he was still occasionally called Briggy at the end of his life, it was done affectionately; usually he was called Brigham Young. He had walked through the tunnel behind his father but had won the esteem and respect of his people.

If there was a challenge to which he did not measure up, it was the challenge of change. His life had spanned the Mormon experience from the Missouri persecutions to the era of accommodation after the Manifesto. In a certain sense, therefore, the ordeal of Briggy was the ordeal of the Mormon Church. Representing the old guard, he clung to the old ways and shook his head at the new ones. He may even have welcomed death when it came. The Church as an institution, capable of absorbing new blood and having more than the three score years and ten allotted to an individual, continued on, making adjustments while retaining the most basic principles of the Restoration.

Notes

1. Andrew Jenson, *Latter-day Saint Biographical Encyclopedia* (Salt Lake City: Andrew Jenson History Company, 1901), 123. Jenson based these biographical sketches on material supplied by the subjects; hence it seems that the details came from Brigham Young, Jr., himself. Susa Young Gates, "Lives of Our Leaders—The Apostles: Brigham Young," *The Juvenile Instructor* 35 (1 May 1900): 258.

2. Gates, "Lives of Our Leaders," 260.

3. *On the Mormon Frontier: The Diary of Hosea Stout, 1844–1861,* 2 vols., ed. Juanita Brooks (Salt Lake City: University of Utah Press, 1964), 2:536.

4. Ibid. 2:553.

5. William Jennings, "Material Progress of Utah," *Utah Historical Quarterly* 3 (Jan. 1930): 89–90.

6. Dean C. Jessee, ed., *Letters of Brigham Young to His Sons* (Salt Lake City: Deseret Book, 1974), 34.

7. Ibid., 45.

8. From age fifteen, in 1851, he was a member of the Valley Tan Boys or minute men (Gates, "Lives of Our Leaders," 261). He held the rank of major during the Utah War.

9. "Give my love to Lott Smith and tell him that I am not So afraid to Stand up before a congregation as I once was in Farmington where I was called to the Stand and instead of going I ran out of doors" (Brigham Young, Jr., to Brigham Young, 13 Oct. 1862).

10. In Washington he was in the company of senators elect William H. Hooper and George Q. Cannon, both of whom were elected by the legislature as "United States senators" from the proposed "State of Deseret." John M. Bernhisel was territorial delegate.

11. Brigham Young, Jr., Diary, Church Archives. All information in the present essay is derived from the diary unless otherwise indicated. It was his father who started Brigham Jr. keeping his personal record (Jessee, *Letters,* 22).

12. Ibid., 22–25.

13. Brigham Young, Jr., to Brigham Young, 7 August 1862. In a later letter he noted that his father would enjoy visiting the exhibition, where he could see "the elements which God has provided for the use of man, organised, and brought into Subjection to his will, but do they thank God for these blessings, and give him the prise, no they do not, they take all the glory to themselves, therefore God will give it to those who will give him the rightful owner of it, the praise" (Brigham Young, Jr., to Brigham Young, 4 Sept. 1862).

14. For details about this arrest see B. H. Roberts, *Comprehensive History of the Church of Jesus Christ of Latter-day Saints,* 6 vols. (Salt Lake City: Deseret News Press, 1930), 5:28–30.

15. These letter and diary quotations are all from Jessee, ed., *Letters of Brigham Young to His Sons,* 45.

16. The visit to the Isle of Man is described in a letter, Brigham Young, Jr., to Brigham Young, 22 April 1863. The tour of the Continent is described in letters from Lyons, Rome, Geneva, and Copenhagen, Brigham Young, Jr., to Brigham Young, 9 June 1863, 21 June 1863, 5 July 1863, and 20 July 1863.

17. In 1864 Brigham Jr. assisted President Daniel H. Wells in presiding

over the European mission. In 1865, when Wells returned to Utah, Young assumed full charge (Gates, "Lives of Our Leaders," 262–63). Although the names of both Wells and Young appeared on all official statements, there seems to have been a division of labor, with Brigham Jr. handling financial matters (*Millennial Star* 26). At first Brigham Jr. worked under Wells but tried to assume most of the "business transactions" (Brigham Young, Jr., to Brigham Young, 3 Aug. 1864).

18. For indications of moral problems in the British Mission, see *Millennial Star* 27:777–79 and 28:25–26. See also Brigham Young, Jr., to Brigham Young, 27 October 1864, 9 October 1865, 23 October 1865, and 25 November 1865. This last letter summarized the problem vividly if not tastefully: "I find that the greatest trial the brethern have to meet is to keep their skirts clear of women, that class of people being very plenty, and from the customs of the country, they have come to think every man they meet wants to ride them and about two thirds of the females keep an open shop day and night." See also 15 January 1866.

19. Orson Pratt took charge of the mission by early June 1866. See also this statement in a letter to his father: "when bro. Cannon was here I have understood that he said, the mission was growing less each year. I must say that I concur with him. Inspite of all that I can do, backed as I know that I am by the brethern, baptisms are growing more seldom, and in some instances the people exhibit an apathy that is almost unaccountable" (Brigham Young, Jr., to Brigham Young, 3 April 1866).

20. During his trip to the States his wife remained in England at 53 Vine Street, a house he had rented for her. Boarding there were Franklin D. Richards and John W. Young. "Manuscript History of the British Mission," 21 September 1866.

21. Brigham Young's use of ghostwriters was not substantially different from that of modern political leaders. Assistants prepared drafts; he went over them and made necessary changes, if any. The Governor's message of 1867 was for Brigham Young in his position as Governor of the ghost state of Deseret.

22. On the significance of the Council of Fifty, see Klaus Hansen, *Quest for Empire: The Political Kingdom of God and the Council of Fifty in Mormon History* (East Lansing: Michigan State University Press, 1967).

23. Further good description of the visit to Washington and the postbellum Congress is contained in Brigham Young, Jr., to Brigham Young, 28 March 1867.

24. John Bright, a liberal member of Parliament, was a major proponent of Parliamentary reform and may well have been occupied with the reform bill of 1867. A letter modifies the description of Bright: "We chatted on several subjects for ten or fifteen minutes, when he appointed to meet us at

his residence Hanover Square next day at 12 M. We kept the appointment to a minute and were soon in the presence of the peoples mouthpiece. He seemed exceedingly dull at first, and received us rather coldly, but pretty soon he began to undbend, and in the hours conversation which followed he learned that Mr. Bowles book which he had just been reading, was untrue in many places where he had formerlly believed it correct. We were well suited with our visit and bro. Franklin [Richards] thought as I did that the visit would be productive and good" (Brigham Young, Jr., to Brigham Young, 18 April 1867).

25. "The specimens I was enabled to get into the exhibition building and some of them assigned to their proper places, but the very small part of the building which has been appropriated to the use of the United States made even our small collection seem a superfluity" (Brigham Young, Jr., to Brigham Young, 5 June 1867).

26. Adah Isaacs Menken was the stage name of an American actress and dancer noted for her daring unconventionality.

27. Brigham Jr. was not more impressed with British royalty. After seeing Prince Albert in 1863 he wrote to his father: "If I had meet them in the street I should have taken no notice of them. Prince Albert might have attracted a little notice perhaps, and, a person not knowing who he was, would think he was not the brightest Jonny man they had ever seen, or maybe have gone a little further, and said that he was not right in the uperstory, but he is a Prince and so perforce must be smart and perfectly capable of assuming the reins of Government" (Brigham Young, Jr., to Brigham Young, 14 March 1863).

28. The dates of his ordinations are: apostle and assistant counselor, 4 February 1864; Quorum of Twelve, 9 October 1868; and assistant counselor, 8 April 1873. D. Michael Quinn, "Organizational Development and Social Origins of the Mormon Hierarchy, 1832–1932: A Prosopographical Study" (M.A. thesis, University of Utah, 1973).

29. Brigham Young, Jr., to Brigham Young, 18 December 1869.

30. When Benson died in 1869, Peter Maughan served as acting president for two years. William B. Preston then was "acting presiding bishop in Cache." Brigham Young, Jr., became stake president in November 1871 and served until May 1877. Joel E. Ricks, ed. *The History of a Valley: Cache Valley* (Logan: Cache Valley Centennial Commission, 1956), 279–80. He was officially sustained as stake president in 1872. Journal History, 1 September 1872. This is a huge, multivolume compilation of newspaper clippings and other primary sources located in the Church Archives.

31. A popular lecturer, Victoria Woodhull championed women's suffrage, spiritualism, and other reforms regarded as radical at the time.

32. On the failure of the United Order efforts in 1874, see Leonard J.

Arrington, Dean May, and Feramorz Fox, *Building the City of God: Community and Cooperation among the Mormons* (Salt Lake City: Deseret Book, 1976). Brigham Young, Jr., was elected president of the Cache Valley United Order on 2 May 1874. He was also one of the assistant vice-presidents of the United Order "in all the world wherever established." Journal History, 10 April 1875.

33. The authoritative study of Mormon colonization in Arizona is Charles S. Peterson, *Take Up Your Mission: Mormon Colonizing along the Little Colorado River, 1870–1900* (Tucson: University of Arizona Press, 1973). See also James H. McClintock, *Mormon Settlement in Arizona* (Phoenix, 1921); and George S. Tanner and J. Morris Richards, *Colonizing on the Little Colorado* (Flagstaff: Northland Press, 1977).

34. William Mulder, "Prisoners for Conscience' Sake," in Thomas E. Cheney et al., *Love of Faith and Folly* (Salt Lake City: University of Utah Press, 1971). See Leonard J. Arrington, "The Settlement of the Brigham Young Estate," *Pacific Historical Review* 21 (Feb. 1952): 1–20. For details on the contempt case see *Deseret News*, 30 July 1879–28 August 1879. The "executors" served a prison term of twenty-four days before being released by the Territorial Supreme Court. Eventually the suit was settled out of court.

35. Peterson, *Take Up Your Mission*, 173, 243–44.

36. Henry J. Wolfinger, "A Reexamination of the Woodruff Manifesto in the Light of Utah Constitutional History," *Utah Historical Quarterly* 29 (Fall 1971): 328–49.

37. Jessee, ed., *Letters of Brigham Young to His Sons*, 59.

38. Peterson, *Take Up Your Mission*, chap. 5.

39. Lawrence Coates, Professor of History at Ricks College, is doing research on this theme.

40. See Quinn, "Organizational Development," 289.

41. As early as 1865, Brigham Young, Jr., had considered the winding-up scene and the building of the New Jerusalem to be close at hand. *Millennial Star* 27 (16 Dec. 1865): 793–96.

42. The most important such statement was before the Master in Chancery. *Deseret News*, 24 October 1891 and 31 October 1891.

43. Information on number of children per wife is from D. Michael Quinn, "Organizational Development," 289. From the Family History Library, Salt Lake City, Utah, I have obtained charts showing the children of Catherine and Abigail.

44. Entries in the Journal History of the Church for 19 January 1899 and in the April 1899 general conference report indicate the beginning of a policy of advice to European Saints to remain in their own countries. James R. Clark, ed. *Messages of the First Presidency* (Salt Lake City: Bookcraft, 1965–75), 5:199. See also William Mulder, "Immigration and the Mor-

mon Question: An International Episode," *Western Political Quarterly* 9 (June 1956): 416–33.

45. The following year Brigham Young, Jr., was unable to attend the National Irrigation Congress at Lincoln, Nebraska. He sent his scheduled opening address to be read. Interestingly, it contains a proposal for public ownership: the government should "purchase all the reservoirs and other means of water storage" in the arid regions of the country. Journal History, 28 September 1897.

46. Jean B. White, "The Making of the Convention President: The Political Education of John Henry Smith," *Utah Historical Quarterly* 39:4 (Fall 1971): 350–69.

47. D. Michael Quinn, "The Mormon Hierarchy, 1832–1932: An American Elite" (Ph.D. diss., Yale University, 1976), chap. 4.

48. Stanley S. Ivins, "Free Schools Come to Utah," *Utah Historical Quarterly* 22 (Oct. 1954): 321–42.

49. D. Michael Quinn, "The Mormon Church and the Spanish-American War: An End to Selective Pacifism," *Pacific Historical Review* 43 (Aug. 1973): 342–66.

50. This sermon was given in the October 1898 general conference. *Conference Reports* 1898 (Salt Lake City: n.d.), 48–51.

51. *Deseret Evening News*, 10 June 1901. A firm sense of the dwindling importance of this theme awaits a systematic content analysis of sermons.

52. *Salt Lake Tribune*, 11 June 1901.

53. The issue was not merely vaccination but compulsory vaccination. That Young was not alone in opposing it is indicated by the passage of a bill in the state legislature forbidding compulsory vaccination. The symbolism is suggested by the following entry: "I do look upon this case as Gentile doctors trying to force Babylon into the people and some of them are willing to disease the blood of our children if they can do so, and they think they are doing God's service."

8

The Exclusion of
B. H. Roberts from Congress

ON JANUARY 25, 1900, the House of Representatives by a vote of
268 to 50, refused to seat Brigham Henry Roberts, congressman-
elect from the newly admitted state of Utah. The events leading up to
that exclusion illustrate a period of significant transition, for the last decade of the nineteenth century in Utah was one of momentous change,
a period in which were caught up together the problems and conflicts of
the nineteenth century and the promise of the twentieth. The transition
from pre-Manifesto to post-Manifesto social orientations, the mollify-
ing of the bitter Mormon-Gentile conflict, the mass shifts in political
loyalty accompanying the rise of national parties in Utah, the advancement from territorial status and carpet-bag government to statehood
and self-government—all these threads converge in the B. H. Roberts
case of 1898–1900.

» «

Roberts was born in Warrington, Lancashire, England, on March 13,
1857. His parents were converts to the Mormon Church, and in 1862 his
mother with two of the youngest children left for Utah. He followed in
1866 and joined the family in Bountiful, Utah, where he worked on the
farms and in the mines of the territory. At the age of seventeen Roberts
was apprenticed to a blacksmith, thus following the trade his father had
practiced in England. In 1877, with only a modicum of secondary school
background, he entered the University of Deseret, from which he gradu-
ated as valedictorian in 1878. That same year he married Louisa Smith.

For most of the 1880s Roberts was engaged in missionary work. At
the age of twenty-three he was called on a two-year mission to the Mid-
western and Southern states. When this mission was completed, he

was immediately called on another mission, and, still in his twenties, was named as mission president. In 1885, just before he was transferred to the British Mission, he took as his second wife, Celia Dibble, with whom he was to have eight children. In the British Mission he edited the *Millennial Star* for two years. Upon his return, at the age of thirty-one, Roberts was named to the First Council of Seventy.[1]

This return from England coincided with perhaps the darkest days of the Church in Utah. According to the provisions of the Edmunds-Tucker Act of 1887, the Church was disincorporated; much of its property was seized; and a new test oath, by which voters were to deny the practice or advocacy of polygamy, resulted in a denial of the franchise to thousands of Mormon voters. Many prominent Mormon leaders went into hiding; others were tried and consigned to the penitentiary. Among the latter group was Roberts, who on April 29, 1889, was arraigned and pleaded guilty to the crime of unlawful cohabitation. He was sentenced to four months in the penitentiary.[2]

It was in reaction to these trying conditions that the Woodruff Manifesto, which formally brought to an end the contracting of polygamous marriages in Utah, was unanimously sustained at the October 1890 general conference of the Church.

The Manifesto resulted in significant political changes in Utah. Until this time the political parties in the territory had been divided along religious lines, with the People's party constituted primarily of Mormons and the Liberal party representing the Gentile element. In June 1891 the People's party disbanded and its members were divided along national party lines. Although the Liberal party, suspicious of Mormon intentions, hung on until 1893, it too finally disbanded. Thus was introduced a new era in Utah politics.

Roberts was among those who allied themselves with the Democratic party. The Democrats at this time were clearly the strongest party in Utah, and Democratic leaders, attempting to gain support for statehood from the national party, confidently promised that Utah would be a Democratic state. Democratic optimism was short-lived, however; for when the Liberal party disbanded in 1893 and its leader, Judge O. W. Powers, on whom little love was wasted by the Mormons, assumed a place of leadership in the Democratic party, many Mormons were loathe to support the Democrats. Also contributing to a mass exodus from the Democratic party were the economic collapse of 1893 and the commercial policies of President Grover Cleveland.[3] Thus it was that the Republicans, who had polled only 6,613 votes in the election of 1891, doubled their support in 1892 and by 1894 had 21,343 votes, which were sufficient to elect the Republican delegate to Congress.

The following year Roberts was selected as the Democratic candidate for Congress. It was during this campaign that a great deal of excitement was caused by the Thatcher-Roberts incident. The incident began when Roberts and another high Church official, Apostle Moses Thatcher, were censured by the presiding officials of the Mormon Church for seeking public office without first consulting their colleagues about the advisability of dividing their energies between church and state affairs. The Democrats were quick to raise the cry of "church influence," but as Roberts later said:

> Undoubtedly President [Joseph F.] Smith was right in reproving these brethren for their dereliction of duty in the respect named; for the right he claimed for the church authorities to be consulted under such circumstances and by such men holding such relationship to the organization as did the two candidates criticized, was reasonable. The dereliction of the two brethren undoubtedly arose, however, not through wanton disregard of their superior officers or disrespect for the church, but through the confusion which at the time prevailed in regard as to what was to be the attitude of high ecclesiastics of the church respecting political office holding.[4]

Although defeated in this election, Roberts ran well ahead of his party and also was encouraged by the fact that his marital affairs did not become a campaign issue.

Utah became a state in January 1896, but it was not until two years later that Roberts again expressed interest in becoming a candidate. In the summer of 1898 he paid a visit to James H. Moyle, a prominent Utah Democrat and next chairman of the state party. When Roberts indicated that he again had ambitions for Congress, Moyle opposed the idea. But when others in the party who thought that he planned to nominate Roberts threatened him, Moyle angrily reversed his position and decided to go ahead with the nomination. Later, at a Democratic dinner in one of the Salt Lake City hotels, Roberts was discussed and, with the exception of Moyle and U.S. Senator Joseph L. Rawlins, was unanimously opposed as a candidate. Rawlins thought that the clouds had blown over and that the marital status of Roberts would not be an important issue.[5] Perhaps he too had been encouraged by Roberts's comparative smooth sailing in the 1895 campaign.

But times had changed since 1895. During the summer of 1898, a Salt Lake City lawyer by the name of A. T. Schroeder had published articles in the *Kinsman*, a small anti-Mormon newspaper in Utah, charging that the Mormons had reverted to polygamy. This same man published a small sheet called *Lucifer's Lantern*, in which he harassed the Mormons and insinuated that they were practicing polygamy as strongly as ever.[6] Even more important than these periodicals was the meeting of the State Presbytery at Manti on August 29. The Presbytery drew up a list of six charges against the Mormon Church,[7] the most important of which were (1) that unlawful cohabitation had resulted in more than one thousand births since statehood, and (2) that polygamy was flourishing, with no attempt being made to enforce the law. Although the *Deseret News* did not hesitate "to deny in toto the assertions made,"[8] the charges received wide publicity.

Most of the problem, as the Mormons saw it, was the continuation of plural relationships already entered into before 1890. Charles W. Penrose humorously expressed the frustration: "It is related of 'Christian' missionary work in heathendom that a polygamous chief, converted to one of the numerous modern religious sects, was instructed that he could not receive baptism until he had separated from all his wives but one. After a time he returned to the minister and announced himself a monogamist. Being questioned as to what he had done with his plural wives, he promptly replied, 'Me eat 'em.' Do our Christian friends (?) expect the Mormons to summarily dispose of their plural families to please the Presbytery?"[9] The Mormon response did deny that new plural marriages were being solemnized in Utah.[10]

When Roberts's desire for the Democratic nomination became known, there were omens of trouble. In Cache County the old "church influence" controversy threatened to erupt.[11] The *Tribune*, which during the campaign of 1895 had never mentioned Roberts's marital status, served notice that its position too had changed. In a September 6 editorial, it said that "if men are nominated of whom nothing can be said except they are prominent for nothing except positions in the Mormon church, and who are believed to be law-breakers every day, that will be a notice not only to the people of Utah, but to the United States, that conditions have really not changed, but that one purpose has been adhered to from the first, and that the rank and file of the Saints are ready

not to carry it out." This time the *Tribune* was not planning to deal
gently with Roberts.

»   «

It was in this climate of opinion, with feelings high and charges of
reversion to polygamy coming from all sides, that on September 13,
Moyle rose to his feet in the state convention and nominated Roberts.
His closing words were: "It is our bounden duty to place in nomination
only the best, the strongest, the most eloquent, the best-equipped man
that can be found in the State. If such are our desires, if such are the lofty
purposes that animate us, if such are the considerations that animate
us, then I say, fellow delegates, that there is but one man in all Utah that
so perfectly fills the place as does that favored son, stalwart, peerless,
matchless speaker, the 'Blacksmith orator' of Utah, B. H. Roberts."[12]

The nomination was applauded by the Democratic *Herald,* which
said, "in all probability the opposition will make a personal fight upon
Mr. Roberts, for which he is doubtless prepared. The *Herald* will defend
his democracy and the political rights of the people he represents."[13] On
September 16 the *Tribune* jubilantly inserted the *Herald* statement in
about five places throughout the paper, commenting that "it will defend
what is not going to be attacked, but won't defend him from 'personal
attacks,' knowing apparently that there is no defense. . . . It is a prudent
limitation, and one whose prudence will become more and more evident as we progress with the campaign."

Thus began a furious and incessant campaign on the part of the *Tribune* that was not to abate until the eve of the election. Not a day
passed that the editorial page did not carry an article against Roberts; on
some days there were two or even three such articles on the same page.
The front page was decorated with vicious, sometimes hilarious political cartoons that, capitalizing on the recent birth of twins to Roberts's
plural wife Celia, portrayed the candidate in all sorts of embarrassing
situations. The *Tribune* left no stone unturned in its search for reasons
why Roberts should not be elected. The chief reasons, as they developed
through the campaign, were as follows:

    1. Roberts owed a "higher fealty" to the Mormon Church.
"Were he in Congress, a desire on the part of the church chiefs
would be more to him than any claim of the Government of the
United States. A request by ten thousand of the business men of

Utah would, at a single intimation from the head of the dominant church here, be ignored by him."[14]

2. Roberts was a law-breaker and, if elected to Congress, "could not take the prescribed oath without committing perjury."[15]

3. Roberts had devoted almost all of his time to church affairs and therefore was deficient in his knowledge of government.[16]

4. Roberts had opposed women's suffrage.[17] It was for this reason that a letter from Susan B. Anthony, published in the *Tribune* on November 3, urged the women of Utah not to vote for him.

5. Roberts had opposed an eight-hour day for labor and therefore should be opposed by Utah labor.[18]

6. The election of Roberts would be considered a breach of faith by those who granted Utah statehood.[19]

7. The election of Roberts would influence public opinion against Utah and dissuade business interests from establishing in Utah.[20]

8. The election of Roberts would have a disastrous effect on Mormon missionary work.[21]

This last point was mentioned only once, but it shows how far the *Tribune*, which was anything but interested in the success of Mormon missionaries, was willing to go in its attempt to influence Mormon voters.

What was being done meanwhile to defend Roberts from these blasts? One turns in vain to the *Deseret News* for a defense. In contrast to the vigorous, outspoken editorial policy of the *Tribune*, the *News* tried to remain aloof in the campaign and let the "party organs" argue it out. Its milk-and-water editorials had little appeal. That some of its readers were impatient with its refusal to take a stand is indicated by a *Herald* statement: "The News seems to be in mortal terror of mentioning the Tribune by name. It beats around the bush, soars in the clouds, does everything but say in words what it hopes its readers will infer."[22]

The *Herald*, on the other hand, not only raised its voice in a vigorous defense but took the offensive against the Republican candidates. With reference to Roberts's supposed "higher fealty," it asked why the same charge would not apply to John Henry Smith, an apostle, and Alma Eldredge, president of Summit Stake, both of whom were supported by the *Tribune*.[23] With reference to the charges of unlawful cohabitation, it reminded its readers that during the constitutional convention, it was the *Tribune* editor who was loudest in declaring that the only requirement for statehood was that the contracting of plural marriages should cease.[24] About Roberts's supposed inability in government, the *Herald* quoted previous *Tribune* editorials in praise of Roberts and criticized its "forked tongue."[25]

But newspapers were not the only antagonists. During the campaign Protestant churches became more and more vociferous. The Presbyterian Synod of Utah, meeting at Ogden in October, made charges of reversion to polygamy and included in their resolution a call for agitation and a memorial to Congress.[26] Later that same month the Congregational Association of Utah drafted a bold resolution that made indirect but unmistakable reference to Roberts. The people were urged to elect only candidates who were "law-abiding and whose private lives are in accordance with the laws of the State and in agreement with the pledges made to Congress leading to the admission of Utah."[27] It was such agitation that, in the long run, had the greatest influence on the ultimate outcome of the case.

Early in the campaign the opponents of Roberts began thinking of possible courses of action should he be victorious at the polls. Warren Foster, the Populist candidate, indicated "a possible fight in Congress . . . in the event of Mr. Roberts' election."[28] On October 5, the *Tribune*, fearful of a Roberts victory, editorialized: "If Mr. Roberts is elected he will be denied a seat in Congress. Mr. [George Q.] Cannon was denied that seat 18 years ago, though the Southern members in that House were disposed to help him on the grounds that the Saints were being persecuted by carpet-baggers. There will be nothing of that kind in this case. The record will be the thing to judge by, and there will be protests from every outside church in the Union against his admission, and Congress will not seat him." Protesting the election was therefore not a last-minute maneuver adopted only after the votes were counted.

Just before election day, two influential Mormon Republicans in Utah tried to sway the voters from Roberts. Governor Heber M. Wells stated that "a vote for Roberts is a vote against Utah."[29] And not less a Mormon leader than George Q. Cannon, first counselor in the Church's First Presidency, stated that "any man who cohabits with his plural wives violates the law."[30] With frequent charges being made against Roberts at this time, such a statement could hardly be calculated other than to decrease public support for him.

But all efforts of Republicans, Congregationalists, Presbyterians, and the *Salt Lake Tribune* to the contrary, on November 8, 1898, Roberts received 32,316 votes, compared to 27,108 for the Republican Alma Eldredge and only 2,025 for the Populist Warren Foster. The following day a *Tribune* cartoon, showing Roberts dancing into Washington, was accompanied by the following jingle: "Ha! Ha! Ha! / There's My Pa, / He'll Go to Washington, / But He Won't Take Ma."[31] The battle was ostensibly over. Popular opinion had decided the issue; Roberts was victor.

The campaign issues were too deep-rooted, however, to be resolved so easily. The former intimations of protesting the election were more than "sounding-brass." On December 6, 1898, a body of prominent Salt Lake City clergymen joined in a lengthy protest of the election. Making specific charges against Roberts and deploring his election as a breach of promise by Utah, they called "most earnestly upon the people of the United States to join us in a strong protest to Congress against the admission of the member-elect from this state."[32]

During the next year or more, a vigorous national program to muster popular opposition to the seating of Roberts was organized. Its most active participants were members of the Salt Lake Ministerial Association, whose "protest and petition to the Honorable Speaker and Members of the House of Representatives," dated January 6, 1899, was filed by Reverends C. T. Brown, W. M. Paden, and T. C. Iliff. The Reverend William R. Campbell, clerk of the Presbytery of Utah, was also very busy. Not only did he write a pamphlet entitled *Reasons Why B. H. Roberts, or Utah, Should Be Expelled,* he also sent a typewritten letter all over the country to newspaper editors, asking that they print it on a certain day and that they write anti-Roberts editorials.[33] The wealthy philanthropist Helen Gould provided influential backing.

On the other side were a few newspaper or magazine statements, such as *Harper's Weekly* for December 24, 1898, to the effect that since Roberts could not really, that is, legally, be married to more than one person, if he would leave his families in Utah, "it seems as if Congress might get along with him." In the same periodical Finley Peter Dunn's Mr. Dooley had some fun with the question:

"How manny wives has this here man Roberts that's thryin' to break into Congress?" Mr. Dooley asked.
"I dinnaw," said Mr. Hennessy; "I niver heerd iv him."
"I think it's three," said Mr. Dooley. "No wondher he needs wurruk an is fightin' hard f'r th' job! I'm with him too, be hivens!

Not that I'm be taste or inclination a marryin' man, Hinnissy. They may get me to th' altar some day. Th' best iv us fails, like Cousin George, an' there ar-re designin' women in this very block that I have me own throubles in dodgin'. But anny time ye hear iv me bein dhrawn fr'm th' quiet miseries an' exclusive discomforts iv single life ye may know that they have caught me asleep an' chloroformed me. But f'r thim that likes it it's all r-right. . . . Th' Mormons thinks they ar-re commanded be th' Lord f'r to marry all th' ineligeable Swede women. . . .

"But no. Th' minyit a Mormon thries to break into a pol-itical job, a dillygation rises, an' says they: 'What!' they says, 'permit this polluted monsther f'r to invade th' chaste atmosphere,' they says, 'iv th' House iv Riprisintatives!' they says. 'Permit him f'r to parade his fam'ly down Pinnsylvania Avanoo an' block thraffic!' they says. 'Permit him, mebbe, to sit in th' chair wanst occypied be th' laminted Breckinridge!' they says. An' they proceed f'r to hunt th' poor, crowded man. An' he takes a day off to kiss his wife fr'm house to house, an' holds a meetin' iv his childer to bid thim good-by, an' r-runs to hide in a cave till th' dillygation ray-mimbers that they have husbands iv their own, an' goes home to cook th' supper."[34]

But such joshing was not typical. Most newspapers came out sternly against Roberts.[35] And in churches and Sunday Schools throughout the country, petitions were circulated and signed. Ministers took advantage of the case, Roberts later noted, "to proclaim their great holiness and inpeccability in relation to loyalty to monogamous marriage, etc., and each sought to proclaim his own sanctity by throwing stones at the member from Utah."[36]

When Congress convened on December 4, 1899, it was greeted by petitions that were later described as "piled up there in front of the Speaker's desk 7 or 8 feet high, wrapped about with the national colors, said to contain 7,000,000 names."[37] To estimate the effect of such a public demonstration, one needs only to realize that a petition signed by a like percentage—nearly ten percent—of the national population today would contain some 25,000,000 signatures.

»   «

On December 4, 1899, when Roberts presented himself for swearing in as representative from Utah, Robert W. Tayler (R) of Ohio arose and objected on the grounds of Roberts's previous conviction for unlawful cohabitation. He also indicated, although he did not wish to defend the point, that there was some doubt about Roberts's naturalization. As an indication of the gravity of the question, Tayler pointed to the memorials "from over 7,000,000 American men and women, protesting against entrance into this House of the Representative-elect from Utah."[38] Thomas C. McRae (D) of Arkansas also objected. In addition to attacking polygamy as an institution, he charged that Utah by electing Roberts had violated "the fundamental compact made by his State with her Government." This question of compact was later to become one of the fundamental issues in the controversy.

The next day provision was made for three hours of debate, half to be controlled by Tayler and half by James D. Richardson (D) of Tennessee. Tayler discussed the following questions: Can Congress impose qualifications other than those listed in the Constitution? Has Congress imposed such qualifications? Has Congress, independent of any previously enacted law, the right to impose a qualification when a member-elect comes to the bar? Can the question of his eligibility be raised when he comes to the bar to be sworn, and can he be required to stand aside until the House shall have investigated the question of his right to take a seat? In a lengthy argument from precedents, Tayler answered all these questions in the affirmative.[39]

Richardson did not seek to establish Roberts's ultimate right to retain his seat in the House. He argued that Roberts was entitled to be sworn in, and then "if found guilty as charged, he can be removed from the House in an orderly and becoming fashion."[40] The main issue, as it was now developing and that later was to divide the committee, was not a choice between accepting and rejecting Roberts, but a choice between means of rejecting him. Tayler stood for excluding, Richardson for expulsion after swearing in.

When Richardson yielded thirty minutes to the gentleman from Utah, Roberts asserted that, although he had in fact pleaded guilty to the charge of a misdemeanor twelve years earlier, two presidential amnesties and statehood had removed any disqualifications that hindered him then. He called attention to the fact that members of the House, as part of their congressional immunity, could not be arrested for a misdemeanor, yet they were seeking to deny him admittance to the House "upon allegation of some one that I am guilty of a misdemeanor."[41] Referring to the charged breach of compact, he said that since statehood the administration had appointed to federal offices in Utah men against whom charges of unlawful cohabitation had been made; and so the administration was just as guilty as anyone of breaking the compact. Referring to the mammoth petition, he suggested that most of the signatures had been collected in Sunday Schools. He also read a letter used in collecting signatures for the petition indicating that those who had signed could sign again. "In asking for my political rights upon the floor of this House," Roberts concluded, "I do not champion the cause of polygamy. . . . I am not here to represent polygamy, I am not here to advocate it, I am not here to ask a repeal of the provision in the constitution of my State which places that practice now under the ban of constitutional provision as well as under statutory law."[42]

The arguments had been on a rather high plane, confining themselves to the legality of the case, until Fitzgerald of Massachusetts indignantly condemned Mormonism as "the curse of this country to-day. . . . nothing else than legalized licentiousness and corruption." For several minutes he lashed out at the Mormons in this manner.[43]

It was finally decided to create a special committee on the case of Brigham H. Roberts, which would examine the case in detail and then report back to the House. Included on the committee were representatives Robert W. Tayler (R), Charles B. Landis (R), Robert P. Morris (R), Romeo H. Freer (R), Smith McPherson (R), Samuel W. Lanham (D), Robert W. Miers (D), Charles E. Littlefield (R), and David A. De Armond (D). The party affiliation of these committee members has little significance to the case. Indeed, neither the voting in committee nor the final voting in the House was along party lines.

It was in the committee, meeting January 4 and 5, 1900, that the case received its most thorough investigation. Roberts was not represented by counsel but sat in on the hearings himself, asking questions of others and presenting his own case. Although not a lawyer, he spared no energies in studying the precedents and qualifying himself thoroughly to discuss the issues as they would arise. His twenty-two-page "Brief on Demurrer," dated December 12, 1899, was filed with the committee and provided the basis for his testimony before it.

Chief counsel for the opposition was Salt Lake City lawyer and editor of *Lucifer's Lantern*, T. S. Schroeder. Roberts on one occasion showed his contempt of Schroeder and his supporters in these words:

> I call your attention to the class of people who are, I will not say persecuting, because I have a sort of contempt for that word, and

do not propose to plead persecution, to those who have hounded me to the threshold of the House of Representatives? Who are they? Are they the bankers, the merchants, the lawyers, the representative people of the State of Utah, or are they confined exclusively, with the single exception of a tenth-rate lawyer who is without standing in his own state, to missionaries sent from the Eastern States to convert the "heathen Mormons," and having been opposed by one native to the faith of the Mormon religion now pursue him to the doors of the House of Representatives? Is not the class entirely confined to them? Where are the petitions from the representative classes of the State of Utah? [44]

The questionability of Roberts's naturalization, though mentioned repeatedly during the hearings, was never urged as a sufficient reason for excluding him. The committee did, however, seek to determine the truth of the basic charge that Roberts had been living in open violation of the law. Affidavits were collected, witnesses were called. One of the witnesses reported seeing a picture of Roberts in the home of one of his polygamous wives. A Dr. Wishard reported that Roberts had introduced one of the wives to him as "Mrs. Roberts"—to which Roberts replied that relations were such between himself and Wishard that he would hardly have introduced anyone, let alone his wife, to Wishard. [45] When one of the memorials charged not only three but four marriages, Roberts replied, "I challenge name, place, and all there is connected with it, because it is not true in any particular." [46] The charge was frequent that Roberts did not deny his guilt, but he did in fact specifically deny contracting any plural marriages since the 1890 Manifesto. If he had in fact lived with any or all of his plural wives, he would be guilty of the misdemeanor of unlawful cohabitation, but since he had not been charged with or convicted of such in a court of law, he argued, his innocence must be presumed.

Roberts insisted that vindication of the law had never been the object of his opponents. If he were guilty of the charges, he said, then he was equally guilty during the election of 1895. Yet no one had sought to indict him then. Also, since the campaign of 1898, during which the charges were made, he had been constantly before the public, had walked the streets of Salt Lake City in broad daylight. Yet no one had sought to indict him. Only in the fall of 1899, when he had left for New York, did someone enter charges of adultery against him. Roberts immediately wrote a letter to the prosecuting attorney, expressing his willingness to return to Utah if necessary. That he had not been required to do so was proof to Roberts that there was not sufficient evidence for conviction.[47]

Perhaps more important, however, were the basic legal issues that developed during the hearings. Chief of these were the following: (1) How did Section 8 of the Edmunds law affect Roberts's eligibility? (2) How was the eligibility affected by the presidential amnesties? (3) How was it affected by the enabling act and statehood? (4) What was the compact between the United States and the people of Utah, and was that compact violated in the election of Roberts? In an attempt to give a fair presentation of both the Schroeder and Roberts positions, each of these issues shall be discussed separately.

1. *The Edmunds law.* Section 8 of the Edmunds law, which during the hearings was quoted and requoted, reads as follows: "Sec. 8. That no polygamist, bigamist, or any person cohabiting with more than one woman, and no woman cohabiting with any of the persons described as aforesaid in this section, in any Territory or other place over which the United States have exclusive jurisdiction, shall be entitled to vote at any election held in any such Territory or other place, or be eligible for election or appointment to or be entitled to hold any office or place of public trust, honor, or emolument in, under, or for any such Territory or place, or under the United States."[48]

The contention of Schroeder was that under the provisions of this section the citizenship of Roberts had been impaired and that it had never been restored to its former condition. The phrase "under the United States" came in for considerable discussion. Although he recognized the difference between a territory and a state, Schroeder maintained that since Congress had "exclusive jurisdiction" in Washington, D.C., any office held there would still be included in the intent of the Edmunds Act.[49]

Roberts maintained that the entire Edmunds law was limited to territories. Senators and representatives were not, he contended, offices "under the United States" and therefore would not be affected by the Edmunds law.[50]

2. *The presidential amnesties.* In 1893, as a result of a plea from the general authorities of the Mormon Church, an amnesty proclamation in behalf of those imprisoned for unlawful cohabitation was issued by President Benjamin Harrison. They were granted amnesty "upon the

express condition that they shall in future faithfully obey the laws of the United States, hereinbefore named, and not otherwise." This proclamation was reaffirmed by President Grover Cleveland in a similar statement.[51]

Schroeder held that since both amnesties were "expressly conditioned on compliance with the law," Roberts's eligibility remained just as though they had never been issued.[52]

Roberts agreed that the amnesties required compliance with the law. But those pardoned were not required "to set the town crier at work," nor were they required to go before a court and make a statement. How, then, was compliance with the terms of the amnesty to be judged? There were two evidences: (1) If there had been no accusations before the courts, or prosecutions, the fair presumption was that the law had been observed; (2) If an individual had enjoyed publicly the advantages that would come from the amnesty, the presumption was that he had complied with its terms. Both of these evidences applied to Roberts.[53]

3. *The enabling act and statehood.* The enabling act of 1893, which allowed Utah to prepare a constitution for statehood, provided for a new registration of voters to be administered by the Utah Commission. In doing this the commission changed the oath taken by voters and left out any reference to polygamy. This not only enabled such men as Roberts to vote, but also to act as delegates to the constitutional convention. Whereas Congress could justifiably prescribe qualifications for territorial elections, Utah, when admitted as a sovereign state, prescribed the qualifications for its own electorate. Again there was no such disabling clause as that of the Edmunds law.

Schroeder held that the enabling act required citizenship as one of the prior qualifications for voting, and if the citizenship of Roberts had previously been impaired, statehood was hardly calculated to restore it. In this connection, it should be remembered that Schroeder had made a distinction between citizenship in a state and in the United States. The Utah laws might make it possible for Roberts to exercise some of the rights of citizenship, but as far as the United States was concerned, his citizenship was still impaired.[54]

Roberts insisted that the intent of Congress in the enabling act was "to remove disabilities that had been created by the Edmunds law."[55] He sighted an attempt to make the enabling act inclusive of those disabilities and concluded that in rejecting that attempt Congress showed its intent.

4. *The compact.* Schroeder indicated that there were two interpretations as to the nature of the compact between the United States and Utah. One was that only new polygamous marriages were to be prohibited. The other maintained that unlawful cohabitation also was included in this compact. In an attempt to establish that Congress was led to believe that Utah promised to cease both new polygamous marriages and unlawful cohabitation, Schroeder quoted statements from the following Mormon leaders: S. F. Richards, Wilford Woodruff, Joseph F. Smith, George Q. Cannon, Lorenzo Snow, and Anthon H. Lund. All these statements taken together constituted the "promise" of Utah. The sending to Congress of Roberts, an open and flagrant violator of the law, was a distinct breach of "these promises." That the enabling act itself did not mention unlawful cohabitation was accounted for, said Schroeder, by the fact that Congress believed such relations to have been discontinued.[56]

In Roberts's view the discontinuation of unlawful cohabitation was not at all part of the compact. The best way to find out what a compact is, he said, is to go to the compact, whereupon he reread the crucial clause of the enabling act: "Provided, that polygamous or plural marriages are forever prohibited." He noted that there is no clause requiring the disruption of family relations and at the same time rejected Schroeder's explanation for that omission. For if it were believed that unlawful cohabitation had been discontinued, it was also believed that the contracting of new polygamous marriages had been discontinued. The omission of reference to the former, therefore, was expressly so as not to press "too hard upon the people who were involved in those relations."[57] He quoted from the proceedings of the constitutional convention to show that the Utah legislators understood the enabling act to pertain to future marriages only: "That part of the law that would tend to disrupt the relations of the past was knowingly, purposely, and publicly omitted from the provisions that were meant to meet the demands of the United States on the part of the people of Utah."[58] That these proceedings were available to the president of the United States and that he nevertheless accepted the Utah Constitution as fulfilling the requirements showed conclusively that the people of Utah had satisfactorily met the demands of Congress.

With rare exceptions Roberts was treated cordially by the committee. Some of his views were favorably received and eventually found their way into the minority report. By the same token, Schroeder was at times hard pressed by members of the committee. The end result of the deliberation, however, was to split the committee simply on the means of sending Roberts back to Utah.

On January 23, 1900, the Roberts case was again opened on the floor of the House. Tayler, representing the committee majority, asserted that Roberts should be excluded for three reasons: (1) his violation of the Edmunds law; (2) his declarations, words, and acts showed that he considered himself to be above the law; and (3) in sending Roberts as representative-elect from Utah the people of that state had violated the compact with the United States. The majority rejected Roberts's plea of innocence to the charge of unlawful cohabitation since 1889. (Actually, he simply said he had not been convicted and should therefore be presumed innocent.) Referring to the second wife, Celia Dibble, whom Roberts married "about 1885," Tayler said, "With her he has lived ever since. She has borne him six children, the last of whom were twins, born in 1897. This woman he married with full knowledge of the law, openly, publicly, notoriously holding her out as his wife and rearing children by her."[59] Roberts also was charged with marrying a third wife, Dr. Margaret Shipp, although he claimed that this marriage occurred before the 1890 Manifesto.

The minority of the committee, comprised of Littlefield and De Armond, took direct issue with two of the above three charges. The Edmunds law, they said, applied only to territories and since Utah had become a state had no application to Roberts. As for the supposed violation of the compact, the minority replied: "The idea of a compact or contract is not predicable upon the relations that exist between the State and the General Government. . . . The condition upon which Utah was to become a State was fully performed when she became a State. . . . No power was reserved in the enabling act, nor can any be found in the Constitution of the United States, authorizing Congress, not to say the House of Representatives alone, to discipline the people of the State of Utah, because the crime of polygamy or unlawful cohabitation has not been exterminated in Utah."[60]

The minority also attacked the basic assumption of the majority that the House could add qualifications for membership to those listed in the Constitution. The minority conclusion, however, was simply that Roberts should be admitted and then immediately expelled.

When Roberts was given the floor for the last time, although he certainly realized the hopelessness of his case, his sense of humor was still
intact.

> I find myself in a position where one could say, with some pro-
> priety, perhaps, "a plague on both your houses" [laughter], since
> the propositions of both minority and majority reports equally
> propose my undoing.
>
> The situation, however, may not be altogether without its ad-
> vantages; for if the minority can convince the House, as I confess
> it has me, that I ought not to be excluded, and, on the other hand,
> if the majority can convince the House, as it has me, that I can not
> be expelled [laughter], it seems to me that matters would fall out
> about as I would have them, and I think substantial justice would
> be done [laughter and applause].[61]

He said that he was not there as a representative of the Mormon
Church. To think that he was elected by the Mormon vote as against the
Gentile vote was erroneous. "I carried," he said, "every gentile strong-
hold in the State of Utah."[62]

Roberts's concluding remarks, although not concerned with the fundamental legal aspects of the case, provide a good example of the ora-
torical flourishes he was capable of rendering.

> Some of the papers in discussing the Roberts case have said,
> "Brand this man with shame and send him back to his people."
> Mr. Speaker, I thank God that the power to brand me with shame
> is something quite beyond the power of this House, great as that
> power is. The power to brand with shame rests with each man
> and nowhere else. I was reared and am sensible of no act of shame
> in my life. Brand me with shame! Why, if you finally determine
> either to exclude or expel me, I shall leave this august Chamber
> with head erect and brow undaunted and walk God's earth as the
> angels walk the clouds, with no sense of shame upon me. [Ap-
> plause on the floor and hisses from the gallery.] And, if in response
> to the sectarian clamor that has been invoked against the member
> from Utah, you violate the Constitution of your country, either in
> excluding or expelling me, all the shame that there is in this case
> will be left behind me and rest with this House.[63]

The affectionate appellation, Utah's "blacksmith orator," was not misapplied.

The House, however, was little swayed by Roberts's remarks. Not to be outdone by the Utahn, H. Henry Powers (R) of Vermont replied to Roberts's reference to the Constitution as follows: "Well, if that sermon had been preached to us by somebody who was not himself trying to break down those bulwarks, it would have a great deal more force. For one I am perfectly willing to risk the ship of state. . . . It is true, sir, that in sailing over these troublesome waters the timbers of the old ship may creak, the cordage may in some parts of it snap, the crew may murmur, but of one thing I feel well assured, that the old ship of state will never be swallowed up in the miry waters of Salt Lake [laughter and applause]."[64]

When a vote was finally called, the minority resolution to admit and then expel Roberts was defeated by a vote of 244 to 81 with 29 not voting. The majority resolution to exclude him from the House passed resoundingly—268 ayes, 50 nays, and 36 not voting.

In retrospect it is easy to chide Roberts for attempting the impossible. To the modern reader, gifted with hindsight, the outcome of the Roberts's case was never in doubt. It must be remembered, however, that Roberts's decision to run for office was made in the wake of the 1895 campaign, during which no charge of ineligibility had been made. He was encouraged also by Senator Rawlins, who, experienced in politics on the national level, was confident that Roberts would have no difficulty in taking his seat in Congress. Roberts's decision to run occurred before his Utah opponents had set off the national agitation that culminated in the flood of protests to Congress. Such public pressure, impossible as it is to assess precisely, must have been tremendous. Had it not been for this irresistible tide of public opinion, the position of the minority might well have prevailed. And had Roberts once been seated, under those circumstances, the necessary two-thirds vote for expulsion may have been difficult to muster. From the mid-1898 perspective, therefore, Roberts's hopes seemed not entirely without foundation.

Roberts returned to Utah, continued his ecclesiastical activities, became a much-loved speaker at Mormon conferences, wrote theological manuals and a six-volume history of the Mormon Church, loyally stuck to his Democratic political position, occasionally ruffled the feathers of his colleagues among the Church's general authorities, and in 1933 died, being old and full of days. In 1966, when Congress was debating whether or not to seat Congressman-elect Adam Clayton Powell, the Roberts case was noted as an interesting precedent.[65] It seems safe to predict that any time a Representative or Senator is accused of a crime (if such a situation can be imagined in Mr. Dooley's chaste halls of Congress) and the question of seating or expulsion is raised, lawyers will scour the Roberts case for relevant parallels.

Notes

An earlier version of this chapter appeared in *Utah Historical Quarterly* 25, no. 1 (Jan. 1957).

1. This biographical information was taken from the article "Roberts, Brigham Henry," in Dumas Malone, ed., *Dictionary of American Biography*, 16 vols. (New York: Scribners, 1935), 16:3–4. The standard biography is now Truman G. Madsen, *Defender of the Faith: The B. H. Roberts Story* (Salt Lake City: Bookcraft, 1980).

2. Records of the Third District court of Utah Territory as cited by the *Salt Lake Tribune*, 12 October 1898.

3. Glen Miller, "Has the Mormon Church re-entered Politics?" *The Forum* 20 (1895): 501–2.

4. B. H. Roberts, *A Comprehensive History of the Church of Jesus Christ of Latter-day Saints*, 6 vols. (Salt Lake City: Deseret News Press, 1930), 6: 331.

5. From Moyle's diary as quoted in Gordon B. Hinckley, *James Henry Moyle* (Salt Lake City: Deseret Book, 1951), 230–32.

6. On Schroeder see David Brudnoy, "Of Sinners and Saints: Theodore Schroeder, Brigham Roberts, and Reed Smoot," *Journal of Church and State* 14 (Spring 1972): 261–78.

7. The Presbytery's full statement is given in the *Salt Lake Tribune*, 1 September 1898.

8. *Deseret News*, 1 September 1898.

9. Ibid., 3 September 1898.

10. The wording of the denial of new marriages is interesting in view of recent studies demonstrating post-1890 plural marriages in Mexico: "If polygamous marriages were being solemnized in Utah. . . . everybody knows that such unions have ceased in this State." *Deseret News*, 3 September 1898. See Kenneth L. Cannon II, "Beyond the Manifesto: Polygamous Cohabitation among LDS General Authorities," *Utah Historical Quarterly* 46 (1978): 24–36; and Victor W. Jorgensen and B. Carmon Hardy, "The Taylor-Cowley Affair and the Watershed of Mormon History," *Utah Historical Quarterly* 48 (1980): 4–36.

11. *Salt Lake Tribune,* 1 September 1898.

12. Ibid., 15 September 1898.

13. *Salt Lake Daily Herald,* 15 September 1898.

14. *Salt Lake Tribune,* 17 September 1898.

15. Ibid., 11 October 1898.

16. Ibid., 18 September 1898.

17. Ibid., 22 October 1898.

18. Ibid., 28 September 1898.

19. Ibid., 5 October 1898.

20. Ibid., 1 October 1898.

21. Ibid., 4 October 1898.

22. *Salt Lake Daily Herald,* 30 September 1898.

23. Ibid., 1 October 1898.

24. Ibid.

25. Ibid., 8 October 1898.

26. *Salt Lake Tribune,* 18 October 1898.

27. Ibid., 27 October 1898.

28. Ibid., 18 September and 16 October 1898.

29. Ibid., 5 November 1898.

30. Ibid., 7 November 1898.

31. The same, or virtually the same, words had been used in the campaign of 1884 against Grover Cleveland.

32. *Salt Lake Daily Herald,* 7 December 1898.

33. A typed copy of one of Campbell's letters is in the LDS Church Library, Salt Lake City, Utah.

34. *Harper's Weekly,* 18 November 1899.

35. *Literary Digest,* 9 December 1899, quotes from several newspapers, with only *The Christian Register,* a Unitarian publication, in favor of seating Roberts.

36. *The Autobiography of B. H. Roberts,* ed. Gary James Bergera (Salt Lake City: Signature Books, 1990), 218.

37. Thetus W. Sims of Tennessee in the *Congressional Record,* 56 Cong., 1st sess. 1900, Vol. 33, pt. 2, p. 1176.

38. Ibid., 5.

39. Ibid.

40. Ibid., 38–40.

41. Ibid., 44.

42. Ibid., 48.

43. Ibid., 49.

44. "Special Committee to Investigate the Eligibility of Brigham H. Roberts, of Utah, to a Seat in the House of Representatives," (Washington, D.C.: Government Printing Office), 206.

45. Ibid., 184–86.

46. Ibid., 192.

47. Ibid., 194–95.

48. As quoted in ibid., 128.

49. Ibid., 135.

50. Ibid., 200–201.

51. Amnesties cited in ibid., 165–66.

52. Ibid., 164–66

53. Ibid., 204–5

54. Ibid., 124–26.

55. Ibid., 206.

56. Ibid., 140–42.

57. Ibid., 216.

58. Ibid., 221.

59. *Congressional Record*, 56 Cong., 1st sess. 1900, Vol. 33, pt. 2, p. 1074.

60. "Case of Brigham H. Roberts, of Utah," House of Representatives, 56 Cong., 1st sess. 1900, Report No. 85, pt. 2, pp. 71–73.

61. *Congressional Record*, 56 Cong., 1st sess. 1900, Vol. 33, pt. 2, p. 1101.

62. Ibid., 1103–4. In *Lucifer's Lantern*, September 1899, Schroeder claimed that the Gentiles who supported Roberts were: those who wanted to raise the issue; those who thought that his election would do harm to the Mormon Church; those whose zeal for the silver cause was greater than their hatred of Roberts; and those who considered Mormon polygamist Roberts to be less of an evil than his opponent Eldredge, a Mormon and former Danite.

63. *Congressional Record*, 56 Cong., 1st sess. 1900, Vol. 33, pt. 2, p. 1104.

64. Ibid., 1125.

65. *The Reporter*, 15 December 1966.

9

The Ritualization
of Mormon History

IT IS EASY for historians to assume that people maintain their links
with the past primarily through reading histories. Without denying
that written histories have enormous influence, especially those used
in the schools, it should be recognized that a pervasive, ultimately more
important influence in fostering a sense of the past is ritual. I am using
this term in a broad sense to refer to the forms and symbols whose
function is not primarily the communication of knowledge but rather
the simplification of the past into forms that can be memorialized,
celebrated, and emotionally appropriated.[1] In this sense a ritualized approach to the historic past has been promoted, consciously or uncon-
sciously, by churches, political parties, labor unions, and other groups.
Most dramatically, nations have stimulated national consciousness by
developing a pantheon of heroes, monuments, ceremonies, and even
standardized narratives reminiscent of morality plays in their insistent
simplification.[2] Although not yet studied from this point of view, Mormonism provides an instructive case study of the ritualizing of the past
by a modern group with an unusually acute self-consciousness.[3]

Émile Durkheim said, "There can be no society which does not feel
the need of upholding and reaffirming at regular intervals the collective
sentiments and the collective ideas which make its unity and its personality. Now this moral remaking cannot be achieved except by the
means of reunions, assemblies, and meetings where the individuals,
being closely united to one another, reaffirm in common their common
sentiments."[4] It is not surprising, therefore, that the Mormons, who
shared with other Christians such anniversaries and festivals as Christmas and Easter, formed their own calendar of annual celebrations. It
was such celebrations that Harvey Cox described as "a human form of
play through which man appropriates an extended area of life, including the past, into his own experience."[5]

Almost immediately the date of April 6, the day in 1830 when the Church was officially organized, was given special recognition. Apparently there was no particular notice given to the date in 1831 or 1832, but in 1833 a meeting of about eighty took place on the Big Blue River near the western limits of Jackson County, Missouri. According to Joseph Smith's history, "It was an early spring, and the leaves and blossoms enlivened and gratified the soul of man like a glimpse of Paradise. The day was spent in a very agreeable manner, in giving and receiving knowledge which appertained to this last kingdom—it being just 1800 years since the Savior laid down His life that man might have everlasting life, and only three years since the Church had come out of the wilderness, preparatory for the last dispensation. . . . This was the first attempt made by the Church to celebrate the anniversary of her birthday, and those who professed not our faith talked about it as a strange thing."[6]

There was no such "birthday" celebration in 1834, 1835, or 1836 apparently, but in 1837 a solemn assembly was held in the Kirtland Temple over several days, including April 6, when special instructions were given. In 1838, April 6 saw the beginning of a "general conference" at Far West, Missouri, to transact church business and "to celebrate the anniversary" of the Church.

The following year the Prophet was in jail, but in 1840 at Nauvoo, Illinois, another general conference was held. The pattern was now established, and from then until 1977 the annual conference was always scheduled so as to include April 6 as one of its days. Thus a need for a regular annual conference was met while at the same time commemorating the founding day.[7]

Another day with some potential, it would seem, was December 23, the birthday of the Prophet Joseph Smith. Some attention has been given to it from time to time; in fact, usually some special mention of the Prophet's contribution is made on or about that day. The circumstance that the date is close to Christmas, however, made it difficult to celebrate. After the Prophet's death those who wanted to give him a day of special remembrance sometimes chose June 27, the date of his martyrdom in 1844.[8] This, however, is only about a week before July 4. Furthermore, martyrdom is not really a time of rejoicing; only, as at Easter, when accompanied by something unique and glorious like the resurrection can it be celebrated happily.

For festive purposes the day that came to be the annual Mormon celebration par excellence was July 24, the official day of entry into the

Salt Lake Valley in 1847. Long enough after July 4, the 24th was still in the summer and seemed to be a time after sowing and before harvest when a day of celebration could be afforded. The day was not celebrated in 1848 due to the harsh conditions, but in 1849 an elaborate celebration was held. Included in the procession, for example, were:

> Twelve bishops, bearing banners of their wards.
> Twenty-four young ladies, dressed in white, with white scarfs on their right shoulders, and a wreath of white roses on their heads, each carrying the Bible and the Book of Mormon; and one bearing a banner, "Hail to our Chieftain."
> Twelve more bishops, carrying flags of their wards.
> Twenty-four silver greys [older men], each having a staff, painted red on the upper part, and a branch of white ribbons fastened at the top, one of them carrying the flag.

After parading around to the tune of band music, the people settled down to a round of addressees, poems, and toasts. There were more speeches. It was quite an extravaganza for a young, precariously established frontier community.[9]

Besides the annual celebration, there are longer intervals that seem to lend themselves to commemorative purposes. On July 24, 1874, for example, a "jubilee" was held celebrating the twenty-seventh anniversary of the arrival of the Saints in the Valley. It was a Sunday School program held in the Tabernacle, featuring bands, a special hymn entitled "O Lord Accept Our Jubilee," prayers, and sermons. The "grand Sunday School jubilee" featured some eight or ten thousand children.[10]

Celebrations were also held in the individual settlements throughout Mormon country. In 1874, for example, there was a celebration in Bloomington, Idaho:

> At sunrise this morning silence was broken by a volley of twenty-four guns.
> The people assembled at the schoolhouse at nine o'clock A.M., formed a procession and marched to martial music through the principal streets then back to the schoolhouse in the following manner—twelve fathers of Israel, twelve mothers of Israel, twelve daughters of Zion dressed in white, and twelve sons of Zion, the citizens and Sunday School children following in line.
> The services consisted of an oration by James H. Hart, George

Osmond read an address in behalf of the daughters of Zion, John Walker spoke in behalf of the fathers of Israel, Christian Madsen in behalf of the sons of Zion, Sister Jarvis in behalf of the mothers of Israel. A number of toasts were given.

At two o'clock all were seated at table, spread with viands, including strawberries, sugar, and cream.

At four o'clock the dance opened for the small children, and in the evening for larger children and parents.

All was joy, peace, and unity. The whole was gotten up under the auspices of the Relief Society.[11]

The fiftieth anniversary was emphasized even more than the usual annual celebration or that of the twenty-fifth anniversary. Now there was a sense of historical continuity and distance. While a few of the original members and leaders remained, a new generation had come to the fore. Besides, the celebration of fifty years had Old Testament precedent as a time of "jubilee." Such an opportunity presented itself in 1880, fifty years from the organization of the Church. Coinciding with general conference, this date was mentioned by many of the speakers, including especially Church Historian Franklin D. Richards, who reviewed the history of the Church during the preceding decades. He mentioned Stephen A. Douglas, Senator Thomas Hart Benton and the Mormon Battalion, the coming of Johnston's Army, and the fate of government officials. "In all these things we recognized the hand of the Lord," he said, "and we should reflect on his providences and be stirred up to individual righteousness, and to battle against the drunkenness and whoredoms and various forms of evil now being introduced by our enemies for our overthrow." Other sermons followed the same theme, as did a lengthy prayer by Apostle Orson Pratt.[12]

In July 1880 the jubilee was continued in a mammoth celebration. In the parade or procession were the following:

The surviving Pioneers of 1847 in five wagons. Portraits of Brigham Young on both sides of the first wagon with the inscriptions "Gone Before Us" and "Absent But Not Forgotten." Above them was the "old pioneer banner," on which were the names of all the pioneers and a picture of Joseph Smith blowing a trumpet. Also the U.S. flag.

Surviving members of Zion's camp.

Surviving members of the Mormon Battalion and wagon with "Women of the Mormon Battalion."

The "Minute Men."

Wagon with representatives of the various countries of the earth. On the side were various mottoes.

24 couples. "The ladies looked lovely in cream-colored riding habits, with white silk caps and white feathers, and the young men presented a fine appearance in black dress suits, white neckties, and white gloves."

Education was represented by a car containing five ladies personifying Religion, History, Geography, Science, and Art.

The parade continued with representation of different church auxiliaries, school children, and industry of Utah. The whole procession extended over three miles. It was as part of this 1880 celebration that Wilford Woodruff told of Brigham Young's "This Is the place" statement that has since become an icon in the Mormon public memory.[13]

The Mormon parades we have described were squarely in the mainstream of American public ceremony. The parade in its classic American form had been "invented," or at least assumed its definitive form, roughly between 1825 and 1850. In the latter half of the century major American cities punctuated their temporal existence with celebrations that included parades. Trades or occupations, immigrants or ethnic groups, voluntary societies, along with symbolic representations of concepts like liberty, characterized these parades. In the large cities, Mary Ryan has said, parades "made order out of an urban universe that teemed with diversity and change." Again, "the disorder and cacophony that reigned most of the year was ordered into reassuring, visually and audibly pleasing patterns."[14] There has been no full-scale study of Mormon or Utah parades to itemize the changes across time, but clearly there are profound similarities with the developments elsewhere. In their remote location and faced with their own challenges of identity and increasing diversity, the Mormons used parades to help propagate the community ideals and did this in part by symbolic references to past achievements or events.

Often the celebrations paid tribute to special groups, especially the surviving members of Zion's Camp, the Mormon Battalion, and the Pioneers of 1847. They were given places of honor in the processions and seated together on the stand during programs. Wilford Woodruff's keynote address in 1880 recounted the stories of these three groups, who were becoming something like canonized saints in the Mormon hagiography. Reunions of such groups were held. Like meetings of high school graduating classes, such gatherings served social purposes, but they also included speeches, orations, songs, and prayers that celebrated the past. Needless to say, the past events seen through the eyes of nostalgia were simplified, romanticized, and in the broad sense of the term, ritualized.

An especially important celebration occurred in 1855, the proceedings of which were reported by the stenographer J. V. Long and published in a rare pamphlet, *The First General Festival of the Renowned Mormon Battalion* (St. Louis, 1855). In addition to refreshment, music, and dancing, there was a general setting decorated with banners. One of these showed an eagle with the word "order" on one side and "justice" on the other and "Great Salt Lake City" across the bottom. Another showed the all-seeing eye, the united hands, a representation of pioneers at the Crossing of the Platte, and the motto "Blessings follow sacrifice."

After toasts honoring such men as Battalion leader Colonel Philip St. George Cook and Brigham Young, there were speeches by David Pettegrew, Dimick B. Huntington, Thomas S. Williams, Jedediah M. Grant, Heber C. Kimball, Brigham Young, William Hyde, James Brown, and others. Despite the differences, there is a common interpretation running through their remarks: the courage and dedication of the Battalion members, the conspiracy theory of the circumstances behind the muster, the providential overruling power of God, and rededication to their leaders. In a ritualized setting a sense of group consciousness was being formed by a simplified remembering of their history.

The Mormon Battalion story is a good example of what typically happens as the historical event is ritualized. Without going into the complex history of the Battalion, we can safely say that the decision to call it was made at least in part at the instigation of the Mormons, who saw it as a means of obtaining government help for the journey west. Some of the Battalion's pay did find its way back to the main body of the Latter-day Saints, where it doubtless was of help. As for the journey itself, there were few noteworthy events in the grand military tradition.[15] Remarkably soon, however, this whole experience was transformed into a symbol of federal oppression, Mormon heroism, and the overruling omnipotence of God. It was told and retold in these terms; participants even started remembering it in these terms. The men of the Battalion (and later their descendants) were lionized as representatives of truth in a heroic struggle.

It should be noted that the ritualization did not require invention out of whole cloth. From the beginning some Mormons saw the venture as an onerous obligation; some did not know about the previous requests and negotiations; others who did know resented the timing of the call and the number demanded. The ritualization was not invention; it was a selecting out of certain aspects, dramatizing them, memorializing them, and giving to the whole the simplicity of a morality play.

It was but a short step from meetings of groups of survivors, like those of the Mormon Battalion, to the organization of descendants. This occurred, as might be expected, about the time the actual survivors were disappearing in the 1890s and the first two decades of the twentieth century. There were meetings of Sons and Daughters of the Pioneers in 1894 and 1898. In 1901 the Daughters of Utah Pioneers (DUP) were incorporated and have continued as an active group of women ever since. Later the Sons of Utah Pioneers, especially in the 1930s, performed some of the same functions. In addition to these two most important of such societies, there have been at different times Daughters of the Mormon Battalion (1909), Daughters of Utah Handcart Pioneers (1915), and Sons and Daughters of the Indian War Veterans (1916). With the enlargement of membership in the DUP to include all female descendants of pioneers who came to Utah before the railroad in 1869, the other organizations were readily dissolved into the larger group.[16] Such societies, analogous to the Daughters of the American Revolution, perform many functions, social and even political. But their main raison d'être is to celebrate and honor the past not primarily on the level of scholarship but on the level of ritual commemoration and rededication.[17]

A physical example of the ritualizing impulse is the historic site or shrine, examples of which can be found almost from the beginning of Mormon history. In New York the Hill Cumorah and the Sacred Grove, for Mormons sites of sacred events, were visited with interest by Mormon missionaries and converts, who doubtless gained inspiration as they contemplated the surroundings.[18] The Kirtland Temple, completed in 1836, also early became a kind of shrine that could be visited by Mormon pilgrims. It was significant on two counts: it was the scene of heavenly manifestations; and persecution forced its builders to abandon it after a short use. Thus it had the aura of the past and was an appropriate symbol of the sacrifice of those who erected it, of the divine power manifested in it, and of the persecution that had forced the Mormons to move away. The Nauvoo Temple, an edifice with similar monumental potentialities, was destroyed by arson within two years after the Mormon exodus from Nauvoo and hence lost most of its value as a site. (In a sense the entire city of Nauvoo might be thought of as a monument, and Mormons going through the area often visited the city and reflected on the events associated with it.) But there were no monuments, properly so called, during the first generation of Mormonism's history.

The work of erecting historical monuments and markers coincided with the generation following the death of the original Mormon leaders, the rise of the organizations mentioned earlier, increased prosperity, and the increase of leisure time and travel in the twentieth century. Even before the turn of the century, signs of such memorialization could be seen. A monument was erected at Mount Pisgah in 1888, and the Brigham Young monument was unveiled in 1897 as part of the jubilee celebration of that year. In 1905 a granite shaft was dedicated at Sharon, Vermont, Joseph Smith's birthplace. The Sea Gull monument, the work of Mahonri M. Young, was dedicated in 1913, the original "This Is the Place" monument in 1921, and the Mormon Battalion monument on the Utah Capital grounds in 1927. The 1930s and 1940s were a time of almost feverish activity in the erection of monuments and historical markers. The Daughters of Utah Pioneers placed more than 300 of these, while at least 120 were the work of the Utah Pioneer Trails and Landmarks Association, led by George Albert Smith and John D. Giles. The culmination of this monument building was reached in 1947, the centennial year, with the dedication of the new "This Is the Place" monument. The work did not cease, however, and continued attention to such recognition of historical sites has continued.[19]

One activity in the making of historical sites that deserves mention is restoration—the attempt to restore homes and buildings to their appearance of a hundred or more years ago. The groundwork was laid for such restoration by the acquisition of important pieces of property and some early efforts in Manchester, Liberty Jail, and Utah. Perhaps because of the rise of historical preservation as a discipline (connected with the success of Colonial Williamsburg) and perhaps because of the need of fairly large expenditures, it was not until after mid-century and mainly in the 1960s that the restoration of the Beehive House and the Lion House in Salt Lake City and, even more impressive, the work of

Nauvoo Restoration, Inc., at Nauvoo showed what could be done in restoring the physical surroundings of the past.[20]

A powerful means of capturing and "monumentalizing" the historic past was through visual representation—in monuments, bas-reliefs, stained-glass windows, and paintings. One aspect of the ritualizing process was to commission portraits of the leaders of the past: Joseph Smith, Brigham Young, Heber C. Kimball, and other leaders of the first generation. D. Rogers, W. W. Major, Dan Weggeland, George M. Ottinger, and others created portraits of the heroic, the equivalent of equestrian statues on canvas. Even daguerreotypes and engravings were important parts of the idealization. See, for example, the great engravings by Frederick Piercy of the Mormon leaders in the 1850s. Later in the century beautiful metal engravings were found of many of the leaders.[21] In 1855, Charles W. Carter copied a daguerreotype of a painting of Joseph Smith, made prints, which he had heavily retouched by the artist Dan Weggeland, and then rephotographed, copyrighted, and distributed the "portrait." Quite unlike the profile portrait that community leaders of the 1850s considered authentic, the Carter portrait was preferred by most people. It was "aesthetically superior," closer to a recognizable standard of male attractiveness. The Carter portrait enjoyed a wide distribution and was often framed and hung in homes and ward buildings.[22] Each of these works has its own tradition, of course, and a subject matter by no means confined to history, but each contributed to the ritualization by transforming events and personalities of the past into something fixed, heightened, and to a greater or lesser degree, standardized.

The most powerful contribution of art to the ritualization process came when events were frozen into graphic scenes that could be visualized by successive generations. Quite early there were visual representations of the assassination of Joseph Smith and other dramatic historical episodes. The Charley Mackay history was full of such drawings, as, for example, was Fanny Stenhouse's *Tell It All*, which went through several editions in the 1870s and 1880s.[23] For the Mormon audience, however, the two great creators of the visual image were Philo Dibble and C. C. A. Christensen. As early as 1847 Dibble, an amateur, self-taught painter, had produced scenes of the events that he showed on many occasions through the second half of the nineteenth century. These enjoyed a kind of official endorsement.[24] Other speakers used pictures to supplement their lectures about Mormon history.[25] The most skilled of these early artists was Christensen, who by 1878 had completed eight huge canvases of past scenes and later added to them. His manner of using these is described by the following:

> in 1878, he had sewn the first group of eight together, rolled them on a long wooden pole and placed the whole package in his wagon. Then, using the pictures as illustrations for a lecture on Mormon history, he drove through the Utah country advertising his appearance as a lecturer on the Mormon story. In 1888 it was reported that nineteen paintings were being exhibited in Sanpete County and other areas of Utah. For Christensen's lectures, the roll of paintings was hung over loops of rope suspended from portable tripods, and the individual scenes were rolled out as he spoke.[26]

In later generations, the process culminated in impressive sculptured monuments (Mahonri Young's *This Is the Place* monument in 1947; Torlief Knaphus's work *The Handcart Pioneers*, and so on) or in murals, such as those by Lynn Fausett. Branching out, the Church presented standardized, "prettified" versions of history through movies produced by the BYU Motion Picture Studio. Working powerfully in the same direction were graphic arts as mediated by manuals, official periodicals, and brochures prepared by public relations firms. By mid-century the visual representations of Mormon history numbered in the thousands— all contributing to the process of ritualization by establishing a sense of the past that was primarily emotional, appropriable, and not primarily concerned with accuracy. Accurate or inaccurate, it was certainly selective. There are, for example, no marble monuments to polygamy.

Combining the verbal and the visual were pageants. David Glassberg has described the emergence of pageants as a way of commemoration.[27] Drawing upon some antecedents, specific individuals and organizations in the early twentieth century developed the forms of pageantry, borrowed from one another, published newsletters and periodicals. Mormons got on this same bandwagon. In 1930, for example, it was *The Message of the Ages*, with a "poetical text" by Bertha A. Kleinman. Perhaps "historical" is the wrong word to describe such a work, but it unquestionably sets forth simplified images about the past. After reviewing the different biblical dispensations, the pageant reaches its great culmination in a series of episodes on the restoration. Kirtland, Nauvoo, the martyrdom, the exodus to the Great Basin—the key scenes are all sharply etched. After the death of Joseph Smith an important scene was given in the following words:

> So fell Elijah's mantle from the skies,
> So Priesthood girded Israel's newer Seer,
> A Moses to emblaze the sunset trail,
> A Joshua to lead his people there:
> Of such as this the olden Exodus,
> That routed teeming legions in a night,
> Of such as this the migratory surge
> That swept the Pilgrims over unknown seas;
> Of such the consummations of the past—
> The message of the ages to inscribe.

The organ played a brief interlude on the theme from "Come, Come Ye Saints," after which the reader proclaimed: "List! the Marseillaise of the Latter Days / At the battle line of toil, / Where sang they litany of praise / From the heart of the stubborn soil."[28] After getting the Saints established in the tops of the mountains the pageant continued with tableaux depicting home, church, education, work, play, and the coming of the nations. The work concluded with a ringing "praise for the centenary of truth."

A similar pageant was presented in 1947, another centennial year. Pageant-like in some ways, too, are Grace Johnson's *The Mormon Miracle*, presented annually at Manti, and Roland Parry's *All Faces West*, presented for a few years in Ogden. The westward trek was the subject of Crawford Gates and Arnold Sundgaard's *Promised Valley*, which combined words and music in the manner of Rogers and Hammerstein. Presented at the 1947 centennial, *Promised Valley* was repeated every year and until recently has been shown, in shortened form, free to tourists. These are all vehicles for perpetuating a romanticized, ritualized, version of the Mormon past.[29]

A dramatic episode in *Promised Valley* (and most of the other pageants and plays) is that of the crickets and seagulls. This famous miracle, which every Mormon child learns in Primary or Sunday School if not at his or her mother's knee, is a classic example of how the ritualization of history works. Although William G. Hartley has demonstrated that some contemporaries did not view the incident as particularly providential, at least if we are to judge from their diaries, it would be idle to

deny the historicity of the event—that is, there were crickets, and seagulls did devour them.[30] There were of course crickets on many other
occasions, and at other times seagulls or other birds must have helped
to fight the invading hordes. The point is not the event itself but what
the people did with it in later years. Seized upon as a useful symbol of
the struggle of darkness against light, of the triumph of the latter, and
of God's providential care over his Saints, the incident was simplified,
dramatized, and commemorated. It was told and retold to successive
generations of Mormon children. It was reenacted in pageant and drama.
It was pictured in paintings, engravings, journalistic art, and finally in
the famous monument to the Seagull on Temple Square. All this is the
process of ritualization.

Such simplified presentations of the past as parades, monuments, and
pageants were contributing to nation building in many American cities.
Especially poignant as a case study of conscious simplification of a ritualized past is the American South.[31] Mormons were faced with a similar
challenge and understandably employed similar means. One problem
for them was the need for group cohesion in the face of ridicule and
persecution. New converts, as part of their assimilation into the body
of the faithful, could easily master the simplified history and accept it
as their own.[32] If one of the reasons for the creation of the "mythic history" by early Americans was, as Major Wilson believes, their sense of
being "orphans in time and space," the Mormons had the same need in
their own new communities.[33] "Any people in a new land," says Wallace
Stegner, "may be pardoned for being solicitous about their history: they
create it, in a sense, by remembering it."[34] More important, perhaps, the
Mormons had their own special problems of orphanage. Cut adrift from
the moorings of orthodox Christianity, and even, at times, from a sense
of belonging to the American nation, they needed ritualistic supports
for their legitimacy. Robert Flanders has observed that the ritual incan-
tations of restoration, priesthood authority, unity of the faith, patriotism, and so on, may be, in part, cases of protesting too much. In any
event, the value of a standardized, moralized sense of the past during
the Mormons' long identity crisis is unmistakable.

It is significant that the rituals have tended to focus on the "centrist
nucleus" by giving attention to people and events near the center. The
cohesion of the group is enhanced, the lines of traditional identity maintained. Selecting only those events clearly related to the doings of hierarchy, however elitist it appears, may be unavoidable, just as national

heroes are usually figures high in the government or national military circles. But there is some regional and local de-emphasis, some distortion, some loss of richness and variety. As Mormonism entered its period of expansion outward after World War II, there was bound to be some tension between the need to establish a sense of Mormon identity and the desire to respect local traditions or at least avoid imposing Wasatch Front or American mores—the covered wagons of the 24th of July parades, for example—in places like Japan and Bolivia. Perhaps it is ritualization of the *religiously* significant—Joseph Smith's vision, the restoration of the priesthood, even the first missionaries of different countries—that will best respond to the needs of a worldwide movement.[35]

Ritualized history is not satisfactory for all purposes. By definition it is simplified. It celebrates that which is celebratable, ignoring much of the past as it was. Those who probe more deeply are bound to discover that men and women of the past were not that flat and, more essentially, that the past was not that simple. Historians have a duty to criticize and correct inaccurate, inadequate, or oversimplified versions of the past. Part of their social role is to go over the record more thoroughly than the average person can do, subject each other's scholarship to scrutiny and criticism, and produce works of richness and complexity. Students in history classes, especially as they advance in years and experience, will hopefully learn a history that rings true. But it will not be the one true history or the only possibly history. It would be pedantic of historians to ridicule all ritualization of the past. Indeed, awareness of the way in which ritual has created and perpetuated public memory in many different settings should leave the historian unsurprised to find the same icons being employed within Mormondom. The fact is that most people are not historians—which is to say that most of us will possess our history ritualistically or not possess it at all.

Notes

An earlier version of this chapter appeared in *Utah Historical Quarterly* 43 (1975): 67–85.

1. See also Robert Middlekauff, "The Ritualization of the American Revolution," in *The Development of an American Culture*, ed. Stanley Coben and Lorman Ratner (Englewood Cliffs, N.J.: Prentice-Hall, 1970). As applied to history the concept is closely related to myth, but the emphasis

of ritual is not on beliefs about the past but on behavior commemorating it. See Ellen Marie Litwicki, "Visions of America: Public Holidays and American Cultures" (Ph.D. diss., University of Virginia, 1992).

2. Some random examples of the use of simplified history in creating a sense of group consciousness are C. E. Black, *Rewriting Russian History: Soviet Interpretation of Russia's Past,* 2d ed. rev. (New York: Vintage Books, 1962); David D. Van Tassell, *Recording America's Past: An Interpretation of the Development of Historical Studies in America, 1607–1884* (Chicago: University of Chicago Press, 1960); Wesley Frank Craven, *The Legend of the Founding Fathers* (New York: New York University Press, 1956); and Maurice Agulhon, *Marianne into Battle: Republican Imagery and Symbolism in France, 1789–1880* (Cambridge: Cambridge University Press, 1981).

3. "Apart from the veneration of certain idealized episodes from the past—the first visions, the martyrdom of the Prophet, the crossing of the plains—we have forgotten our past. As far as such features of the past as plural marriage are concerned, some of us would appreciate not being reminded of them" (Richard D. Poll, "God and Man in History," *Dialogue* 7 [1972]: 102). In the present frame of reference, I would prefer to say that Mormons, like other groups, have simplified and ritualized their past.

4. Émile Durkheim, *The Elementary Forms of the Religious Life* (New York: Free Press, 1965), 474–75, as cited in Conrad Cherry, *God's New Israel: Religious Interpretations of American Destiny* (Englewood Cliffs, N.J.: Prentice-Hall, 1971), 7.

5. Harvey Cox, *Feast of Fools* (Cambridge: Harvard University Press, 1969), 7.

6. Joseph Smith, *History of the Church of Jesus Christ of Latter-day Saints,* 7 vols., 2d ed. rev. (Salt Lake City, 1951), 1:337.

7. A survey of the April general conference finds frequent references to the anniversary of the organization of the Church. There were rare occasions when regular conferences were not held. See Jay R. Lowe, "A Study of the General Conferences of the Church of Jesus Christ of Latter-day Saints, 1830–1901" (Ph.D. diss., Brigham Young University, 1972).

8. *Diary of Charles Lowell Walker,* ed. A. Karl Larson and Katharine Miles Larson, 2 vols. (Logan: Utah State University Press, 1980), 2:78 (entry for 27 June 1859).

9. *Deseret News,* 24 July 1849; B. H. Roberts, *A Comprehensive History of the Church of Jesus Christ of Latter-day Saints,* 6 vols. (Salt Lake City: Deseret News Press, 1930), 3:493–97; *Frontier Guardian,* 19 September 1849. See also Philip A. M. Taylor, "Pioneer Day," *Millennial Star* 120 (1958): 164ff., 193ff., and Dale Beecher, "Pioneer Day in Salt Lake City: The First Fifty Years," unpublished paper. Richard Burton, traveler to Utah in 1860, observed that the Mormons treated July 4th "with silent contempt;

its honors are transferred to the 24th of July, the local Independence Day of their annus mirabilis 1847" (*The City of the Saints* [New York, 1862], 251). Burton exaggerates, but his basic point, the importance of the 24th, is sound.

10. *Deseret News*, 21 July 1874.

11. Ibid., 5 August 1874.

12. Ibid., 14 April 1880.

13. A detailed description of the procession and program is in the *Deseret News*, 28 July 1880. See also *The Utah Pioneers: Celebration of the Entrance of the Pioneers into Great Salt Lake Valley* (Salt Lake City, 1880).

14. Mary Ryan, "The American Parade: Representations of the Nineteenth-Century Social Order," in *The New Cultural History*, ed. Lynn Hunt (Berkeley: University of California Press, 1989), 139, 152. See also Susan G. Davis, *Parades and Power: Street Theater in Nineteenth-Century Philadelphia* (Philadelphia: Temple University Press, 1986).

15. John F. G. Yurtinus, "A Ram in the Thicket: The Mormon Battalion in the Mexican War," 2 vols. (Ph.D. diss., Brigham Young University, 1975).

16. On Zion's Camp and Mormon Battalion reunions, see Journal History of the Church, 9 April 1907, Church Archives. On Daughters of the Mormon Battalion, 24 July 1909; on Sons and Daughters of the Blackhawk and Walker Indian War Veterans, 17 August 1916, 10 February 1922, 16 January 1923, 13 August 1924; on Daughters of Utah Handcart Pioneers, 2 November 1915, 3 October 1916; on Sons and Daughters of the Pioneers, 29 October 1898, 31 October 1898, 24 March 1894, 30 March 1933; on Daughters of Utah Pioneers, 11 April 1901, 21 May 1901, 24 October 1901, 11 April 1903. See also James T. Jakeman, *Daughters of the Utah Pioneers and their Mothers* (n.p., n.d.).

17. A partial impression of the interests of the Daughters of Utah Pioneers can be gained by examining the "lesson" materials compiled in the following multivolume sets: *Heart Throbs of the West*, 12 vols. (Salt Lake City: Daughters of Utah Pioneers, 1939–51); *Treasures of Pioneer History*, 6 vols. (Salt Lake City: Daughters of Utah Pioneers, 1952–59); *Our Pioneer Heritage*, 20 vols. (Salt Lake City: Daughters of Utah Pioneers, 1958–77); *An Enduring Legacy*, 12 vols. (Salt Lake City: Daughters of Utah Pioneers, 1978–89); *Chronicles of Courage*, vols. 1–4 (1990–93, series continuing). Uncritically compiled and inadequately documented, these works still have some value to scholars, especially for leads that can be verified elsewhere. See also Wallace Evan Davies, *Patriotism on Parade: The Story of Veterans and Hereditary Organizations in America, 1783–1900* (Cambridge: Harvard University Press, 1955).

18. Two of the earliest examples of visits to Palmyra by Mormons who viewed the place, including the Hill Cumorah, are described in John S. Carter Diary, September 1883, and Jonathan H. Hale Diary, 30 May 1835,

Church Archives. On historic sites and other topics related to this chapter, see Paul L. Anderson, "Heroic Nostalgia: Enshrining the Mormon Past," *Sunstone* 5 (July–Aug. 1980): 47–55.

19. Larry C. Porter, "Twentieth-Century Monuments to Mormonism," unpublished paper, Historical Department of the Church. Marilyn Seifert and Albert Zobell, Historical Department of the Church, helped supply information on monuments and organizations.

20. Anderson, "Heroic Nostalgia"; and Janath R. Cannon, *Nauvoo Panorama: Views of Nauvoo before, during, and after Its Rise, Fall, and Restoration* (n.p.: Nauvoo Restoration, Inc., 1991).

21. Frederick H. Piercy, *Route from Liverpool to Great Salt Lake Valley* (Liverpool-London, 1855; ed. by Fawn M. Brodie for Harvard University Press, Cambridge, 1962). See also Mary M. Powell, "Three Artists of the Frontier," *Missouri Historical Society Bulletin* 5 (1948): 33–43.

22. Information supplied by Catherine Gilmore, Church Archives.

23. See Leonard J. Arrington, "Charles Mackay and his 'True and Impartial History' of the Mormons," *Utah Historical Quarterly* 36 (1968): 24–40.

24. "I spent part of the day in council with the Presidency and others upon the subject of the Paintings got by Philo Dibble, the work was finally sanctioned by the Presidency & Twelve who signed their names to it" (Wilford Woodruff Diary, March 1847, Church Archives). See also *Millennial Star* 11 (1848): 11–12. Dibble also had casts of Joseph and Hyrum Smith's death masks, which he exhibited. In the 1880s he contracted with an artist to make copies for sale. Information supplied by Catherine Gilmore, Church Archives.

25. Others giving "panoramic" lectures were a Brother Kirkham on the Book of Mormon and a Brother Smith on the seven wonders of the world. George Goddard Diary, 4 March 1884 and 9 February 1885, Church Archives. Dealing specifically with Mormon history were the lectures of Edward Stevenson. Edward Stevenson Diary, pass., microfilm, Church Archives. Three pictures used by Edward Stevenson in his illustrated lectures are reproduced in Joseph Grant Stevenson, "The Life of Edward Stevenson" (M.A. thesis, Brigham Young University, 1955), 185.

26. Carl Carmer, "A Panorama of Mormon Life," *Art in America*, May–June 1970, 52–71. See also L. F. Wheelwright and L. J. Woodbury, eds., *Mormon Arts: Volume One* (Provo, 1972), 44–49.

27. David Glassberg, *American Historical Pageantry: The Uses of Tradition in the Early Twentieth Century* (Chapel Hill: University of North Carolina Press, 1990).

28. *The Message of the Ages: A Sacred Pageant* (Salt Lake City: Deseret News Press, 1930), 27.

29. Historical pageants include *The Message of the Ages: A Sacred Pag-*

eant Commemorating the One Hundredth Anniversary of the Organization of the Church of Jesus Christ of Latter-day Saints (Salt Lake City, 1930); *The Message of the Ages: A Sacred Pagent Presented in Honor of the Pioneers to the Valleys of the Rocky Mountains* (Salt Lake City, 1947); Grace Johnson, *The Story of the Mormon Miracle* (Salt Lake City, 1973); William A. Morton, *Joseph the Seer in Song and Story: A Cantata* (Salt Lake City, ca. 1920); John Karl Wood, *The Exodus: A Pageant of the Pioneers* (Logan, 1940). Musicals include Arnold Sundgaard (music by Crawford Gates), *Promised Valley* (Salt Lake City, 1947); R. Don Oscarson (music by Crawford Gates), *Sand in Their Shoes: A Musical Play* (Provo, ca. 1958).

30. William Hartley, "Mormons, Crickets, and Gulls: A New Look at an Old Story," *Utah Historical Quarterly* 38 (1970): 224–39.

31. Charles Reagan Wilson, *Baptized in Blood: The Religion of the Lost Cause, 1865–1920* (Athens: University of Georgia Press, 1980).

32. Jan Shipps's observation is relevant. A friend, she writes, "told me of having heard a new convert describe, at a meeting the evening before, the mobbings and persecutions at Kirtland, Far West, Nauvoo, and of how this convert's account failed to make any reference to the possibility that the Saints might have been in some measure responsible for the way they were treated. . . . The convert's rehearsal of this highly ritualized version of Mormon history is an integral part of the process of his becoming a Mormon, acquiring an identity as a Latter-day Saint—of taking the Mormon heritage as his own. It seems to me that what an experience like this does for the individual convert, the ritualization of Mormon history has done for the entire Mormon community—it has helped them acquire an identity and pride in that identity." Jan Shipps to Davis Bitton, 25 January 1974.

33. Major L. Wilson, "The Concept of Time and the Political Dialogue in the United States, 1828–1848," *American Quarterly* 19 (Winter 1967), as cited in Robert Flanders, "To Transform History: Early Mormon Culture and the Concept of Time and Space," *Church History* 40 (1971): 108–17.

34. Wallace Stegner, *The Gathering of Zion: The Story of the Mormon Trail* (New York, 1964), 2.

35. A handbook of potentially celebrated events is Andrew Jenson, *Church Chronology: A Record of Important Events*, 2d ed. (Salt Lake City, 1899).

Index

DAVIS BITTON is professor of history at the University of Utah. With Leonard J. Arrington he coauthored *The Mormon Experience: A History of the Latter-day Saints* (1979) and *Mormons and Their Historians* (1988). He also has expertise in early modern European history, teaching courses in the Renaissance and Reformation. His earlier work, *The French Nobility in Crisis, 1560–1640* (1969) was published by Stanford University Press. He is a charter member and past president of the Mormon History Association.